# THE COMPLETE INSERVICE STAFF DEVELOPMENT PROGRAM

## A STEP-BY-STEP MANUAL FOR SCHOOL ADMINISTRATORS

# THE COMPLETE INSERVICE STAFF DEVELOPMENT PROGRAM

## A STEP-BY-STEP MANUAL FOR SCHOOL ADMINISTRATORS

R. Lloyd Ryan

Prentice-Hall, Inc.
Englewood Cliffs, N.J.

Prentice-Hall International, Inc., *London*
Prentice-Hall of Australia, Pty. Ltd., *Sydney*
Prentice-Hall Canada, Inc., *Toronto*
Prentice-Hall of India Private Ltd., *New Delhi*
Prentice-Hall of Japan, Inc., *Tokyo*
Prentice-Hall of Southeast Asia Pte. Ltd., *Singapore*
Editora Prentice-Hall do Brasil Ltda., *Rio de Janeiro*
Prentice-Hall Hispanoamericana, S.A., *Mexico*

© 1987 by

PRENTICE-HALL, INC.
Englewood Cliffs, N.J.

All rights reserved

Library of Congress Cataloging-in-Publication Data

Ryan, R. Lloyd (Ronald Lloyd),
  The complete inservice staff development program

  Bibliography: p.
  Includes index.
  1. Teachers—In-service training—Handbooks, manuals,
etc. I. Title.
LB1731.R93  1987    371.1'46    87-1321

ISBN 0-13-161316-2

Printed in the United States of America

*This book is dedicated to my children:*

*Patrick*
*Rachel*
*Justin*

*and to the memory of*

*Thurza Anthony (née Oxford)*
*(1879–1960)*
*who helped me through some pains of youth.*

# ABOUT THE AUTHOR

R. Lloyd Ryan was born and lives on the island of Newfoundland, part of the province of Newfoundland and Labrador, on the northeast coast of Canada.

For his undergraduate degrees of Bachelor of Science in Mathematics and Bachelor of Education, he attended Memorial University of Newfoundland and Queen's University at Kingston, Ontario. He also earned a Master of Education degree (Administration) at Memorial University. He began a doctorate in continuing education at the University of Toledo and is now completing work on that degree at the University of Southern Mississippi.

In addition to some time spent in the forest industry, he has been an educator for more than 20 years, as elementary and high school teacher of mathematics, science, English, and art in Newfoundland and on a Cree Reserve in James Bay, Ontario; as elementary and high school principal; and now as assistant superintendent of a rural school district on the northeast coast of Newfoundland.

He has a number of articles published in professional journals and is working on a number of manuscripts on educational topics.

With his wife and three children, he lives in the coastal town of Lewisporte, Newfoundland, where he is active in church and social affairs, dabbles in art, and is writing a novel in his spare time.

# ABOUT THIS BOOK

*The Complete Inservice Staff Development Program: A Step-by-Step Manual for School Administrators* has been written for school principals, administrators, and other educators who are responsible for teacher inservice and staff development. School administrators are sometimes guilty of attempting to bring about change by mandate, change requiring significant readjustment by subordinate administrators, supervisory personnel, and classroom teachers. Yet, frequently, our mandates lack the needed practical components for implementation. We might justly be accused of using stereotype statements and making vague generalizations—statements that sound good, perhaps, but frequently lack practical meaning and don't get the job done.

This book can provide you with an understanding of at least some of the processes that have to be considered. It also provides some direction for appropriate planning. By following the principles and directions outlined here, you should be able to achieve a greater degree of cooperation and approval from teachers and a reduced degree of resistance and animosity. You will also become more aware of the administrative roles which you must specifically address if your inservice efforts are to be successful.

It usually falls to supervisory personnel and subject area consultants to prepare and conduct the actual teacher inservice and staff development activities. This group sometimes includes school-based administrators and department heads. It is nothing short of amazing to witness the crudeness with which this function is sometimes handled. The "Tell, go do" approach is still too prevalent and almost universally unsuccessful. Furthermore, it is abhorred by teachers, who expect and deserve something much more supportive and useful.

The literature is full of accounts of inservice efforts that have failed. Simplistic models of staff development lead to frustration for the personnel whose responsibility it is to deliver the staff development, and to even greater frustration and stress for the teachers who are expected to implement change at the classroom level consistent with the new expectations. The two-step process of "tell, go do" has frequently been the operational assumptions, when a multistep process has been needed.

If your efforts are to be successful, then a much more sophisticated research-based process is required. This book can be the basis for that process because it is practice oriented and can give you the confidence to proceed and succeed with change requiring teacher inservice. It cuts through, without ignoring, the abstractions and theory and research, and it applies the synthesized basics by demonstrating how to proceed at the practical, day-to-day, classroom-level of operations.

*The Complete Inservice Staff Development Program* is not presumed to be a recipe book. It cannot be taken, flipped open, and mindlessly applied. It does address some of the theory, it is based on the research, and it gives the implications of both for highly professional, comprehensive, and practical approaches to inservice staff development. Moreover, you will know not only what might be appropriate to do in a particular staff development circumstance, but also why it is appropriate. Enough guidance is provided to permit you, whatever your responsibilities, to tailor-make a staff development process to fit the specific needs of your particular school situation.

This book is meant to be read more or less completely before bits of it are extracted for use. To use it otherwise would be to contradict the underlying principle of the book, which is that, in order for inservice staff development to be successful, it must occur within a holistic and organic conceptualization of educational management. That is, every facet of school operation affects every other facet, and all aspects have to be considered whenever change is introduced into any one of the components. This is one of the "secrets" of the successful Japanese management techniques that we have heard so much about in recent years.

Fantasy and wishful thinking, which characterize so much educational literature, has been avoided. What something "should" be like or what it "might" be like has been left out. Attempts have been made to describe what the situation *is like*, pretty or not. Also, I have tried to be aware of my personal ideologies and have attempted to prevent them from coloring the presentation.

Inservice staff development for teachers receives a large share of supervisory energies, time, and, in some school districts, substantial funding. Yet, the literature seems to indicate rather strongly that inservice activities are seen by teachers almost uniformly as disasters. Very few teachers have good things to say about their staff development experiences. Furthermore, school principals and other supervisory people are frustrated and are obtaining few satisfying results expect in very specific and localized instances. Something, obviously, seems to be terribly wrong.

Inservice teacher education is not successful primarily because we tend to conceive of it and to perceive it in overly simplistic terms. We tend to see the inservice process as an isolated factor in the school workplace rather than as only one of many elements in an interactive mixture. Not only do inservice activities have a complex relationship with other school-based factors, they may also have

## ABOUT THIS BOOK

even more complex relationships with factors external to normal school and district operations. A teacher's interrelationships with family members, for example, can be extremely important and can have an impact not only on staff development activities but also on almost all a school's operations. Consider the effect of scheduling inservice sessions after school, for example, on the teacher whose teenage sons were expecting "Mom" or "Dad" to provide them with a ride to some sports competition that afternoon.

We don't have a lot of control over very many of the external factors impinging on inservice. However, we do affect many of the school-specific factors whether we choose to do so or not. The effects can be positive ones if we become aware of those factors most amenable to our influence and if we learn appropriate methods of manipulating them to our advantage. The fact is that by doing so, we can provide satisfactory and satisfying staff development experiences.

For example, the notion that adult, mature teachers might be different as learners from what they were as postadolescent or young adult college students seems to have received little notice in the general school-focused literature. This is surprising in light of the fact that considerable related research has been available in the "nonschool" journals. Even a cursory examination of the behaviors of teachers in your own school will support this contention. Notice, for example, the difference in enthusiasm for after-school, evening, or weekend staff development activities between beginning teachers and more senior teachers who have young families. It's quite striking, isn't it? And we are not hard pressed to see why.

It's unfortunate that preparatory programs for supervisory and administrative personnel are so narrowly conceived and so often mutually exclusive. "Staff development" is usually a supervision course and "personnel" an administration course. This gives rise to the phenomenon characterized by few of us realizing that the inservice process is an intervention in the workplace and is, as such, an element, an important component of educational change and is subject to the influence of factors influencing any change effort in the educational setting. But, generally, this fact has not received very much attention.

There are other relevant factors, the most important of which may be that the careful curricular and instructional processes needed for successful staff development activities have been given very little attention. If we don't see the enterprise of continuing education for teachers in its proper complex, interrelated context, then we probably won't be very confident that the planned inservice activity rests on a reasonably complete foundation or that it has a fair chance of success.

The remainder of this work provides some rather specific guidelines for planning your staff development activities. With the exception of Chapters One and Two, which provide some necessary but brief background materials, the other chapters deal with the various aspects of deciding on, planning for, and implementing teacher inservice staff development.

Included are numerous useful forms, checklists, and other practical tools, all of which have been proven valuable by various schools, school districts, and other educational agencies. If you decide that these tools don't quite fit your situation, don't hesitate to modify them for your own purposes. Cut and paste as you please to produce useful instruments tailor-made for your situation. They are not sacred, so use them in your school as you see fit.

It is advisable to at least skim the total book before attempting to utilize specific materials. One of the major reasons for the failure of change efforts is the attempt to utilize materials in inappropriate sequences or in ways unintended by the developers. It pays to be aware of the time and energy requirements and of the sequencing of the various components of staff development planning and implementation before beginning any of them. It's probably better not to begin a project unless you are fairly confident that you know how you are going to see it through. If you have to abandon a project because of inadequate planning, it may be just another bad inservice experience for your teachers. If that happens, teachers may lose confidence in you, and your task will be even more difficult next time.

But if the guidelines and advice provided in *The Complete Inservice Staff Development Program* are taken into account in your staff development planning, then your teachers will be able to anticipate satisfying and meaningful inservice staff development.

*R. Lloyd Ryan*

# ACKNOWLEDGMENTS

This book could not have come about without the support, encouragement, and understanding of a number of people.

I wish to acknowledge the initial encouragement and direction of two learned gentlemen and scholars, Dr. George Dixon, dean emeritus, College of Education, and Dr. Newton Rochte, professor ereritus, Department of Higher Education, University of Toledo.

During the writing of the book, I also received technical assistance and advice from colleagues, namely, Norman Paddock, Alister Mesh, Wayne Pardy, Michael Roth, and Dr. Michael Jackson. And I wish to express my appreciation to those numerous authors, organizations, and publishers who gave me permission to use both previously published and unpublished materials.

I also have to acknowledge the many colleagues, superintendents, supervisory personnel, other administrators, and teachers who have contributed unwittingly to the substance of the book. In particular, I wish to acknowledge the debt I owe to those teachers with and for whom I have conducted inservice staff development. I wish to mention the teachers of Junior High Art in the Notre Dame Integrated School District—Edgar Hunt, Bertram Brown, Scott Andres, Cordell Small, Delmon Reid, Jim Troke, Chris Vincent, Byron White, David Morrison, and Kevin Head—the practicing teachers from whom I have learned most about inservice staff development.

Finally I wish to acknowledge the support of my wife, Patsy, and our three children. I will try to make up for all those evenings "down in the study."

# CONTENTS

About This Book ix

CHAPTER ONE   What Is Inservice Staff Development and Why Is It Needed? 1

What's in a Name? 1

*A Matter of Definition 2*

Why Inservice? 3

*The Rationale for ISSD 3*
*What All This Means 4*

Academic Professional Training Versus Teaching Assignment 5

*Demands Made on Teachers 6*
*The Present Status of Teaching as a Profession 7*

A Final Word 8

## CHAPTER TWO  What Research Tells Us About Inservice Staff Development 9

Lessons from Research 9

The State of the Art? Defects! 11

A Final Word 17

## CHAPTER THREE  Planning for Inservice Staff Development 11

A Staff Development Model 18

The Phases of Staff Development 21

*The Context 18*
*Foundations 21*
*Impetus and Initiative 22*
*Commitments 22*
*Needs Assessment 23*
*Program Development 23*
*Program Delivery 23*
*Evaluation 24*

A Final Word 24

## CHAPTER FOUR  Preliminaries to Needs Assessment 25

Who Decides the Teacher Needs to Be Addressed? 25

ISSD and Teacher Training Institutions 30

A Final Word 32

# CHAPTER FIVE   Effective Schools and Effective Teachers 33

The Effective School 33

Effective Schools Require Effective Teachers 39

The Ineffectiveness of "Effective Schools Research" 45

*Argument Sounds Reasonable, But...* 45
*The Process of Learning Is Ignored* 46
*The Importance of Needs Assessment* 47

A Final Word 53


# CHAPTER SIX   Orientations Toward Inservice Staff Development 54

Various Approaches to Inservice 54

A Final Word 59


# CHAPTER SEVEN   The Process of Needs Assessment 60

Delimiting Needs Assessment 60

Errors in Needs Assessment 64

Planning for Needs Assessment 66

Methods of Data Collection for Needs Assessment 69

*Personal Interviews* 70
*Response Forms* 71
*Observations* 73
*Archival Research* 74

*Small-Group Meetings* 76

*Committees* 76

*Case Studies* 76

A Final Word 76

## CHAPTER EIGHT   Needs Assessment Instruments 77

School Social Climate Questionnaire 77

Michigan School Improvement Project 77

A Telephone Survey 78

Needs Assessment Survey for Instructional Staff 78

Instruments from the Koll and Cozad Collection 78

Portland Consortium Training Complex: Teacher Survey Instrument 78

Staff Development Survey 79

A Specific Need Instrument 79

Staff Assessment of Principal 79

## CHAPTER NINE   Implementing Inservice Staff Development 124

Setting the Stage 124

*Preliminary Notions* 125

*Scheduling Inservice* 127

Addressing the Issues 128

*Relative Effectiveness of Inservice Staff Development Methods* 128

*Teacher Involvement in Planning for Inservice Staff Development* 130

*Teacher Preferences in Staff Development 131*
*Preferred Composition of Inservice Staff Development Groups 133*
*Preferred ISSD Trainers 133*
*Preferred Content for Inservice Staff Development Activities 134*

A Final Word 135

## CHAPTER TEN  Preventing Failure 136

A Critical Perspective 136

*Assumptions, Beliefs, and Premises 137*
*Putting Theory into Practice 138*

Why Do Staff Development Efforts Fail? 139

Research Implications for Improving Inservice Staff Development 142

A Final Word 145

## CHAPTER ELEVEN  Presession Considerations 145

Inservice Prerequisites 147

*Awareness 147*
*Readiness 147*
*Commitment 148*
*Delivery Systems Prerequisites 148*
*Incentives 149*
*Interfaces 149*
*Staff 149*

Determining the Nature of the Inservice Experiences 151

> The CBAM: Stages of Concern 151
> Levels of Experience Impact 154
> Level of Use 159

A Final Word 166

# CHAPTER TWELVE   The Sessions and Follow-Up 167

Objectives and Expectations 167

The Components of an Inservice Experience 169

> Theory 169
> Modeling or Demonstration 170
> Practice Under Simulated Conditions 170
> Feedback 171
> Coaching for Application 171

The Importance of These Components 171

Consolidation and Long-Term Maintenance 172

> The Classroom Implementation Stage (Consolidation) 173
> Long-Term Maintenance 176
> The Refining Phase of Inservice 177

A Final Word 178

# CHAPTER THIRTEEN   Evaluating Your Efforts 179

Preparing for Evaluation 179

Assumptions and Beliefs About Staff Development 181

Guidelines for Staff Development 182

In Conclusion 194

## Appendices 199

A: Addresses of Agencies Having a Staff Development Focus 201
B: Resources 204

## Notes 207
## Index 221

# CHAPTER 1

# WHAT IS INSERVICE STAFF DEVELOPMENT AND WHY IS IT NEEDED?

This chapter has two objectives. The first is to examine very briefly what might be meant by the phrase "inservice staff development." The other is to determine some of the rationale that might be advanced for engaging in this educational activity.

## WHAT'S IN A NAME?

There may be some inclination to say, "Why bother with definitions? Everybody knows what inservice is!" I am not disputing the notion that practically every person connected in a professional manner with the teaching profession "knows" what inservice is, and they frequently cling to what they "know" in a fundamentalist way. However, we must realize that people "know" different things about inservice. They may even seem to know mutually contradictory and incompatible things about inservice. And, of course, people will naturally define a concept according to what they think they know about that concept. That is, a definition will depend on the person defining it. If we have a dozen people, we will get a dozen definitions! Besides that, not only does the definition depend on who defines it but, as Nicholson and Joyce state "the choice of words depends upon one's view of teaching,"[1] and, naturally, one's view of teaching will influence, and maybe determine, what one thinks "inservice" should be. Furthermore, one's definition of inservice, or at least one's concept of inservice, will determine what is undertaken in the name of inservice.

To complicate matters further, there are a number of synonyms for inservice: staff development, professional renewal, inservice teacher education, professional development, and others. The simple terminology "inservice teacher education" has fallen into disrepute in some quarters because it seems to be undignified, derogatory, meaningless, or out of date. Nicholson and Joyce suggest the possibility that the term "has become repugnant because most of what is done in its name is so terribly boring."[2] Some synonyms seem to be more acceptable than others, with "continuing staff development" enjoying some popularity.

I have decided to use the term "inservice staff development" (ISSD) in this book, probably because "inservice," in spite of its unpopularity, is still the most widely used term and because "inservice staff development," the marrying of the two most popular terms, seems to me not only to "tell it like it is" but also to be a mildly new term probably able to extricate itself from some of the negative sentiment and unpleasant reactions associated with the other terms. However, I fully realize that past unpleasant experiences that have been foisted upon teachers in the name of inservice make almost any term suspect.

**A Matter of Definition?**

The terms used are otherwise not important as long as a definition is agreed upon. Without agreement about meanings of words, communication simply cannot take place. (Do you remember what Humpty Dumpty said to Alice? "A word means exactly what I want it to mean."[3] If we are guilty of such an arrogant linguistic attitude, then we don't get very much communication done!) Furthermore, there is some doubt that staff development can ever be a successful undertaking if we are unable to define it in some kind of mutually agreeable way. It is in the interest of promoting communication that I have looked for some contemporary definitions of this concept. I have looked at numerous definitions and I have considerable difficulty in isolating significant consistency between them.

Instead of defining inservice teacher education or one of its synonyms, some writers have made lists of inservice activities. The National Education Association, for example, compiled a list of nineteen different types of ISSD:

> classes and courses, institutes, conferences, workshops, staff meetings, committee work, professional reading, professional association work, cultural experiences, individual conferences, visits and demonstrations by outside parties, field trips, travel, camping, work experiences, teacher exchanges, research, professional writing, and community organization work."[4]

In any practical terms, such lists are virtually useless since almost anything a teacher does (a visit to a nudist beach?) or experiences (constipation?) seems to constitute inservice. But later on another author, Edelfelt,[5] gave a list and included such things as microteaching and televisions. But it is still nothing more than a list and again, for practical purposes, is of very little utility.

To proceed, for communication to take place, some definition has to be established and, at least while reading this book, that definition has to be accepted. Therefore, in the present context, ISSD will be used with roughly the following meaning:

> Those activities planned for and/or by teachers designed to assist them in more efficiently and effectively planning and attaining designated educational purposes.

However, let's not delude ourselves. No one definition is likely to be satisfactory, and any one definition is unlikely to connote more than a part of what inservice education is or should be. As a matter of fact, we might even say that if we were able to formulate "the" one absolutely correct and universal definition, then there would be no difficulty in engaging in the process. As it is, let's attempt to avoid the danger of focusing on the delimiting aspects of the definition that I've given because if we do, we will probably perceive ISSD in narrow and simplistic terms. A definition is merely a particular instance of a concept; it can't be the concept itself. Yarger, in writing in *The Journal of Teacher Education*, says in this regard that "any attempt to rename [ISSD] is likely to underestimate [its] potential, thus having the effect of being harmful."[6]

Now that we have a term and some kind of definition suggesting at least examples of the kinds of concepts and notions that the term connotes, and having avoided Humpty Dumpty's linguistic problems with at least some small degree of success, we can now have some confidence that meaning will be conveyed and that communication will occur.

## WHY INSERVICE?

A great deal of energy, at all levels of the educational enterprise, is expended in inservice activity, in the preparation of it, in its delivery, and in participation in it. The scope of this activity may be indicated by the huge sums of money spent on it. Estimates range up to $2 billion spent in the United States annually on staff development activities for teachers.[7] This activity also results in significant levels of disruption of and intervention in children's schooling as teachers take time away from their classes. A number of authors have commented on the extent of such activities. Hite and Howey, for example, say that "apparently inservice is on everyone's agenda,"[8] and Wood and Thompson say that "nearly all teachers and administrators see inservice education as crucial to improved school programs and practice."[9]

### The Rationale for ISSD

What rationale can be advanced for an endeavor requiring such commitment and commanding such attention? A number of reasons can be advanced as providing support for the current emphasis on ISSD.

*Declining Enrollments* Probably the most significant of the current reasons for the high need for inservice activities are rooted in the phenomenon called "declining enrollments," at least in some parts of the United States and Canada. Because of seniority clauses in collective agreements, teachers are reluctant to relinquish the security of seniority and, at least partially for that reason, are not seeking new positions in other school districts since the likelihood of layoff would be higher because of their resulting lack of seniority. Teacher mobility has slowed down considerably, making it difficult for schools and districts to obtain new people with new expertise. The declining enrollment problem is also resulting in layoffs of the less senior but perhaps better qualified teachers and forced transfer of teachers to positions for which they have little or no teacher preparation.

*Educational Changes* School districts are trying to cope with these problems while still attempting to accommodate a number of other highly significant educational changes: new curricula at all levels, preschools, mainstreaming, remedial education, industrial education, and music, to name only a few. These changes require new expertise, and that expertise must come from currently employed teachers.

*Teacher Shortages in Some Areas of the Country* But some parts of the continent have a problem for the opposite reason. A veritable baby boom and population displacement (such as the general movement of population from the Northeast to the South and West) have caused a shortage of teachers, necessitating the hiring of people who have no teacher training at all. A policeman in Philadelphia, for example, has joined the teaching force along with a pharmacist and an advertising executive,[10] none of whom had prior teacher training. Some states (e.g., California and New Jersey) and cities (e.g., New York City) have introduced alternate teacher certification regulations, admitting thereby to the profession many people with academic degrees but with no teacher training whatever.

*Teacher Attrition* Attrition rates among teachers are very low in some areas, partially because the bulk of the teaching force is some years away from retirement. Additionally, pension benefits promise future security and provide another reason why relatively few teachers are leaving the profession. But again, this general statement does not have universal application. New York State, for example, is one notable exception. There, it is estimated that at least 20 percent of its teaching force will be eligible for retirement by 1990,[11] and there is concern that teacher colleges will not be able to produce the required teachers in the desired quantity and quality.

## What All This Means

The situation developing primarily as a result of these factors is exacerbated by the fact that most teachers received their initial training a decade or more ago, and many of them have done little or no upgrading since. (A colleague of mine, a superintendent, has made the statement that 75 percent of the 450 or so teachers in his district have not taken a course in fifteen years!) A great many of them are at the top of their salary grid, and many have advanced degrees. Returning to college for more teacher training holds no financial incentive. It would be an unrecoverable expenditure—an unwise financial venture—and it would take the funds that they have been putting aside for the education of their own children. In those cases where teachers might, in fact, get a raise in salary if they did additional upgrading, the increment is so small that when the loss of salary for a year, tuition, and family maintenance costs, sometimes in a new city, are all considered, it is quickly realized that the total accumulated increase in salary, never mind the inconvenience, would never compensate for the expenditure. Sometimes, too, teachers have difficulty obtaining the necessary educational leave and could lose their jobs or seniority or both. Teachers have done their analyses! The system itself is a disincentive.

Even if teachers were to return to college, many of the college courses offered are perceived by teachers to be irrelevant to their needs. In one study in Newfoundland,[12] for example, it was concluded that "[education] courses are not seen [by teachers] as bearing much relationship to the day to day problems of teachers."[13]

While numerous authors (most of whom are professors of education at colleges and universities) advocate collaborative arrangements with colleges of education for the provision of inservice education, the idea is considerably weakened by the admission of some colleges of education that their offerings may be irrelevant. The researchers in the study just quoted, for example, say that "In fact, it may be impossible to design a course that would offer to teachers anything that they would consider relevant to teaching."[14]

It must also be recognized that teacher education may have little prestige or "snob appeal." Professors of some institutions prefer to see their institutions as a "university" rather than as a lowly teacher training school or (heaven forbid!) as a "normal school." Teacher training may not be its purpose. This is illustrated by the statement "it is possible that relevance to teaching may not be a proper basis for judging the quality of a course [at a university or college of Education]."[15] This is consistent with statements I have heard from professors of education that go something like this: We don't try to train teachers; we try to give them a university education because ours is a university, not a vocational training institute.

## ACADEMIC PROFESSIONAL TRAINING VERSUS TEACHING ASSIGNMENT

Many teachers are in somewhat unusual teaching situations. There seems to be a high degree of mismatch between academic professional training (i.e., preservice) and teaching assignment.[16] One teacher, for example, who has undergraduate qualifications to teach high school science may also have a master's degree in administration but may be teaching an elementary class; another teacher with a social studies major and initial certification in elementary education may be teaching secondary mathematics, without any further preparation. Since many jurisdictions pay salary based on "qualifications" determined by number of years of college or university education, regardless of teaching assignment, there is no incentive for such "mismatched" teachers to seek formal preparation consistent with their professional responsibilities. This situation is worsened by certification regulations that require teachers to do certain unspecified "academics" to meet degree or certification requirements. The result of this is that teachers who are "upgrading" are more or less forced to take courses available to them in summer sessions or nearby cities but that they know have little or no relevance to their classroom situations. Yet these are the courses that will give them the higher certification and, hence, a higher salary. The courses that they would like to take, the courses that would have relevance to their teaching responsibilities, are not open to them because these courses do not satisty certification requirements. One kindergarten teacher whom I know has taken over sixty semester hours of abnormal and sexual psychology at the undergraduate level and library science at the graduate level to attain higher certification. She readily acknowledges that these components of her preparation are "virtually useless" to her as far as teaching kindergarten is concerned.

This mismatch problem was highlighted by the 1983 report of the U.S. General Accounting Office "New Directions for Federal Programs to Aid Mathematics and Science Teaching," which quoted the statistic that approximately one-half of recent college graduates then teaching mathematics and science were not certified to teach in these fields.[17]

We must also recognize that however extensive the preservice training, it is still only a foundation for actual teaching service. A number of authors have addressed this issue. In particular, Nicholson and Joyce state that "the bulk of teacher competence acquisition has to be accomplished while the person is in service."[18] (This realization should cause school districts to take a second look at how they are introducing novices to the teaching profession. But the issues surrounding beginning teachers are topics for another discourse.)

A most troublesome realization is that many schools have defeated, apathetic, and cynical teachers—a poor environment, not only for children but also for beginning teachers. Again, Nicholson and Joyce can be quoted. They state, "it has turned out...that forces operating in the schools and colleges have socialized the young teachers to the preceding norms, thus subverting the idealism with which they supposedly entered their careers."[19] It is with some chagrin that I can illustrate this statement. A young lady I know (a close relative) was consulting me on how to obtain a teaching position. My advice respecting the importance of lesson planning was flatly rejected as being of value only if she knew that she was going to be evaluated. It was something that only professors wanted. Teachers at the school where she had completed her practicum had assured her that experienced teachers were wise to that sort of thing and that they didn't need such time-consuming crutches.

With respect to this issue of cynical teachers, even as I write I have another illustration at hand. The teachers in my jurisdiction have just rejected the last attempt to achieve a contract settlement and a strike vote is about to be taken. My discussion with teachers have caused me to conclude that the issue is not really about salaries, although that is the focus of the dispute. It is evident that these teachers are bitter and are exhibiting signs of "burnout." It is obvious that these problems will remain even if a settlement on salary is reached. These teachers are badly in need of inservice sessions in conflict management, interpersonal relations, and interpersonal communications.

**Demands Made on Teachers**

Teaching seems to make unique demands upon its practitioners. Champaign says, "There is no more complicated, enervating, or frustrating job in the world than teaching. To keep at it, most of us need help and encouragement; staff development is an effective means to provide this encouragement."[20]

Over the past decade or so there have been tremendous advances in knowledge about how children learn and the contexts conducive to child learning. One could argue that teachers and their school and district administrators have an obligation to the children in their care to familiarize themselves with this new knowledge and to utilize it in their classrooms. Inservice education is the obvious vehicle for providing such "updatings" to mature, tenured people.

The public is making demands for accountability, and the term "educational malpractice" is more and more frequently heard. If districts and schools are going to avoid the embarrassments (and worse!) associated with such charges, then they probably are going to have to engage in a program of systematic and planned staff development activities. So, it is interesting to note that the courts are already ordering school districts to provide staff development and are taking some policy-setting authority away from school districts.[21] Rather than having the courts mandate school reform, schools and districts would be much better off if they planned for staff development long before the situation arises that would force them into it.

## The Present Status of Teaching as a Profession

Finally, teaching is supposed to be a profession. The then president of the National Education Association, John Ryor, said in 1979 that "any professional is a constantly developing person. The never-ending challenge of educational growth is one of the significant attributes of professional life."[22] Further, the NEA supports the position that one mark of a profession is that its practitioners shall have a high level of preparation according to standards set by the profession itself. In its platform, the NEA states that there should be "In every classroom a teacher with...a zeal for continued learning"[23] and that "The competent teacher is a growing teacher. The professionally minded teacher seeks opportunities for continuous growth."[24]

Maybe we might be inclined to suggest that it would be cheaper, more convenient, and more efficient simply to fire "outdated" teachers and hire new ones with the desired specific expertise to meet our needs. After all, there is an oversupply. But, we would find ourselves at odds with the literature. As early as 1975, Calhoun addressed the argument: "Even if summarily replacing unsatisfactory incumbents with eager candidates were feasible, the simple truth is that the surplus of teachers is a quantitative, not a qualitative oversupply."[25] Champaign further countered the notion in 1980, saying that, even if we decided to hire people with the skills we need rather than to become engaged in inservice education, we would quickly find ourselves needing it. He says, "these people do not exist. No preparation program could ever be that specific and, even if you find the people with the skills you need today, by tomorrow they would be partly incompetent and in five years they would have to be fired because your needs would be different."[26]

Even though the notion of an oversupply of teachers persists, it appears to have little support in fact. For example, the National Science Teachers Association[27] conducted a study in 1981 and discovered that science and math teacher graduates from U.S. colleges and universities *dropped* about 65 percent from 1971 to 1981, and a similar study conducted by the National Council of Teachers of Mathematics reported a decline of 77 percent from 1972 to 1982.[28] The situation was so severe that Georgia imported math and science teachers from Germany.[29] Also, according to a Rand Corporation report, a 30 percent shortfall in the teacher supply can be expected by the end of the 1980s. This is supported by the Council of Chief State School Officers (CCSSO) in its report *Staffing the Nation's Schools: A National Emergency*, which states that "Fewer college students than ever want to teach and those who say they do are from the bottom of the academic barrel."[30] In fact, there is a virtual chorus of outcrying by school districts and educational organizations over this phenomenon. Detroit, Dallas, and Denver,[31] for example, reported severe shortages of math teachers in the early 1980s; the Governor's Task Force on Higher Education in Houston indicated that Texas had a critical shortage of math and science teachers.[32] This seems to be only the tip of the iceberg since the National Council of Teachers of Mathematics report that "43 states have reported a 'critical' shortage of mathematics teachers."[33] Added to this is a report of the National Center for Educational Statistics (NCES), which emphasized concern over the decreasing numbers of high school seniors who were planning to pursue teaching as a career,[34] a finding corroborated by a study conducted by the American Council on Education in 1982, which showed declining numbers of college freshmen indicating teaching as a career choice. The situation is further exacerbated by the situation discovered by a National Institute of Education study that indicated that more of the academically talented teachers leave the classroom before age 30.[35] There is the growing realization that the "Teacher shortage in all subjects...is becoming more severe"[36] and that "fewer than half [of today's teachers] intend to teach until they retire."[37]

## A FINAL WORD

There seems little doubt that inservice education is a badly needed commodity. In fact, with a young, degree-holding, tenured static faculty, it appears that inservice education and staff development are needed more now than at any time in the past. Wood and Thompson say that "if schools are to install...improved plans, and perhaps even to strive, the 1980s must be the decade of staff development."[38] It is probably fair to say that conditions will persist such that a similar strong need will continue into the 1990s, especially if there is no change in the academic quality of the young people entering teaching, if they "are near the academic bottom,"[39] as the National Institute of Education claims, or if, as *The New York Times* reports, because of low teacher pay, education students are "pursuing the skilled trades they were trained to teach."[40] These factors combine to create a situation that will need immediate and long-term effort.

# CHAPTER 2

## WHAT RESEARCH TELLS US ABOUT INSERVICE STAFF DEVELOPMENT

The purpose of this short chapter is twofold: to present a very brief survey of some of the general research related to inservice staff development and to give some reasons for the failure of many inservice staff development efforts. This is a stage-setting chapter, a jumping-off point for the remainder of the book.

### LESSONS FROM RESEARCH

Since practically all the rationale for ISSD, given in Chapter One, came from a review of the literature, we might be able to expect that the arguments for inservice staff development are also founded on a solid research base. Surprisingly, perhaps, this expectation is ill-founded! Very little research on either the positive or the negative effects of staff development activities is reported in the literature. The support for inservice education seems to be founded more on feeling and hope than on solid research!

Most of us like to feel that those behaviors that we exhibit in performing our professional functions have some substantial basis, something other than mere whim or personal experience. One of my objectives in this book is to provide you with not only some guidance with respect to planning for and implementing inservice staff development activities, but also some understanding and appreciation of the research support that exists for this aspect of our professional responsibilities. This chapter does not contain an exhaustive review of the research. However, it will give you some appreciation of the research that is being done. And the research results provided in this chapter and those quoted later on in support of suggested methodologies are representative of the totality that exists.

In assessing the impact of ISSD, it is of some considerable benefit to determine what would be acceptable as evidence of success of inservice and staff development activities. Some researchers, such as Kelly and Dillon, suggest that both indirect and direct outcomes should be considered. Indirect outcomes, according to them, are represented by change in the behavior of staff members, and direct outcomes are changes in pupil outcomes attributable to experiences of staff members in a staff development program or activity.[1] Let's first look at some of the indirect effects.

There seems to be strong support for the potential value of inservice staff development activity. For example, from a survey of over two hundred pieces of related research, Joyce and Showers state positively that "nearly all teachers can acquire new skills that 'fine tune' their competence. They can also learn a considerable repertoire of teaching strategies that are new to them."[2] In a related study of junior high school teachers, one researcher, James,[3] concluded that continuous individualized inservice tends to be effective in improving (teacher) sensitivities, understandings, abilities, and attitudes about those aspects of instruction for which they can perceive support in their instructional setting. You will notice the key words "continuous" and "individualized." A somewhat similar positive finding has been reported by Steele and Caffey.[4] From their study of the effectiveness of inservice for six teachers in designing and developing reading in content area classroom materials, they concluded that there existed a high level of satisfaction with the use of the materials and that teachers exhibited more positive understanding of the relationships between teaching of reading skills and students' ability to grasp textual materials in the content areas.

As is the case with many research conclusions, what these researchers didn't say is probably more important than what they did say. They didn't, for example, make any mention of whether teachers did, in fact, change their classroom and teaching behaviors subsequent to their staff development activities.

The positive research results are not consistent, either. Heeney and Ashbaugh, for example, found variable results in their study of 389 teachers in twenty school districts. In this study, only academic teachers benefited significantly from a long-term inservice (eighteen to forty-eight hours of instruction over an average of eight and one-half sessions) that included lectures, discussions, laboratories, case studies, and clinical studies. They determined that special education teachers benefited only slightly and that vocational teachers did not benefit from their inservice activities at all. These researchers concluded that "regardless of the mode of training, other variables contribute as much or more to the implementation of...[ISSD]."[5]

There tend to be as many negative conclusions as positive with respect to the benefits of ISSD for teachers. Scriven says with respect to inservice activities that "their ultimate value in terms of teacher development is suspect. And even more suspect is their ultimate effectiveness in terms of improving classroom performance."[6] Another researcher, Smith, is much more candid. He says, quite frankly, that "much inservice activity has been a disaster."[7]

Wade (utilizing "meta analysis," a sophisticated form of averaging) gives a much more positive assessment to inservice activities. She states that "attempts to increase participant learning through inservice teacher training are highly effective"[8] while she perceives that attempts to change teacher behavior are less effective.

The range of conclusions varies as much when direct effects are investigated. Kelly and Dillon suggest that it is the direct effects in terms of student outcomes that should constitute evidence of success or failure. However, they go on to say that "realistically, it is very difficult to show that substantial change in student performance does in fact occur"[9] and can be directly attributed to specific prior inservice activities.

In contrast, Champaign[10] seems not to have had Kelly and Dillon's difficulties. He concludes, from his research, that inservice activity results in lower rates of incidence of vandalism, truancy, and tardiness and higher test scores. He also concluded that by using project I/D/E/A/, the relationship between teachers and students improved and teacher absenteeism decreased. From another study using management by objectives with a group of Connecticut administrators in 1974 and 1975, he reported lower levels of written complaints and lower negative response to supervision. Aspy and Roebuck[11] report similar positive results. Their study with teachers trained to create "facilitative conditions" supports the conclusion that ISSD can show specific cognitive, affective, and behavioral results with students.

There is little consistent professional opinion in the literature about the efficacy of inservice education. Berman and McLaughlin[12] acknowledge that some staff development can have a lasting difference in schools. However, Woods and Thompson, from a perspective two years later have no such apparent delusions. They state, without a shadow of doubt, that "inservice teacher training, as it is now constituted, is the slum of... contemporary education. It is disadvantaged, poverty-stricken, neglected, and has little effect. Most staff development programs are irrelevant and ineffective, a waste of time and money."[13] Wade, apparently comfortable with her conclusions from her meta analysis, would seem to agree that inservice is not very effective in terms of student outcomes. She does say, however, that ISSD is "mildly effective"[14] in this respect.

The inconsistency of the conclusions about the efficacy of ISSD is not necessarily a problem. It may mean only that very different kinds of experiences are being lumped together. If we can isolate the influential characteristics of staff development activities with either positive or negative results, then these characteristics may be helpful in designing activities that are able to produce consistently positive results.

## THE STATE OF THE ART? DEFECTS!

There is a disturbing philosophy that seems to be growing in popularity in educational circles, maybe reflecting Western society as a whole. I see it as the "head in the sand" philosophy. Apparently, it is simply not socially acceptable even to admit to the existence of negatives, let alone examine them. We, apparently, are to "accentuate the positive" and "build on the good things." This is "positive think." Orwell would love it! However, if we ignore the negative, if we don't make an effort to determine what is going wrong, then it is going to be very difficult to remedy the faults. They just keep growing and accumulating. So, we are going to take a look at some of the negative aspects of past inservice staff development experiences to assist us in making the whole enterprise more positive.

As we have already seen, much of the literature makes reference to the general dissatisfaction of teachers with staff development activities. With respect to this, Joyce, Howey, and Yarger, writing for Teacher Corps, state "there is great discontent with [inservice], and many professionals and nonprofessionals apparently regard it almost as though it did not exist."[15] They continue to say "we are led to the unnerving conclusion that one of the largest training enterprises...is an incredible failure!"[16]

The general tone of these sentiments is echoed throughout the literature. There seems to be little doubt that educators generally hold negative attitudes about the actual value of inservice education at least as it currently is practiced. A number of studies conducted since 1974 consistently suggest that the majority of teachers, administrators, and college personnel are not satisfied with current inservice programs. Reference can be made to numerous authors and, in particular, to Brim and Tollet[17]; Ainsworth[18]; Joyce and Peck[19]; Zigarmi, Betz, and Jensen[20]; and Crocker.[21]

Consistently, however, in spite of the general negative attitudes, inservice is seen as crucial and enormous efforts are being made to determine what is going wrong. Wood and Thompson feel that ISSD is ineffective because inadequate resources are allocated to it. They state "we earmark inadequate funds for inservice training and staff development activities. We would never let our equipment and buildings become obsolete and nonfunctional by failing to maintain them, but that is exactly what we do with our professional staff."[22] Joyce and his colleagues seem not to quite agree with this point of view. While they express the general view that "the effort is very weak...even impoverished...and is a relative failure,"[23] they feel that the failure is not the result of lack of investment of time and energy but is due, rather, to structural problems. They feel that too much attention has been given to the process of organizing inservice programming and that too little attention has been given to determining the substance and process of the inservice activity. That is, for example, we may spend more effort on the "trappings" (e.g., planning the coffee breaks) and not enough on planning the actual activities.

From a survey of the literature one is able to glean a number of other defects in inservice identified by a variety of researchers and observers. Twenty of these specific defects are the following:

1. *Poor planning and organization.* Later chapters will show how to prevent this.
2. *Disjointed workshops and courses* focusing on information dissemination rather than stressing the use of the information or appropriate practice in the classroom.[24] James Coleman[25] calls this "information assimilation": the presenting of ideas, principles, and/or skills for use back in the classroom; sometimes providing an opportunity to discuss applications; and having the teacher return to the classroom to implement what was supposed to be understood. This is sometimes called the "tell, go do" method of inservice. It doesn't work!

3. *Principles of adult learning not used.* Woods and Thompson deplore this procedure, saying that it "doesn't fit what we know about adults and adult learning. In fact, the major flaw in staff development appears to be that we have ignored what is known about the adult learner and adult learning, just as we have accused teachers of ignoring the individual child and how [children learn]."[26] (They might have added that individual children have learning rates and styles that may differ markedly from those of their age and classmates. Teachers are really no different in this respect. A discussion of this topic is beyond the scope of this book. I would encourage you to explore the issue in your other professional literature.)

4. *Activities that are impersonal and unrelated* to the day-to-day problems of participants. This sometimes happens when there is no prior consultation of and joint planning with the intended participants.

5. *Inadequate needs assessment.* This book devotes three chapters to this vital and pivotal aspect of the whole process.

6. *Unclear objectives.* Both Ruth Wade[27] and Georgia Sparkes,[28] for example, emphasize the necessity of establishing clear objectives. Numerous authors concur, including this one.

7. *"The lack of follow-up* in the classroom or job setting after training takes place is almost universal."[29] This book contains a chapter on this aspect of the enterprise.

8. *Staff development activities not individualized and not related to learner interests and needs.* They tend to be top-down activities and as such are "doomed to failure" says John Ryor,[30] president of the National Education Association. While Ryor's comments might be suspect, since he was arguing for union rights in staff development, he does, in this case, have a valid point. It's addressed later on in the book.

9. *Options and choices in learning activities within the ISSD programs not provided for.*

10. *Responsibilities not clearly developed.*

11. *Effort not made to promote trust and concern.*
    These three matters (9, 10, 11) are discussed later in the book.

12. *A districtwide or statewide focus, distant from the real (assessed) local needs of teachers and administrators* in their schools. Local school faculty have not been involved in articulating goals or objectives at the planning stages nor have they been involved in the implementation of *their* inservice. This seems to be contrary to the evidence, which, as Woods and Thompson state, "shows the largest unit of successful change in education is the individual school, not the district."[31] Furthermore, as Ryor claims "teachers who know most about their own needs have had too little to say about it."[32] (I want to caution you that while I am quoting particular authors, that does not mean that I am in agreement with their statements or that the weight of research supports their arguments. As a matter of fact, strong exception can be taken to both the immediately foregoing statements, and they enjoy very little research support.)

13. *A decided lack of modeling* in inservice sessions of the kinds of practice that teachers are asked to take back to their classrooms and which principals are asked to take back to their schools. This crucial aspect is addressed in some detail later on in the book.

14. *Resources and efforts for ISSD split* among the various factions wishing to gain control of the inservice enterprise. Unions, for example, want inservice and staff development activities to be a matter of bargaining along with all other conditions of employment[33] and want teachers to decide what they want to do and to have much greater control over the content to which they will be exposed (possibly two mutually contradictory positions). Ryor, for example, states, "teachers should be the principal arbiters of their inservice education."[34] It is my interpretation of research results that they do not support Ryor's contention. His is an ideological statement and must be seen in its proper light. However, this is a very influential view and cannot be ignored.

15. *Naive positions or policy statements* as the underlying assumptions for subsequent inservice activity. Such statements have been more politically motivated than empirically based. Besides, it seems that many people believe a statement to be the paramount of truth simply because they believe it to be so, or because they said it. I call that "the God-almighty I syndrome." (This phenomenon might be described with more sophistication using Freud's notions of the ego and the superego.) For example, the literature produces such statements as:

Teachers know what they want.
Teachers don't want prescription.
Teachers will accept responsibility for their own continuing education.

The literature also offers statements which support a contrary view:

Teachers don't, and in many cases cannot, assess their continuing education needs.

Teachers want how-to-do-it, practical, day-to-day stuff. And so on...

Probably the most unexpected aspect of this phenomenon is that it is not unusual to find individual authors espousing mutually contradictory statements, either openly, by implication, or in assumption. The same author, for example, who advocates letting teachers decide the totality of their own inservice might also espouse the position that teachers should be paid extra for attending. In my opinion, these two positions are mutually contradictory and incompatible.

Those of us who have experience in administrative or supervisory capacities don't have to go to the literature to discover that teachers don't (always) seek help when they need it. Besides, as Joyce and his colleagues state, "there are limits to what teachers can do"[35] [respecting the determination and addressing of their own inservice needs], even if they had the best of intentions. There seems to be some reluctance to face issues. In fact, there may very well be some teachers who do know what some of their needs are and who do seek assistance to satisfy their needs. At the same time, we must realize that there exist teachers who appear not to know what their needs are, can't find out, and, apparently, couldn't care less. Teacher union officials may not like that statement, and I will not be popular for saying it, but no one is being well served, and the needy teacher least of all, if we allow ideology or political stance to cloud our visions as to the reality of what exists. We must realize and admit that some teachers want prescriptions; some are repulsed and rebel at the idea. Some will resist "imposition" but can be enticed to participate in staff development activities; some will have to be compelled or coerced to participate and will be involved no other way. Some teachers accept responsibility for their continued professional development; some don't. This is well documented in the literature, but it sometimes comes disguised. Staff development, in some cases, is being held for ransom while it is used as a bargaining lever. In some jurisdictions there is hostility between school districts and professional associations. Some school districts, for example, refuse to assist teachers to attend inservice activities sponsored by their professional associations, regardless of whether the teachers are in need of the specifically offered activities.

An attempt is being made, here, to take a careful, moderate, and conciliatory position recognizing the partial truths in many views. However, the position of the moderate is very difficult to sustain because the moderate is susceptible to attack from both extremes. (A political analogy may help to explain: communists charge "liberals," say, with being fascist, while proponents of absolute free enterprise charge these same "liberals" with being communists. Both extremes would be wrong, but the moderates would find themselves forced into one camp or another. It is very difficult to maintain a moderate stance. There seems to be some innate human desire consistently to classify into dipolar dichotomies. That is, all has to be black or white; no gray exists!) Maybe a diagram will help. (See Figure 2-1.)

### Figure 2-1

**The moderate view is difficult to maintain. (The moderate is caught in the squeeze between the opposing extremes.)**

| Teachers don't know what their needs are and can't determine them. | Some do; some don't. Some can; some can't. | Teachers know what their needs are and are able to determine them. |
|---|---|---|
| The "negative" extreme | The moderate | The "positive" extreme |

Nothing here is meant to suggest that the vast majority of teachers is not concerned and unwilling to participate in inservice activities. Some teachers may be quite adept at determining their needs and may be quite willing to seek assistance. It needs to be recognized, however, that teachers are being cheated out of quality inservice because of the bickering and jostling for control. More energy is probably going into the battle for control than is going into preparing quality staff development activities in a cooperative manner.

16. *Little follow through and follow-up evaluation.* Without it, we can't even determine what we've been doing right, how well we might have been doing it, or what may need revising. This book contains a chapter on evaluating staff development efforts.

17. *No recognition that ISSD is an aspect of personnel management.* Different people are "coming at" ISSD from a bewildering variety of philosophical positions, but practically no one in the literature has approached inservice as an aspect of management. This may well be one of the missing keys to successful inservice. While this topic is beyond the scope of this book, I would encourage you to review your other professional literature for a related discussion.

18. *Lack of emphasis on the nature of the instruction* that takes place in staff development sessions. While a teacher is expected to construct very careful lesson plans when teaching children, there seems to be no analogous necessity for supervisory personnel to do so when instructing practicing teachers. Oh, there's a bit of "micro teaching," perhaps, and some other limited techniques. But the question has received significant attention from only a few authors, some of whose suggested approaches will be discussed later.

19. *Lack of philosophy and policy.* While I recognize that a school district's instructional strategies ought to arise out of its well-thought-out and carefully articulated philosophy, there seems to be little realization, if any, that inservice education should also be consistent with, supported by, and supportive of that same philosophy. It has been my observation that many school districts either do not have carefully articulated philosophy or have philosophical positions so ill-founded and poorly articulated that, like Washington Irving's Ichabod Crane,[36] inservice activities are flying off in all directions, incoherent and without focus. (That's what I call "The blunderbus approach"—you might hit something; then again, you might not!)

As a matter of interest, it might be worthwhile to determine if, in fact, your school district has a well-thought-out educational philosophy based on what is "known" about children and child learning, or if your school district has statements that are merely clichés. It has been my observation that much that passes for school district philosophy is anything but what it purports to be and that educational practice—in the classroom—is grossly inconsistent with it in any case. If the philosophy and resultant policies are not in place and if the practice of staff development depends on the personal philosophies and whims of individual administrators and supervisory personnel, then how can we really expect effective inservice? There are probably as many unfounded and unanalyzed assumptions determining inservice as there are inservice practitioners, just as many teachers might be engaged in classroom practice founded on equally unfounded assumptions. For example, that "the mind is a muscle and has to be exercised with 'hard stuff'" is a view that can still be heard in one guise or another.

20. *Inservice trainers not carefully selected*. While we very carefully select teachers to teach our children, it appears that the same degree of care is not given to selecting "trainers" used in inservice and staff development activities. As a matter of fact, those responsible for professional development might be legitimately accused of latching onto whatever self-professed experts happened along.

## A FINAL WORD

Yes, these statements do seem negative, don't they? However, I hope you haven't dismissed me as a negative person with a negative view of the profession. I'm not. But I like to know what the enemy looks like.

Now we know at least twenty of the negative aspects of inservice staff development. You have to attempt to change at least these while you strive to maintain those aspects of the process that seem to be useful and productive. This book is designed to help you do just that.

# CHAPTER 3

## PLANNING FOR INSERVICE STAFF DEVELOPMENT

Before you can begin planning for staff development, it will be necessary to have some overview of where you are going. A brief outline of the staff development process will provide just that and will anticipate some of the topics to be discussed in later chapters.

### A STAFF DEVELOPMENT MODEL

There are numerous models of and plans for staff development in the literature. Some of these are rather simple, maybe even simplistic; others are highly abstract and theoretical. What we need is a middle ground, a model that is comprehensive yet simple enough to be practical. In other words, this chapter is designed specifically for the practitioner, the person who needs to use it on the job. This model of inservice staff development suggests eight stages or phases, all of which need to be carefully addressed. (See Figure 3-1.)

Most of the ideas and phrases of the staff development process mentioned here will receive more extensive treatment in subsequent chapters.

It is important to note that this model implies neither a one-time process nor a rigid sequencing. In fact, the process may branch into multiple efforts at almost any phase. For example, at phase C, the impetus and initiative phase, a number of needs may be making themselves felt. Hence, the process may branch into two or more efforts. At any later phase, multiple efforts may be deemed necessary, particularly after the needs assessment phase has gone through one cycle. The planning and activity structure may result in a process mapping that would be similar to that shown in Figure 3-2.

### Figure 3-1
### A Model of the Phases of Staff Development

A. The Context
   1. District philosophy—policy statement respecting continuing education and inservice staff development
   2. School mission statements—statements respecting staff development
B. Foundations
   1. The literature
   2. The research
   3. Consultative and participative decision making
      a. Collaborative planning
      b. Data-based decision making
C. Impetus and initiative
   1. Initial awareness of need
   2. Initial purposes and goals
   3. Problem-raising process
D. Commitments
   1. Overall planning
   2. Communications
   3. Permissions
   4. Commitment of resources
E. Needs assessment
   1. Establishing a committee
   2. Deciding on methods and techniques
   3. Data collecting
   4. Analysis of data
F. Program development
   1. Training objectives
   2. Curriculum development
   3. The teacher is an adult learner
G. Program delivery
   1. The inservice sessions
      a. The teacher is an adult learner
      b. Participants
      c. Resource people
      d. Location
      e. Timing
      f. Incentives
   2. Follow-up and follow through
      a. Support
      b. Guided practice
      c. Feedback mechanisms
H. Evaluation, reassessment, revisions

# Figure 3-2
## Staff Development Planning Decision Tree*

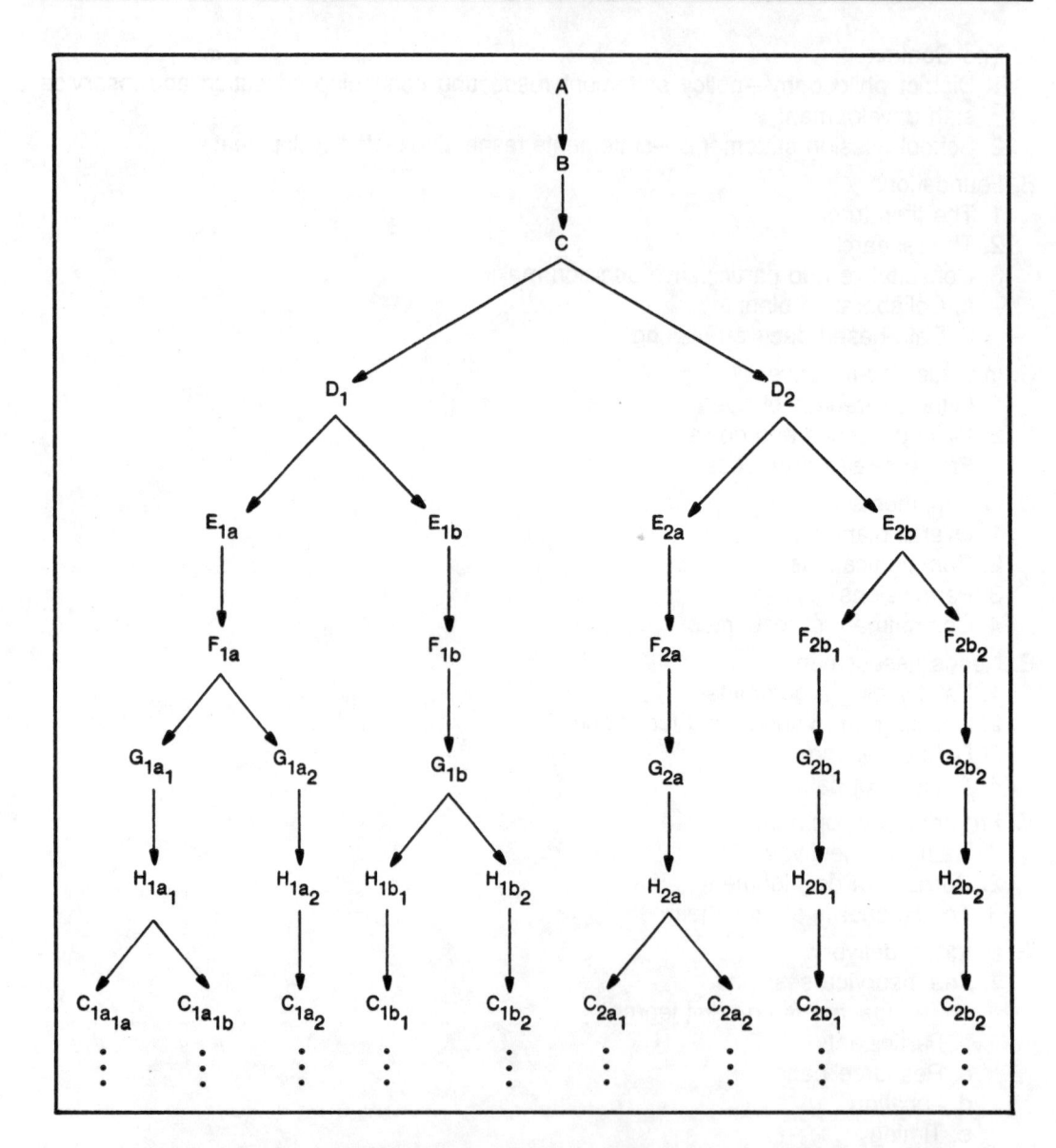

*The phases of staff development are also decision points. For example, the impetus and initiative phase may result in two or more commitments, $D_1, D_2, \ldots$, each of which will require its own needs assessment, program development, delivery, follow-up, and evaluation. Each commitment $D_x$ may result in two or more needs assessments, $E_1$, $E_2, \ldots$ Each needs assessment $E_x$ might result in two or more program development thrusts, $F_{xa}, F_{xb} \ldots$, each of which will require planning for program delivery, follow-up, and evaluation. And so on to the evaluation phase, which will undoubtedly be the impetus for a new series of staff development initiatives.

That is, it is to be expected that any one staff development initiative may result in multiple staff development thrusts.

While Figure 3-2 might suggest that all the phases are in time step, such an eventuality is unlikely. You would be wise to anticipate wide variation in the time required for each phase. Furthermore, depending on the nature and extent of the needs diagnosed and on the material and human resources available to address them, the time for addressing different needs with staff development efforts may vary from a few weeks to several years or more. Additionally, the various stages may have different time requirements for different inservice staff development thrusts.

Staff development has a cyclic structure. There is really no point at which we will be able to say that we are finished. The needs assessment phase may give rise to refined needs assessment with respect to certain needs, while at the same time it may provide clear enough definition of other needs to allow program development to begin. Also, the evaluation stage will probably indicate the need for new staff development thrusts, thus starting the cycle all over again. In fact, new needs may become evident long before summative evaluation has begun.

## THE PHASES OF STAFF DEVELOPMENT

It may be useful to have a brief discussion of each phase of the model.

### The Context

I think that the necessity for philosophy statements cannot be emphasized too strongly. Individual people in an educational institution may indeed undertake and expedite successful and worthwhile staff development activities and projects in the absence of a well-developed and articulated philosophy. However, how are you to know that your staff development thrust will meet with your school district's approval or that it will be consistent with inservice efforts by other people in your district if there are no philosophy statements and resultant policies to guide you? Furthermore, how will you know what the goals are or whether you have reached them, except on a very specific level?

The lack of philosophy and the resultant lack of policy statements and regulations usually contribute to a lack of coordination, a dilution of effort, a waste of resources, and, like Ichabod Crane, people rushing off in all directions. It is the philosophy that provides the unity and coherence and goal structure of any school district. The school-specific situation is a particular application of that of the district. It follows, therefore, that school-level inservice efforts should be consistent with (i.e., not contradictory to or be at cross purposes with) district efforts.

### Foundations

Much effort is expended ineffectively and resources are wasted if people try to reinvent the wheel. Existing literature can provide considerable guidance, and available research, while it has to be read carefully and interpreted cautiously, is beginning to show some clear directions. The person in a position of educational responsibility who attempts to provide staff development in (sometimes willful) ignorance of the literature and of the research has little chance of success. It is efforts of this kind that have caused staff development to be labeled "the slum of American education, disadvantaged, poverty-stricken, neglected, psychologically isolated."[1] There is really no excuse for the administrator who tries to operate a school or district by seat-of-the-pants procedures or for the inservice practitioner who ignores the literature and research or, what is worse, arrogantly and knowingly proceeds contrary to the literature and the research. Deity complexes have no place in schools or school districts!

One other foundation is the necessity of operating in a consultative and participative decision-making mode. This does not mean lowest-common-denominator, "democratic," everybody-making-the-decision-nobody-taking-responsibility decision making. It means, rather, shared responsibility and accountability. Research results in this case seem quite clear! The verdict appears to be in and indicates high effectiveness of inservice staff development efforts if the decision making process is not a unitary, dictatorial, or mandated one.

**Impetus and Initiative**

Many districts and schools operate under the "philosophy" that "if a problem arises, we'll deal with it then." Usually, this results in problems being addressed only after considerable pressure has been applied. A medical analogy would be a middle-aged man who visits his physician only after repeated bouts of pain, when he simply cannot make it to the office or through the day. The diagnosis of advanced coronary problems or prostate cancer may then be of little benefit. The wisdom of regular checkups to identify and isolate problems before they become acute cannot be denied. A school or school district is not essentially different. We should have mechanisms and procedures in place that will identify needs and problems before they surface as full-blown major issues. This is the stage where they can be dealt with much more expeditiously and with excellent chances of success. The male prostate cancer might be kept in mind. Identified in time, it is almost 100 percent remediable. If it is left until the cancer has reached other organs, the probability of survival is considerably reduced.

The competent inservice person, like the competent administrator, will go looking for problems while they are still in the embryonic stage. It would be an exhibition of incompetence not to do so!

**Commitments**

Before you can proceed with staff development, you will need permission to proceed and a commitment that the material and human resources will be available as they are needed. Also, it will be necessary to know whether you are attempting to duplicate an effort already underway, or whether your proposed effort will work at cross purposes with other efforts either planned for or ongoing.

An aspect of the commitments phase is a determination whether the necessary communications avenues are in place and are functioning. The value of adequate communications cannot be overemphasized. If you are not confident that you have adequate communication skills and that you have appropriate procedures in place, you would be wise to consult the professional literature.

**Needs Assessment**

The needs assessment phase is of crucial importance. If a need is to be addressed, then the parameters of the need will have to be identified. It is not a simple process, and it is unlikely to be successful if simplistic methodologies, based on naive assumptions are utilized. It will be necessary to assemble a representative committee of competent people to plan for and execute the decision-making, data collection, and analysis aspects of needs assessment. The success of the staff development thrust depends on competent and expeditious data collection and analysis.

**Program Development**

Your skills in curriculum planning will stand you in good stead during this phase. Keep in mind that you are dealing with adult learners who have characteristics different from children as learners. What is the appropriate mix of theory and "practical" content? What is the appropriate proportion of listening, sharing, and hands-on activity? Who are the most appropriate session leaders? What competencies should they have? What is the appropriate mix of large-group, small-group, and individualized, independent, activity? How much freedom should there be to choose particular aspects of the program? Which delivery modes are most effective? Which components can best be delivered by private at-home study? Curriculum development for adults is every bit as important and complex as it is for children. It cannot be neglected.

**Program Delivery**

The delivery of staff development has two major stages: the training sessions and the activities that occur after these sessions.

With respect to the inservice sessions, you will have to address a number of questions: Where will the sessions be held? Who will attend? How will they be selected? Are the facilities adequate, comfortable, accessible? Do the site facilities lend themselves to a variety of training activities? When will the sessions take place? Will teachers have to give up any of their own time? Will the sessions be cost-free to the participants? What incentives exist to encourage their attendance? Will they have any choice in the matter? Will refreshments be available? These matters certainly have an aura of administrivia, but, if they are not attended to, the total effort can be wasted. Don't become impotent by neglecting to attend to these nitty-gritty details.

A question often going begging in the staff development literature is, "When has staff development been delivered?" As has been stated in Chapter Two, staff development efforts are frequently severely truncated. The process stops at the end of the beginning of the effort. The inservice "session" is only the beginning! Provision has to be made for modeling; for guided practice; for trying out under protected conditions; for individual on-site, in-class attention; for support and assistance; and for long-term follow-up, follow-through, and feedback.

Over time, the specific staff development training sessions may fade in the memory of the individual participants if left alone. However, if the effort is to be successful the priority must remain with the district, probably as the responsibility of designated supervisory personnel who may or may not be the person who instigated the inservice effort. This is a transitional phase where the monitoring of the thrust becomes a part of the regular and ongoing clinical supervision and formative evaluation program. But it must not be forgotten!

## Evaluation

The evaluation phase is not a discrete event. Each phase needs to be evaluated, including the process of evaluation. The foundations and decision-making phases need to be evaluated, as do the impetus and initiative phase. The commitment phase has to be evaluated as well as the needs assessment phase. The effectiveness of program development and program delivery has to be determined, and an evaluation has to be made of the efficacy of clinical supervision and formative evaluation over the long term.

Whenever evaluation is carried out, the results are likely to lead to new initiatives, new efforts, and new thrusts with modification and refinement being normal expectations.

## A FINAL WORD

Later in the book there are checklists and other evaluative instruments to assist you in determining how effectively all phases of staff development have been expedited.

# CHAPTER 4

## PRELIMINARIES TO NEEDS ASSESSMENT

Somehow, decisions have to be made respecting the content and methods of delivery of inservice staff development. These decisions should be based on the needs that exist. That is, staff development programs should be directed toward the clearly articulated goal of satisfying specific diagnosed needs. Two major questions arise in any consideration of which goals to address: Who is to decide what the needs are? and How will the needs be identified or determined? Issues related to the first question are addressed in this and the following two chapters. Issues related to the second question will be addressed in subsequent chapters. That is, Chapters Four, Five, and Six have as a focus preliminary issues related to needs assessment, while Chapters Seven and Eight focus on the needs assessment process after the foundation issues have received appropriate attention.

### WHO DECIDES THE TEACHER NEEDS TO BE ADDRESSED?

There are two major streams of thought with respect to who should determine the inservice needs of teachers. One stream of thought suggests that the substance and process of ISSD should be determined by district-level administrative and supervisory personnel; another stream of thought, held particularly by teacher unions, is that individual teachers should define their own needs.

Joyce and his colleagues state that "The one thing we do know about the retraining of teachers is that retraining should not be separated from teaching itself."[1] While this is a simplistic generality and doesn't help in answering the basic question, it does make another point about the artificial nature of some inservice activities.

Nicholson and Joyce appear to come down clearly on the side of district people determining inservice staff development needs. They say that "the school district can conceive of itself as essential...it sees itself in the best position to define needs and as having the largest potential reservoir of trainers, and of course, as housing the clients of inservice."[2] They go on to say that the district office has the needs assessment authority because it is answerable to the board of education and hence to the public. School districts are seen as being closest to immediate political pressures and pressure to keep costs down and to be responsive to public demands. Furthermore, they strengthen the argument by issuing a caution:

> The school system can be easily so caught up in the day-to-day that it fails to advocate an [inservice system] designed to improve the institution. Improving the institution means changing it, and changing it affects the functions of personnel who have become accustomed to roles in which their spheres of influence are fairly well defined and protected.[3]

The implication seems to be that teachers, the personnel in this case, are not likely to decide on ISSD activities that will threaten their comfortable positions. Since the district has the responsibility and is accountable to the public, then it is its responsibility to determine the needs to be addressed. Some of the choices made by the district may shake the complacency of some of the employees. Another author who sees districts as playing a major role in determining the nature of ISSD is Kelley. He suggests that there should be a "systematic plan for the assessment of achievement, behavioral and attitudinal characteristics adopted by a school or district as evidence of curricular effectiveness and the effectiveness of instruction and teaching."[4] He then suggests that the staff development program should be related to district goals.

Two authors who take a more moderate view are Dillon and Smith. Dillon agrees that ISSD should relate to district goals and to the translation of these goals into improved student achievement. However, he also suggests that ISSD should evolve from a diagnosis of district, building, and individual needs.[5] Smith, while not advocating that teachers determine needs, takes the position that much inservice activity has been a disaster "because of the impersonality of the approach and the virtually complete lack or regard for the day-to-day problems of teachers."[6] He clearly advocates that the staff development emphasis should move away from formal activities that focus only obliquely on classroom practice and that tends to be general and theoretical and toward more functional activities that relate to the specifics of teacher needs in their classrooms. A similar view is expressed by Burello and Orbaugh. They state that "Inservice education has been shaped by outside mandates and initiatives without the collaboration of consumers, clients, or providers."[7]

In general, somewhat in contradiction to these authors, researchers and practitioners in staff development emphasize the importance of basing ISSD activities on the assessed needs of teachers. The emphasis has taken the form of planning programs to address needs that teachers say they have. Furthermore, it appears that more frequently than not, sessions have been conducted in formats preferred by teachers.[8]

There is a crucial question here. Are teachers able to determine their own needs? Jones, analyzing her research results, says no. She says "little relationship was found between expressed needs for knowledge and measured knowledge"[9] Her findings suggest that determining teacher needs and securing statements from teachers concerning their perceived needs are distinctly different operations. Jones and Hayes caution that a person charged with the task of determining inservice needs of teachers must utilize a variety of needs assessment methodologies and must be careful not to establish inappropriate expectations regarding what services will be delivered and how they will be delivered.[10] Jones suggests that questions should be asked in a form that identifies symptoms of needs rather than developmental activities. She suggests that teachers may be able to express symptoms of needs but be unaware of their actual needs. Smith is in agreement with Jones and Hayes on this latter point of view. He suggests that the success of staff development efforts that aim to individualize response to teacher needs must rest upon the recognition that teachers are not very good at self-analysis and that "assistance with problem identification and analysis...would seem to be vital in any move to individualize inservice activities."[11] Burrell is another author who has come virtually to the same conclusion. He contends that it is frequently the case that the immediate and identified problems are only symptomatic of much more basic and long-term ones. He further suggests that these problems can be dealt with, if at all, only through intensive study.[12]

Jones offers some explanation for this degree of unreliability of expressed teacher perception of needs. She suggests that teachers are either unaware of their needs or are reluctant to express them. It is not surprising that she found through her research that teachers preferred "practical" inservice such as workshops and demonstration lessons. Teachers perceive these kinds of activities as being immediately useful to them because they focus on instructional materials and techniques rather than on underlying theory.

The point needs to be made, however, that for demonstration lessons and other "immediately useful or practical" activities to be assumed valid, the staff development participants must already possess the background knowledge required to apply the particular methodology to the general case, that is, to apply "inservice" to the specifics of classroom. That is not always easy to do. Jones suggests that teachers apparently did not possess a solid foundation of knowledge and were unaware of much need for additional knowledge. If this is, in fact, the case, then it should not be surprising that teachers' preference for ISSD activities do not necessarily reflect their "needs" as determined by more objective means. Yet it is at least interesting that the American Federation of Teachers is advocating that teachers be permitted to determine their own inservice needs and that this be made part of their negotiated contracts.[13]

Luke is another author who argues for teacher determination of staff development. He advocates two general principles respecting teacher involvement, clearly supporting the principle of teacher determination. He declares that teachers must be involved in all steps that are part of the needs assessment process. He criticizes the manner in which teachers are sometimes involved and says that sometimes teacher participation is limited to checking a questionnaire or writing additional responses in provided spaces on questionnaires. He says that full involvement implies participating in all phases of the planning process from first conceptualization, contributing to decisions on how data are to be collected, and sharing in the analysis of the assessment data.[14]

Another author who advocates more extensive teacher involvement is Jefferson. She takes the position that if staff development is to be a tool of progress, then staff development personnel must include more participant control over what is learned and over "how that learning is brought about."[15] This apparent advocacy of teacher involvement is supported by Luke, who says that teachers should have a say in determining the "delivery systems" of ISSD, implying that it is imperative that teacher perceptions of the most effective methodologies of delivering skills and information should determine the delivery systems utilized and that what should be delivered is what teachers say they require.[16]

Luke takes the position that since there are different styles of learning, teachers should be able to choose their inservice activities in the learning mode that appeals to them, and that ISSD should be available in a variety of teaching and learning modes for this purpose. This position is strongly advocated by Jefferson who decries the fact that there is a "failure to provide choices and alternatives that accommodate the differences among participants."[17] Luke presents a very strong argument. He says that encouraging teachers to think creatively about their own learning patterns is a strong force against tolerating a conformity of learning in ISSD experiences that would not be considered acceptable in the teachers' own classrooms. He seems to be implying that if teacher individuality is catered to, then teachers will be more likely to cater to the individuality of children in their own classrooms which, we suppose, is a goal of prime importance in most ISSD activities.

There is an issue here that none of the authors has addressed. That is, why should we have teachers involved at all? Jones claims that teachers do not know their own needs; Hayes and Smith agree. Yet Smith and Luke advocate teacher involvement. Is it, then, important to have teachers involved because there is some intrinsic merit or value in their involvement? We might easily argue in this manner, and we could find support for our position in management literature. Or does having teachers involved in decision making contribute to better decisions?

A partial answer to the question may lie in the semipolicy statement of the National School Public Relations Association. The NSPRA took a stand on the issue and rejected what it called "old assumptions": that central administration, colleges, and departments of education knew what was best for teachers; that for teachers to grow professionally, they need basically to learn more about the subject taught; and that experience would take care of the remainder of the problem.

The NSPRA then advocated "new assumptions": that teachers themselves are an important source of information concerning their own professional growth needs; that such information can be gathered in a needs assessment; and that self-awareness and understanding of human interaction are crucial to effective teaching.[18]

We are left to puzzle about what we can conclude from this swirling of opinion about teacher involvement in assessing their own needs. We may be even more puzzled when we realize that only one person offering opinions has any solid research basis[19] and even in that one instance the research was conducted with only one group of teachers with respect to only one teaching responsibility—namely, reading instruction.

Based on what we know about the theory and research respecting personnel management, we might take the position that it is important to have teachers involved in assessing their needs, if they want involvement, simply because it appears that many workers like to be involved in decision-making processes when the decisions concern their workplace. I am assuming that not Smith or Luke or the NSPRA are advocating that teachers be involved in needs assessment against their wills. Yet, in none of the cases was it acknowledged that some teachers would prefer not to be involved, nor was there any indication respecting what the appropriate procedure might be in such a likely eventuality. That is, theory and research[20] suggest that employees' loyalties are strengthened if they *feel* involved, and are made to *feel* that their contributions are important and maybe even instrumental, even though the specific contributions may not be particularly valuable and may not carry much weight in the actual decision making. The involvement and feeling of importance is what is important, not necessarily the value of the contribution, as long as the employee (the teacher in this specific instance) is not made aware of the value that the decision makers perceive in his or her contribution, or the actual weight he or she had in the final decision. An extreme position here would be illustrated by a trainer doing a needs assessment, having teachers involved, and then confining all the documentation to the wastebasket and preparing what he had thought was important all along or utilizing what had been prepared even before the needs assessment took place.

The other important conclusion with respect to teacher (or other employee) involvement in needs assessment is that a great deal of immensely valuable information can be gathered in this manner. After all, teachers are, in most cases, very well educated and intelligent and creative individuals who have a great many ideas to contribute. Their ideas can provide the basis for decisions that can foster more effective, efficient, and pleasurable staff development activities. Besides, as Burello and Orbaugh indicate, one must acknowledge the possibility that for staff development to be of value to a professional, it must be relevant; that is, it must be consistent with the participants' perceived needs.[21]

We would have to suspect the competence and motives of staff development personnel who would ignore the value of such information and who would make all the relevant decisions themselves. The personnel in this case could refer to the collectivity at a school district office or to any group of superordinates or supervisory personnel who are in positions to make or to have made decisions respecting staff development activities.

The logical conclusions that we would deduce from these research reports is that a great deal of valuable information can be gathered with teacher involvement but that the quantity and quality of the information so obtained will depend on the assessment procedures, the instruments, and the analysis.

## ISSD AND TEACHER TRAINING INSTITUTIONS

I am taking the position, here, that ISSD is a continuation of preservice preparation and is founded on it. This is primarily because, as Howey and his colleagues state, "it is obviously impossible for any contemporary preservice teacher education program to equip teachers with all of the skills [demanded]."[22] They go on to state that that would be an impossible set of expectations and that, furthermore, no teacher training program could possibly meet the expectations of all those people who prescribe duties for teachers.

Furthermore, Crocker concludes that teachers believe that many of the available teacher education courses are irrelevant and that teacher training institutions may not be able to provide the desired relevant programming.[23] This conclusion would seem to be supported by the findings of the Howey group that indicate that the empirical base simply does not exist on which the needed preservice programming can be built and that there is limited capacity for change in preservice teacher preparation programs.[24]

Yet a great deal of the bulk of continuing teacher education still takes the form of teachers returning to their alma maters or other teacher training institutions to take more of the standard fare of courses. A refreshing change to this stale method of teacher upgrading may be the developing notions of collaboration between school districts and teacher training institutions. Under these arrangements, teachers are receiving site-specific, needs-based, inservice training, frequently in the form of credit courses on campus or on site (e.g., Teacher Corps). In some instances, inservice staff development is being provided as graduate degree programs like that, for example, developed between the University of Toledo and the Springfield, Ohio, local schools.[25]

But even this admirable effort can have its negative aspects. In my curiosity about these collaborative arrangements, I found an opportunity to discuss the experiences of some of the participants. Several exhibited a degree of anger and resentment that some teachers were merely occupying space in the on-site classroom and getting graduate credit toward a master's degree, with tuition paid by their school board and Teacher Corps. One teacher, citing the example of a lady who brought along her knitting to classes, related that she was totally absorbed in that activity, oblivious to what was going on around her. However, this type of arrangement should not be judged by such anomalies. They merely indicated that refinements have to be made. Several other authors support this type of collaborative arrangement. They support this tailoring of staff development to the teaching roles in specific school districts, thereby qualifying people to work in that specific kind of setting. This may imply that if a teacher so trained takes a new teaching position, additional site-specific inservice may be required. This clinical model preparation, therefore, "would be career long and job specific."[26]

It appears that this kind of college of education/school district collaboration is not yet commonplace. Probably Coleman explains why in his observation that preservice and inservice training have rarely been considered as but two phases of a training continuum. He states that "a fully competent professional"[27] is more likely if collaborative arrangements are utilized.

My intention is not to malign preservice teacher education. Attempts are being made at many institutions to prepare new programs based on thorough analysis of teaching as a task. Competency-based teacher education (CBTE), for example, is one such attempt to improve the preservice foundation. According to Dickson and Saxe, in CBTE programs three types of criteria are used to determine the competencies of the teacher: knowledge criteria, performance criteria, and product criteria. The first set of criteria assesses the teacher's understanding of concepts; the second, his or her teaching behavior; and the third, the achievement of the pupils whom the teacher has taught.[28]

CBTE, however, does not enjoy universal intellectual support. Coleman, for example, says that the research basis for the product criteria simply did not exist when the CBTE programs were being developed.[29] This view is consistent with that of Howey and his colleagues who decry the lack of a sufficient empirical base for programming change.[30] Coleman does, however, concede that the theoretical basis was sound and that the emphasis on performance was appropriate. This empirical basis, required for the development of new teacher preparation programming, is apparently difficult to establish.

Addressing this issue, Borg and his colleagues state that it is difficult to specify the precise elements of teaching behavior that most significantly affect pupil achievement. These people also suggest that we cannot soon expect any detailed set of training specifications simply because the available research base is much too limited.[31]

That is not to say, however, that there is no research base at all. Coleman feels that the pertinent characteristics of effective teaching can be analyzed in terms of in-class teaching behavior on a number of dimensions and that positive changes in teacher behavior can be achieved on these dimensions. He further states that "some inservice programs have demonstrated the ability to change relevant behaviors,"[32] thus allowing us to take heart.

It does appear that some effective teacher behaviors are beginning to emerge through research. Rosenshine and Furst concluded fairly early in the game that they had isolated some of these variables. They listed five instructional variables that they found to have a strong relationship with measurements of student achievement: clarity, variability, enthusiasm, task orientation and/or businesslike behavior, and student opportunity to learn.[33]

Evidence appears to be mounting supporting the conclusion that programs that focus on these variables can change teacher in-class behavior and can positively affect student learning.[34]

## A FINAL WORD

This discussion raises two obvious questions: What are the characteristic behaviors of an effective teacher? And what are the characteristics of an effective school? A synthesis of more recent research can provide valuable information and considerable guidance respecting these questions. Some rather intimate knowledge of both these issues is vital to those who have responsibility for providing inservice staff development. These issues are addressed in the next chapter.

# CHAPTER 5
## EFFECTIVE SCHOOLS AND EFFECTIVE TEACHERS

We hear numerous references to effective schools and effective teachers. We engage in inservice staff development activities so that our schools and our teachers will be more effective. But do we know what our schools and teachers will be like when they are effective? It appears that, even here, there are as many conceptions of effectiveness as there are people working in, being responsible for, or making observations of our schools. The purpose of this chapter is to delineate in some detail those attributes that research suggests characterize effective schools and teachers.

### THE EFFECTIVE SCHOOL

A number of authors have presented the results of research and synthesis respecting effective schools. For the moment I am ignoring the so-called "effective schools research." Because of its insidious nature, I am addressing the associated concepts specifically a little later on in this chapter. I am assuming that you, the reader, subscribe without embarrassment or hypocrisy to the notion of educating the whole child for the long-term good of all that is best in our society. I am not interested in the mere cosmetics or the peripheral and superficial aspects of education, such as scores on narrowly defined standardized tests. My concern is with the fundamentals of living with each other and becoming lifelong creative and learning human beings.

I think that the members of the Commission on Excellence had these long-term notions in mind when they wrote their report *A Nation at Risk*. There, three strong themes emerge: the identifying characteristic of American schools is, in general, not excellence but mediocrity; we cannot have mediocrity and pursue excellence; and if concerted action is not taken to change the current state of affairs, then the future of the nation, as a nation, is "at risk."[1]

Staff development personnel share both the responsibility and the opportunity to enhance the utilization of the five major educational variables addressed in the commission's major recommendations:

1. *Curriculum content:* Are present courses meeting the general objectives of the five new basics (English, mathematics, science, social studies, and computer science)? If not, the curriculum must be changed.
2. *Standards and expectations:* Are expectations high enough and for appropriate ends?
3. *Time:* Is present time utilization efficient, effective, and for appropriate purposes?
4. *Teaching:* How can its status be enhanced? How can disruption be minimized? How can quality performance be recognized?
5. *Leadership:* The superintendent and the school principals are the pivotal people in a school district. How can we ensure that these people have or develop and practice what we know to be good management techniques and processes and administrative practice?

This report also addresses at least four other issues that must provide part of the context in which staff development personnel operate:

1. Educators must become models of lifelong learners. The "learning society" is the ultimate goal.
2. Parents and students must accept their share of the responsibility for student success. How can they be brought to the necessary realization and acceptance of that principle?
3. Quality education implies educational excellence for all students. There are no exceptions.
4. The high school is not the totality of education. Primary and elementary education should provide the necessary foundation. If we don't achieve excellence at the elementary level, then high school education has little chance of success.

The context, then, in which inservice continuing education personnel work should be neither simplistically nor narrowly conceived. The fully functioning student-as-human being is the focus, with the higher good of society being the ultimate goal. The intervening variables (teachers, supervisors, administrators, and other support people) are those with whom staff development people must work to achieve the goals that comprise the *raison d'être* of schools and schooling.

From a survey of a number of listings and compilations of the characteristics of effective schools I have identified six important sources.[2] From them it

*EFFECTIVE SCHOOLS AND EFFECTIVE TEACHERS*

is possible to extract at least twenty significant characteristics that contribute to effective schools. These characteristics are listed in Figure 5-1.

### Figure 5-1
### Characteristics of Effective Schools

- A realistic, articulated, and understood philosophy of education is in place and is used as the guiding principle of the school.

- Both academic and behavioral goals are clearly defined and articulated and are understood and accepted by all. Goals are determined by a process of consultation with all concerned.

- A supportive school climate exists.

- The principal demonstrates qualities and utilizes processes and techniques of good leadership.

- Teachers have high expectations for students and for themselves. They take pride in their work.

- All educational personnel are models of lifelong learners for their students. They have principles and their living exemplifies them.

- Curriculum reflects and is consistent with stated goals of education. It is comprehensive in scope; not narrowly conceived.

- Teacher evaluation and supervision is ongoing, consistent, supportive, and humane.

- Student evaluation is supportive of continued growth.

*Continued*

## Figure 5-1 (continued)

---

School policies and procedures, including disciplinary processes, are workable and consistent with stated educational goals.

---

Parents and other "community" are involved in and are supportive of the school.

---

Teachers and principals care about each other and about the students. They develop a nurturing atmosphere and assist students in developing similar characteristics. Interactions are based on mutual trust and respect. People feel safe and secure.

---

Learning time is used efficiently with few disruptions.

---

There is a conscious, active concern about students' needs, and they are addressed, not merely by lip service. Educating exists within holistic concepts, and explicit efforts are directed toward the development of positive self-concepts, self-worth, and personal pride and integrity.

---

Student activities are well-established components of the total school structure.

---

Necessary levels of student services are provided.

---

Instructional standards are not confused with standardization. Instructional efforts are neither trivialized nor oversimplified but take place in a humanistic and supportive manner.

---

Structuring of schooling components foster the development of student independence, acceptance of responsibility, and positive social living.

# EFFECTIVE SCHOOLS AND EFFECTIVE TEACHERS

**Figure 5-1 (continued)**

> There exists a system of open two-way communications involving administration, faculty and staff, students, parents, and other publics.

> Participative and consultation-based decision-making processes are in place.

Gene Bedley[3], has written an excellent little book called *How Do You Recognize a Good School When You Walk into One?* Included in it is a "'Good' School? Checklist," which you will probably find quite useful. It is given in Figure 5-2.

There have been a number of interesting research studies conducted in an effort to determine the characteristics of effective schools. An excellent synthesis of much of this research has been provided by Squires[4] and his colleagues. Their synthesis (reprinted with permission of the Association for Supervision and Curriculum Development and D. A. Squires, E. G. Huitt, and J. K. Segars, copyright 1983 by the Association for Supervision and Curriculum Development; all rights reserved) seem to indicate that, based on research efforts conducted in the United States and England, effective schools have at least the following thirty-eight characteristics:

1. Students believe that success is related to hard work, not to luck.
2. Students have a sense of control over their destinies.
3. Teachers have extensive contact with a limited number of students.
4. Shared expectations and strong coordination exist respecting school rules.
5. There is consistency in the administration of school rules and in enforcing classroom behavior.
6. Students perceive that discipline is administered fairly.
7. There is an absence of punitive or authoritarian faculty attitudes toward students.
8. Rewards of the school are distributed fairly.
9. Students, faculty, administration, and the community feel that they determine their future by their own actions.
10. The school fosters the understanding that behaviors have effects.
11. Students strive for mastery in their academic work.
12. Students feel that the school is helping them to master their academic work.
13. School faculty have a belief that students are able to master the academic requirements.
14. Teachers and principals spend most of the school day on instructional activities.
15. Rewards are offered for achievement.

16. There are few student differentiations respecting their instructional programs.
17. The principal operates the school with a conscious purpose in mind.
18. The principal emphasizes academic standards.
19. The principal provides support, inservice education, and instructional and disciplinary coordination.
20. The principal regularly observes classrooms and confers with teachers on instructional matters.
21. The school building is well maintained and tastefully decorated and provides pleasant working conditions for students.
22. Staff members are available for consultation by students about their problems.
23. Teachers expect students to succeed and achieve.
24. Nonclass activities allow students and teachers to work together toward common goals.
25. Faculty and administration have arrived at a working consensus on patterns of acceptable behavior for faculty, students, and administrators.
26. There is a working consensus on how school life is organized.
27. There are structured opportunities for faculty and administrators to develop and reinforce consensus.
28. Teachers feel that their interests are taken into account in decision making.
29. A high proportion of students hold responsible positions at school.
30. All students have equal and fair access to academic and co-curricular programs.
31. The principal is perceived by students and faculty as modeling expectations of fair and equal treatment.
32. Teachers provide positive role models for children.
33. Teachers have high expectations for all children, regardless of race or class.
34. Inservice for faculty encourages self-reflection and skill building in areas promoting equal opportunity.
35. The principal actively "sets the tone" of the school by observing classrooms, enforcing the discipline code in a fair but firm manner, and setting faculty-supported goals for the school.
36. The school has a philosophy that provides a focus that is supported by administration, students, and teachers.
37. Time is spent efficiently and directly on academic skills.
38. Teachers usually handle their own discipline problems.

The last eighteen of these characteristics were derived from an extensive longitudinal study conducted in London, England, by Rutter[5] and his colleagues. They concluded that schools do have an effect on student achievement and that the most significant characteristics of schools appeared to be social and institutional, the most salient of these institutional characteristics seeming to be

1. Academic emphasis.
2. Skills of teachers.
3. Teachers' instructional behaviors.
4. The system of rewards and punishments.
5. Students' services.
6. Opportunity for student participation.
7. School organization and administration.

It is important to notice that practically all the characteristics of effective schools mentioned in this chapter *are or can be affected by teachers and their administrators*. In other words, *effective schools are within our grasp. We can have effective schools if we have the will to have effective schools.*

If you wish to pursue the matter of effective schools further or if you are interested in instruments and procedures for assessing school effectiveness, you may wish to refer to the resources appendix (Appendix B).

## EFFECTIVE SCHOOLS REQUIRE EFFECTIVE TEACHERS

The major portion of ISSD activities is directed specifically toward assisting teachers in becoming more effective. Therefore, it seems necessary to have at least some general notion of just what an effective teacher is. If you have some paradigm of the effective teacher, then you will have a much stronger base from which to analyze the results of any needs assessment process. This is even more true if you can be confident that your teacher effectiveness paradigm is supported by research. The last section certainly has set the stage for this discussion since a number of characteristics of effective teachers were implicit in the effective school characteristics.

This discussion is provided primarily for those who may not have experience in teacher evaluation processes. You may have excellent adult teaching technique, but you may not have a ready concept of "the effective teacher." If you are experienced in teacher observation and assessment, you will probably be familiar with the information I have chosen to present here.

This is not meant to be an exhaustive study into either the salient factors related to effective instruction or teaching or of teacher evaluation. It is meant, instead, to be a brief overview for those staff development personnel who have not already had the opportunity to familiarize themselves with and to synthesize this kind of information. From the numerous resources available, I have selected just two sources of information to illustrate this discussion.

The approaches of Dr. Madeline Hunter at UCLA have attracted a great deal of attention and appears to hold much promise for effective teaching. Dr. Hunter

## Figure 5-2
## "Good" School? Checklist

_____ 1. Does the school have a definite philosophical rationale for its professional practices?

_____ 2. Does the school philosophy include persuasion and influence?

_____ 3. Has the school identified the character traits and academic objectives of an educated person?

_____ 4. Does the principal provide leadership to the staff in curriculum and instruction?

_____ 5. Do the personnel have a positive mental attitude?

_____ 6. Are parents not only encouraged to volunteer in the school but also recognized for their service?

_____ 7. Do the personnel in the school have a sense of humor?

_____ 8. Are parents' and teachers' suggestions carefully weighed, considered, and implemented?

_____ 9. Is there a balance between production and satisfaction?

_____ 10. Does the school office have friendly and helpful personnel?

_____ 11. Does the school encourage questions, problem identification, and problem solving by people affected by the system?

_____ 12. Does the school develop criteria for the selection and implementation of each of its programs?

_____ 13. Is there an effort to gather broad community data in the establishment of school goals and objectives?

_____ 14. Does the school program include curriculum at a challenging level while providing the emotional support to accomplish learning tasks?

_____ 15. Does the school have a strong basics program, broadly defined, that includes skill getting and skill application?

_____ 16. Has the school identified the different aspects of relationships that enhance maximum goal attainment?

_____ 17. Has the school identified and shared several indicators of success based on students' progress?

_____ 18. Has the school identified the qualities of effective teachers?

_____ 19. Does the school really value people by celebrating major events in their careers and lives?

_____ 20. Are there numerous interpersonal relationships where people are talking with other people?

## Figure 5-2 (continued)

____ 21. Does the principal encourage an open-door policy for face-to-face communication?
____ 22. Is home/school communication a top priority in the school?
____ 23. Is there a concern about the quantity and quality of papers that funnel through the school?
____ 24. Does the school provide decision-making training for all adults involved in making decisions?
____ 25. Are decision-making alternatives telegraphed to decision-making participants?
____ 26. Are the personnel in the school engaged in ongoing self-renewal and training?
____ 27. Is the teacher's evaluation based on feedback and mutual learning?
____ 28. Does the school provide an open forum for parents to discuss present and future issues?
____ 29. Does the school invest time in parent education?
____ 30. Are the skills of effective parents identified and successes shared with other parents?
____ 31. Does the school have a new parent orientation?
____ 32. Do kids like school?
____ 33. Do the principal and the teachers demonstrate that they like kids?
____ 34. Does the school make an extra effort to get to know kids?
____ 35. Is there careful consideration and quality time given to student placement?
____ 36. Are new students given clear information on the student policies?
____ 37. Is the school's discipline plan carefully developed, implemented, and communicated to teachers, parents, and students?
____ 38. Does the school discipline policy focus on training children to make more appropriate choices?
____ 39. Do the school personnel demonstrate a genuine concern for the human dignity and welfare of all its students?
____ 40. Does the school provide a student handbook?
____ 41. Does the school have a strong student activity program that builds relationships with kids?
____ 42. Is there an interface of love and learning in the school?
____ 43. Does the school actively seek community input as to how it's doing?

From Gene A. Bedley, *How Do You Recognize a Good School When You Walk into One? Hundreds of Practical Ideas,* People-Wise Publications, 14252 East Mall, Irving, Calif. 92714. Reprinted with permission.

emphasizes that teaching has to be objective specific, with objectives and instructional technique adjusted to the learner. Through her program called Instructional Theory into Practice (ITIP), she teaches the application principles of the following teaching strategies:

1. Motivation theory
2. Reinforcement theory
3. Practice theory:
   Meaning
   Modeling
   Monitoring
4. Sequence theory
5. Retention theory
6. Transfer theory

There is really nothing new here. We studied it all in our educational psychology courses, even if we never did feel all that confident about our abilities to apply the principles in our actual teaching. However, Hunter shows how the theory can be effectively applied. If you feel that you need to be refreshed respecting these theories, you may wish to consult some of her books, listed in the resource appendix.

Let's take a look at the approach of one school district with respect to its concept of effective teaching. Of the numerous listings available, I have selected that of the Orange County (Virginia) public schools as representative.[6] That school district holds twelve teaching categories to be indicative of an effective teacher. These categories are given in Figure 5-3.

**Figure 5-3**

**Teaching Categories Indicative of Teacher Behavior**

1. Classroom routines

2. Essential techniques of instruction

3. Provision for individual learning

## Figure 5-3 (continued)

4. Lesson plans and objectives for learning

5. Evaluation of student progress

6. Critical thinking and problem solving

7. Teacher-student rapport

8. Student motivation

9. Management of student behavior

10. Student participation in learning activities

11. Reports and routine duties

12. School and community relations

From Clarence M. Edwards, Jr., and John J. English, "Professional Growth Incentives: A Career Ladder That Works," unpublished paper on 1983–85 Pay-for-Performance and Staff Development Study, Orange County Public Schools, Orange, VA. Used with permission.

Orange County educators have also specified the characteristics that they believe teachers will exhibit if competent instruction is taking place. The district calls the listing "Procedures for Effective Teaching." It is given in Figure 5-4.

**Figure 5-4**

**Procedures for Effective Teaching**

1. A model of courtesy is exhibited.

2. Positive associations are used with enthusiastic or humorous statements.

3. The teacher circulates among students inviting participation.

4. The teacher mediates or redirects incorrect responses.

5. Students are asked to describe the learning objectives.

6. Concrete examples are used to link learning objectives to prior learning.

7. Guided practice with teacher shaped responses is used.

8. The teacher monitors student readiness to proceed to independent practice.

9. Student independent practice without grades is used to determine the success of instruction.

10. Questioning techniques are used to assess fluency and stimulate divergent thinking.

11. Transition strategies for group and class changes are established.

12. Expectations of behavior and routines are explained.

13. The teacher anticipates student behaviors instead of reacting to them.

14. Nonverbal communication techniques are used to encourage appropriate behavior.

15. The teacher makes a statement to the whole group and then directs it to an individual.

Reprinted with permission of Orange County Public Schools, Orange, VA.

If you wish to pursue this matter of teaching effectiveness criteria, contact the district offices of several of your neighboring school districts. Virtually all of them have developed teacher evaluation instruments that, one supposes, are based on criteria of effective teaching. It will probably amaze you that, while there will certainly be many common elements, there are also likely to be many differences. I would also encourage you to explore some of the materials listed in the resources appendix.

## THE INEFFECTIVENESS OF "EFFECTIVE SCHOOLS RESEARCH"

In the last two sections, we have looked at some of the admirable efforts to isolate the defining characteristics of effective schools and effective teachers. However, some of the new thrusts took a somewhat unexpected course, and the decade 1975 to 1985 was characterized by numerous attempts to change education, some of which appear to be regressive. These new directions carried various names (back to the basics, minimum competency testing, competency-based teacher education, and education vouchers, for example) and were accompanied by diverse emphases such as climate improvement programs, clinical supervision, leadership style, teacher stress and burnout, school discipline, high teacher expectations, academic team games, and new grouping strategies.

Probably the greatest challenge, however, was mounted by utilizing that aberration, the so-called "effective schools research" by which it was attempted to demonstrate that the "effective schools model" was a sought-after panacea. Generally built on some extreme and narrowly defined utilizations of Bloom's[7] notions of mastery learning and Mager's[8] educational objectives, the model advocated that students practice a very limited range of precisely defined learning objectives, generally in reading and mathematics, with assessment by means of rigid standardized testing. There was such a public clamoring for results and accountability that school districts and their staff development people succumbed to the pressure. (It is my opinion that those who are pushing such narrow models of excellence are prostituting themselves. In my value system, educational prostitutes or pushers have no more virtue than do any other kind.) They showed that results, educational "highs," could be obtained.

### Argument Sounds Reasonable, But...

The methods utilized in achieving such results may be very attractive, maybe because they are so deceptive—just like other artificially induced "highs." Besides, the model was built on an argument that appeared to be so reasonable. It went something like this:

The major purpose of schooling is teaching and learning. If one believes this, then it necessarily follows that one must also agree that the only basis for determining school effectiveness is in terms of student outcomes. Furthermore, a school or school district's priorities will be evident in which outcomes it measures and how they are measured. Since subjective measures are old fashioned, it follows that modern, standardized (preferably computerized) testing is the only appropriate and valid assessment procedure. This latter argument was supported by statements such as "For educators to know that they have taught effectively and to ascertain that students are learning with efficacy, they must be able to describe the resulting knowledge, skills and behaviors that indicate student mastery."[9] All this was couched in patriotic terms, using such catch phrases as "quality education," "equal educational opportunity," "accountability," "describable results," "benefits accruing to all students," and so on.

It is a very persuasive argument isn't it? But it is not a logical one, and its foundation is seriously flawed. Furthermore, the natural desires of people, especially minorities, for defensible education for their children, and for equal opportunity, were exploited and were used against the people. It was, and is, fraudulent!

If you examine the argument, you will quickly realize that it does not follow that the only basis for determining school effectiveness is in terms of immediately measurable student outcomes. Nor does it follow that a school district's priorities are evident from the outcomes measured or how they are measured. Neither does it follow that subjective measures are invalid. So-called objective testing is deceptive; it is as subjective as any other kind of assessment—if not more so. It merely has the appearance of being nonsubjective. It was a subjective decision, for example, to select particular objectives to be taught and to be tested. The model is very *precise*, but precision should not be confused with accuracy. Furthermore, because something can be easily quantified does not constitute an argument for its virtue, just as being able to provide a "body count" does not make war virtuous.

**The Process of Learning is Ignored**

The model is an outputs-only model of learning, with outputs defined in extremely narrow terms. It is implied, seemingly with no awareness of possible dispute, that only those items of knowledge that can be easily measured, described, and statistically manipulated are valid as learning objectives. Process is almost completely ignored, and affective learnings cannot be countenanced. This model of learning denies the essential humanity of children as learners, denies their very childhood, and cannot even begin to address the value-laden aspirations that we have for our children. It is the antithesis of democracy, the death of creativity, and the fostering of strict, autocratic, mindless regimentation appropriate only for an Orwellian[10] world. What I found even more saddening and surprising was that respected journals were instrumental in promoting the notions associated with the effective schools model, with almost no critical analysis of the claims in its articles.

Even state agencies have fallen victim to the simplistic attractiveness of its promises. The state of Ohio, for example, through its Department of Education, has committed itself to an effective schools model, apparently in an effort to regain public confidence in its schools. Among its statements of rationale is the sentiment that effective schools shouldn't get "bogged down in process at the expense of product."[11] Apparently, any end justifies the means, even if it means turning children into robots—which is precisely what the "effective curricula" require.

**The Importance of Needs Assessment**

If a staff developer, supervisor, or administrator wants to avoid falling victim to the "effective schools" siren song, then any assessment of needs must be conducted in a context of an articulation of the goals of schooling. Are the goals of your school or district limited to the pitifully narrow and oversimplified range of objectives measured by the "effective schools" test instruments? Examine the Chicago Mastery Learning[12] stuff, for example, and then answer the question again. Try to determine if this kind of "educational material" is good for children, or if it is merely a vacuous product?

It might be worthwhile to undertake some assessment of implicit goals of schooling in your school's or school district's client area. What do parents, politicians, business leaders, teachers, principals, students, and district administrators feel are the goals of schooling in nonjargon terms? That is, what are all the goals that your school or district is expected to address and attempt to meet? Where, for example, does respect for all people regardless of race, creed, or color come in? Where does an appreciation of freedom of speech and of religion come in the educational priorities of the school district's clients? The effective schools model cannot begin to address such subjective, value-laden, criteria. These objectives cannot be easily measured by any kind of test, nor can they be measured in the short term.

In one survey of this type, Sapone[13] determined that teachers, principals, and superintendents diverge significantly in their views respecting what characterized effective schools. It might be reasonable to assume that a survey of the goals of schools would reveal an even greater divergency respecting purposes of schooling.

I wish to emphasize that, when we engage in a serious attempt at school change and are utilizing staff development as an aspect of that, we are dealing with an exercise that has a very wide scope. We must keep in mind that, as Professor Theodore Sizer[14] points out, programs for students must be humanistic, not mechanistic, and that we must not confuse standardization with standards. Furthermore, we must not trivialize the process of learning by oversimplifying it.

It is also important to keep in mind that staff development needs assessment has to take place within the context of the school's and the district's developed curricula based on determined philosophy and not on some circumventing of that curricula by overly zealous and simplistic response to truncated educational objectives.[15]

It is also important not to be captivated by the surface aspects of standardized testing. *The Mismeasure of Man* by Stephen Jay Gould[16] convincingly establishes that our faith in standardized testing is ill founded. The weakness of its foundation is further eroded by such lucid discussions of the nature of intelligence as is found in Gardner's *Frames of Mind*.[17] It might be worthwhile to keep in mind that it is easy to be deceived by attractive surface features. We become infatuated by nice clean statistics—but the "ship of education" is being lured on the rocks by the statistical siren song.

If our needs assessment is to be valid, we must be cognizant of the assumptions on which we and our teaching faculties are operating, and we must be satisfied that these assumptions are valid and will stand the tests of time and defensible research.

Furthermore, our perceptions and our assumptions will determine not only how we undertake needs assessment but also how we analyze and interpret the data. If our assumptions are invalid, it is likely that our needs assessment interpretations will be just as invalid. If our perceptions are limited, our interpretations of our needs assessment data will likely be just as limited.

Yes, there is a great demand for accountability and for increased results. But let's not lose sight of the long term in our efforts to satisfy short-term demands. Naisbett[18] argues in *Megatrends* that economic decline is caused by business managers who are preoccupied with short-term results and quantitative performance measures while neglecting the long-term necessities of focusing on investments and innovation. Similarly, we must not lose sight of the long-term view in education as we attempt the short-term aim of satisfying public opinion with inflationary educational "results." As Beegle points out, students need to learn about feeling and valuing and numerous affective dimensions of human living. He says "The world...is too complex, too ambiguous for easy generalizations or simplistic 'quick-fix quarterly reports.' As decisions are made, attention must be given to the long-term consequences."[19]

To begin to stimulate your thinking about school goals and the possibilities of this kind of investigation in your school jurisdiction, consider an instrument developed by the White Bear Lake (Minnesota) School District. That school district developed three instruments based on a listing of eighteen possible goals. Respondents were asked to indicate, first, their perception of the importance of each of the goals; then, the degree of responsibility the school district should accept for developing each characteristic in young people; and, third, the respondent's perception of the school district's effort and success in helping young people develop each of the characteristics.

Figure 5-5 contains the eighteen goals proposed by White Bear Lake School District. Several indicators are provided after each goal listing.

### Figure 5-5

**White Bear Lake
Needs Assessment Instrument**

---

1. Being a good citizen.
    - Awareness of civic rights and responsibilities.
    - Attitudes for productive citizenship in a democracy.
    - Attitude of respect for personal and public property.
    - Understanding of the obligations and responsibilities of citizenship.

### Figure 5-5 (continued)

2. Having respect for and getting along with people who think, dress, and act differently.
   - Appreciation for and an understanding of other people and other cultures.
   - Understanding of political, economic, and social patterns of the rest of the world.
   - Awareness of the interdependence of races, creeds, nations, and cultures.
   - Awareness of the processes of group relationships.
3. Having an understanding of the changes that take place in the world.
   - Ability to adjust to the changing demands of society.
   - Awareness of and the ability to adjust to a changing world and its problems.
   - Understanding of the past, identifying with the present, and possessing the ability to meet the future.
4. Having skills in reading, writing, speaking, and listening.
   - Ability to communicate ideas and feelings effectively.
   - Skills in oral and written English.
5. Having an understanding for practicing democratic ideas and ideals.
   - Loyalty to American democratic ideals.
   - Patriotism and loyalty to ideals of democracy.
   - Knowledge and appreciation of the rights and privileges in our democracy.
   - Understanding of our American heritage.
6. Knowing how to examine and use information.
   - Ability to examine constructively and creatively.
   - Ability to use scientific methods.
   - Reasoning abilities.
   - Skills to think and proceed logically.
7. Having an understanding for and practicing the skills of family living.
   - Understanding and appreciation of the principles of living in the family group.
   - Attitudes leading to acceptance of responsibilities as family members.
   - Awareness of future family responsibilities and achievement of skills in preparing to accept them.
8. Having a respect for and getting along with people with whom we work and live.
   - Appreciation and respect for the worth and dignity of individuals.
   - Respect for individual worth and understanding of minority opinions and acceptance of majority decisions.
   - Cooperative attitude toward living and working with others.
9. Having the skills to enter a specific field of work.
   - Abilities and skills needed for immediate employment.
   - Awareness of opportunities and requirements related to a specific field of work.
   - Appreciation of good workmanship.
10. Being a good manager of money, property, and resources.
    - Understanding of economic principles and responsibilities.
    - Ability and understanding in personal buying, selling, and investment.
    - Skills in management of natural and human resources and the environment.
11. Having a desire for learning now and in the future.
    - Intellectual curiosity and eagerness for lifelong learning.
    - Positive attitude toward learning.
    - Positive attitude toward continuing independent education.

*Continued*

### Figure 5-5 (continued)

12. Being able to use leisure time constructively.
    - Ability to use leisure time productively.
    - Positive attitude toward participation in a range of leisure time activities—physical, intellectual, and creative.
    - Appreciation and interest that will lead to wise and enjoyable use of leisure time.
13. Having an understanding for and practicing the ideas of health and safety.
    - Effective individual physical fitness program.
    - Understanding of good physical health and well-being.
    - Sound physical health habits and information.
    - Concern for public health and safety.
14. Appreciating culture and beauty in the world.
    - Abilities for effective expression of ideas and cultural appreciation (fine arts).
    - Appreciation for beauty in various forms.
    - Creative self-expression through various media (art, music, writing, etc.).
    - Special talents in music, art, literature, and foreign languages.
15. Having the information needed to make job selections.
    - Self-understanding and self-direction in relation to student's occupational interests.
    - Ability to use information and counseling services related to the selection of a job.
    - Knowledge of specific information about a particular vocation.
16. Having a pride in work and a feeling of self-worth.
    - Feeling of student pride in his or her achievements and progress.
    - Self-understanding and self-awareness.
    - Student's feeling of positive self-worth, security, and self-assurance.
17. Having good character and self-respect.
    - Moral responsibility and a sound ethical and moral behavior.
    - Student's capacity to discipline himself or herself to work, study, and play constructively.
    - Moral and ethical sense of values, goals, and processes of free society.
    - Standards of personal character and ideas.
18. Having a general education.
    - Background and skills in the use of numbers, natural sciences, mathematics, and social sciences.
    - Fund of information and concepts.
    - Special interests and abilities.

---

From P. J. Koll and L. Cozad. *Staff Development: A Process Approach*, University of Wisconsin Extension, 1981. Reprinted with permisison of White Bear Lake School District.

Two other instruments may be of value to you at this point. The instruments given in Figures 5-6 and 5-7 were developed by the Arizona State Department of Education and were used as part of its needs assessment program.

## Figure 5-6
## Goal Ranking Instrument I

*Directions:* Ten goals are listed on the left-hand side of the page; two questions appear on the right-hand side. Answer *both* questions for *each* goal.

| GOALS | "NOW" Do schools NOW help every student with the following things? Check One |  |  | "SHOULD" SHOULD schools help every student with the following things? Check One |  |  |
|---|---|---|---|---|---|---|
|  | Yes | No | Don't Know | Yes | No | Don't Know |
| 1. Schools should help every student to understand art, music, literature, and drama in order to enjoy them all through life. | | | | | | |
| 2. Schools should help every student to be a good citizen all through life. | | | | | | |
| 3. Schools should help every student to be a creative thinker and make good judgments. | | | | | | |
| 4. Schools should help every student to feel good about himself or herself. | | | | | | |
| 5. Schools should help every student to gain skills in speaking, listening, reading, writing, and arithmetic. | | | | | | |
| 6. Schools should help every student to know and use good health habits. | | | | | | |
| 7. Schools should help every student to understand family life and be a responsible home member. | | | | | | |
| 8. Schools should help every student to like to learn. | | | | | | |
| 9. Schools should help every student to choose what he or she would like to be in the future and prepare him or her for that choice. | | | | | | |
| 10. Schools should help every student to accept all people, no matter how they look, talk, and live. | | | | | | |

Please add any goals that you feel are important but are not specified: _____

"Arizona Needs Assessment Program: A Report on Phase I," Office of Planning and Evaluation, Arizona State Department of Education, 1971. Reproduced by permission of the publisher, Arizona Department of Education, 1535 West Jefferson, Phoenix, Ariz. 85007.

### Figure 5-7
### Goal Ranking Instrument II

| School Is... | | | | | JOB OF TEACHING OR MANAGING | School Should Be... | | | | |
|---|---|---|---|---|---|---|---|---|---|---|
| very much | much | little | very little | undecided | | very much | much | little | very little | undecided |
| 4 | 3 | 2 | 1 | 0 | Teaching students to distinguish between right and wrong regarding values, morals, and ethics. | 4 | 3 | 2 | 1 | 0 |
| 4 | 3 | 2 | 1 | 0 | Teaching good health habits for physical well-being. | 4 | 3 | 2 | 1 | 0 |
| 4 | 3 | 2 | 1 | 0 | Teaching family life responsibilities. | 4 | 3 | 2 | 1 | 0 |
| 4 | 3 | 2 | 1 | 0 | Providing knowledge and skills to be responsible consumers. | 4 | 3 | 2 | 1 | 0 |
| 4 | 3 | 2 | 1 | 0 | Teaching the rights and duties of responsible citizenship. | 4 | 3 | 2 | 1 | 0 |
| 4 | 3 | 2 | 1 | 0 | Teaching respect for this country. | 4 | 3 | 2 | 1 | 0 |
| 4 | 3 | 2 | 1 | 0 | Developing respect for personal and public property. | 4 | 3 | 2 | 1 | 0 |
| 4 | 3 | 2 | 1 | 0 | Increasing acceptance of people regardless of sex, race, religion, or ethnic origin. | 4 | 3 | 2 | 1 | 0 |
| 4 | 3 | 2 | 1 | 0 | Helping each student to feel worthwhile. | 4 | 3 | 2 | 1 | 0 |
| 4 | 3 | 2 | 1 | 0 | Helping each student to acquire a sense of belonging. | 4 | 3 | 2 | 1 | 0 |
| 4 | 3 | 2 | 1 | 0 | Providing meal services for students. | 4 | 3 | 2 | 1 | 0 |
| 4 | 3 | 2 | 1 | 0 | Offering special services for children who are emotionally disturbed. | 4 | 3 | 2 | 1 | 0 |
| 4 | 3 | 2 | 1 | 0 | Offering special services for children who are gifted and talented. | 4 | 3 | 2 | 1 | 0 |

"Arizona Needs Assessment Program: A Report on Phase I." Office of Planning and Evaluation, Arizona State Department of Education, 1971. Reproduced by permission of the publisher, Arizona Department of Education, 1535 West Jefferson, Phoenix, Ariz. 85007.

## A FINAL WORD

In this chapter you were introduced to and examined some of the criteria we might use in deciding for ourselves what constitutes an effective school and effective teaching. Having made decisions of this nature, we are then in a position to begin a determination of appropriate goals for our schools or school systems. It is information of this type that helps mold our orientations to inservice staff development, a topic addressed in the next chapter.

# CHAPTER 6

## ORIENTATIONS TOWARD INSERVICE STAFF DEVELOPMENT

Since what is undertaken in the name of inservice staff development rests on the perceptions of the enterprise held by those in decision-making positions, I think it is important that some global positions be reviewed. These orientations will, to a very large degree, determine not only the form and process of needs assessment, as noted in the previous chapter, but also the forms and processes utilized in the delivery of the staff development product. We saw, for example, how a standardized test orientation can bias one's view of goals. One way to examine these orientations is to look at how staff development activity has been classified.

### VARIOUS APPROACHES TO INSERVICE

One of the first taxonomies of inservice seems to be that proposed in 1957 by Berge, Harris, and Walden[1] on the basis of a national U.S. survey. They concluded that there were three broad categories of inservice education for teachers:

1. *The centralized approach.* Initiated and conducted by central office personnel.
2. *The decentralized approach.* Initiated and conducted at the local school level utilizing school resouces and people.
3. *The centrally coordinated approach.* Coordinated and assisted by central office personnel with participatory decision making.

Later, in 1966, the National Education Association compiled a listing of nineteen different types of staff development activity for teachers (see Chapter 2),

ORIENTATIONS TOWARD INSERVICE STAFF DEVELOPMENT 55

and in 1975 Edelfelt[2] added a few more activities to the list. Generally speaking, these listings have very little value since it is impossible to distinguish a teacher's everyday activity from those said to be examples of staff development. Still later, however, Edelfelt[3] made a much greater contribution to the literature on the topic. He proposed a taxonomy of staff development activities that included five major categories: (1) degree of licensing related, (2) school improvement, (3) promotion, (4) retraining, and (5) personal development. His taxonomy is given in Figure 6-1.

Edelfelt also provided a concise overview of the preservice-inservice continuum over four aspects of teacher training: staff roles and responsibilities, operational procedure, training programs, and governance. (See Figure 6-2.) Depending on which of these elements seem most important, it can be seen that numerous philosophical positions can be taken by those interested in and concerned about the continuing education of teachers.

A number of authors have taken strong stands respecting what inservice staff development for teachers should consist of. Sobol,[4] for example, proposes the following criteria for teacher inservice:

1. Objectives are closely related to classroom realities.
2. Topics are limited to those that can be extensively treated during a workshop.
3. Skills and information are those that a teacher can use immediately in the classroom.
4. Workshop topics are concerned with teachers' daily problems.
5. Atmosphere is relaxed and unthreatening.
6. Teachers are actively involved in workshop activities; not passive listeners.
7. Demonstrations, guided practice, and follow-up are integral aspects of the inservice.
8. Workshop objectives are clarified to participants before commencement.
9. Self-assessment techniques are included.

While Sobol's guidelines are not exhaustive, they do outline some of the issues that have to be considered before any needs assessment is begun.

One author who is mentioned frequently in recent staff development literature is Joyce. From a review of two hundred research surveys, he and Showers[5] concluded that there were two major purposes for teacher staff development: "tuning," or improving, present skills and learning new skills. They see teachers tuning their skills when they engage in such activities as

1. Trying to become more affirmative.
2. Involving students more.
3. Managing logistics more efficiently.
4. Asking more penetrating questions.
5. Inducing students to be more productive.

## Figure 6-1
## Purposes and Conditions of Inservice Education

| Purpose | Process | Setting | Legal Sanction and/or Administrative Authority | Responsible Agency and/or Standard of Control | Reward | Motivation |
|---|---|---|---|---|---|---|
| Degree, credential, licensure | Formal college or university study | College or university campus, extension center | State law, state board policy, state department regulation, state professional licensure commission regulation | State board policy, state department regulation, state professional licensure commission standard | Degree, credential, license, better job opportunities | Legal and professional requirement |
| School improvement | Workshops, local seminars, analysis of professional practice with help | School district, teacher center, professional development center, training complex, school building, teaching station | Local school board policy, special state or federal legislation | School district policy, collective-bargaining contract | Improved school program, personal satisfaction, parent satisfaction, student satisfaction, salary increment | School board or district requirement, collective-bargaining contract |
| Professional advancement or promotion | Formal and informal study of teaching, administration, counseling (internship, etc.) | College or university campus, extension center, school district, teacher center, professional development center | School district policy, state law or regulation | School district criteria, state certification requirement | Qualification for better position, employment in better position | Requirement set by local and/or state agency |
| Retraining for new assignment | Courses, workshops, institutes, special training in new level or subject | College or university campus, school district | School district policy, state law or regulation | School district criteria, state certification requirement | Qualification for new position, employment in new position | Requirement determined by job, state certification requirement |
| Personal professional development | Choice of individual teacher | Setting appropriate to choice | None: but personal standards and peer pressure influence development | Personal/professional standard | New knowledge, improved competence, self-satisfaction | Personal desire or commitment |

From R. A. Edelfelt, ed., *Inservice Education: Criteria for and Examples of Local Programs* (Bellingham: Western Washington State College, 1977), adapted from "Inservice Education: Alive with Interest, Fraught with Problems" by R. A. Edelfelt, *Inservice* (Newsletter of the National Council of States on Inservice Education), Vol. 1, no. 2 (September 1976), pp. 2–3, 9. Reprinted with permission.

# Figure 6-2
## The Shifting Emphasis to Inservice Teacher Education

| Where We Are or Have Been | Where We Seem to Be Going |
|---|---|
| ***Staff Roles and Responsibilities*** | |
| Inservice education and career development viewed as an individual responsibility | Inservice education and career development viewed as an individual, colleague-to-colleague, and school responsibility |
| College/university personnel functioning as managers | College/university and school district personnel functioning as program facilitators |
| Interns working individually and in teams, usually with one teacher | Teachers, interns, and aides working cooperatively |
| Parents working occasionally on a short-term, voluntary basis | Parents, aides, and interns working in the school as partners on a continuous basis |
| ***Operational Procedures*** | |
| Courses offered primarily on the college/university campus at times established by the college/university | Teachers, the school district, and the college/university collaborating to develop inservice education wherever and whenever needed and desired |
| The college/university independent and autonomous in determining inservice education | Inservice education determined by assessing the needs of school program and school personnel and cooperatively using the information in planning |
| Inservice education programs largely repetitive and stereotyped | Creative models of inservice education developed through infusing new ideas |
| Instructional improvement viewed as an administrative concern and responsibility | Instructional improvement viewed as a professional concern and responsibility |
| Inservice education funded solely by the individual or the school system and controlled by the college/university or school system | Inservice education funded through the college/university and the school district, but controlled by a professional consortium |
| Funds provided to the college/university based on student credits | Funds provided to the college/university or school district based on program needs |
| ***Training Programs*** | |
| Offer isolated courses and workshops or course sequences planned to meet college/university degree requirements | Facilitate individually developed professional programs as part of career-long training |
| Process large numbers of teachers through the same course, with everyone doing essentially the same things | Personalize and individualize programs to improve curriculum or instruction |
| View the individual as the client | View the individual and the organization in which he or she works as clients |
| Often rely on big names as experts | Rely on many people, but particularly on one another in the organization as helpers |
| ***Governance*** | |
| The college/university exclusively autonomous | The college/university teacher organization and school district collaborating |
| The decision-making process closed | The decision making open and shared |
| The college/university staff advising and consulting | The college/university teacher organization and school district operating on a parity basis |
| The college/university having complete and total power | Shared power among cooperating organizations |
| The college/university acting in isolation | The college/university acting within a consortium involving the teacher organization, school district, and community |
| Teacher education viewed solely as a function of the college/university | Teacher education viewed as a cooperative enterprise among the college/university, teacher organization, school district, and the profession |

From R. A. Edelfelt, ed., *Inservice Education: Criteria for and examples of Local Programs* (Bellingham, Western Washington State College, 1977), pp. 6–7. Reprinted with permission.

6. Increasing the clarity and vividness of lectures and illustrations.
7. Understanding better the subject matter taught.

That is, teachers tune their skills when they work on their craft, consolidating their competence, and attempt to increase their effectiveness.

These authors concluded that for teachers to learn new skills or to master a new approach, three conditions needed to be satisfied: (1) the rationale of the new approach has to be explored and understood, (2) the ability to carry out the new strategies has to be developed, and (3) fresh content has to be mastered.

They concluded that fine tuning existing approaches is easier than mastering and implementing new ones, because the magnitude of change in the former is smaller and less complex. When one changes one's repertoire, one has to learn to think differently, to behave differently, and to help children adapt to and become comfortable with the new approaches. Therefore, the mastery of new techniques requires more intensive training than does fine tuning.

Joyce, in collaboration with Nicholson[6] proposed an inservice staff development taxonomy that had five categories: job embedded, job related, credential oriented, professional organization related, and self-directed. A brief description of each category follows:

1. *Job embedded*. Committees, team teaching, interaction with consultants, professional reading, and curriculum analysis. Since it has been determined that teachers do relatively little professional reading, teacher libraries at schools are recommended. The ready availability of appropriate books and other professional literature may be an inducement to more professional reading.
2. *Job related*. Inservice education activities that cannot be classified strictly as being a part of the teacher's job, for example, workshops, college courses, teacher exchanges, visits, teacher centers, training packages, computer-assisted instruction.
3. *Credential oriented*. Generally college courses. They state, however, that "both the literature and our survey of teachers have revealed that college courses have little relevance to [teacher inservice]."[7]
4. *Professional organization related*. Union conventions and workshops, specialized journals. They state that "The AFT has suggested an inservice plan which would be achieved through negotiated contracts...based on the individual teacher's self-diagnosis, self-development, and self-evaluation."[8]
5. *Self-directed*. The teacher as self-motivated artisan or professional who is interested in maintaining the currency of his or her skills and knowledge.

Joyce and his colleagues proposed an additional orientation. Because of lack of teacher mobility, it seems that teacher education competencies (and, hence, inservice staff development activities) "have to be related to and defined in terms of the roles which teachers and other school personnel are presently playing, rather than serving as stepping stones to other kinds of positions within the organization."[9]

Nicholson and Joyce outline three philosophical orientations to teacher education, including inservice education. They see these distinct philosophies or "value orientations" as being implicit rather than explicitly stated. The three chief value orientations that they see evident in the literature tend to describe teaching as

1. An act of mutual development and self-discovery.
2. Program implementation.
3. Skill and knowledge.[10]

## A FINAL WORD

While some attempt has been made to categorize approaches to inservice staff development for teachers, there is at present no generally accepted taxonomy. The philosophical positions are fluid and are not yet established on a sufficiently broad empirical basis. It is within this context that you have to decide on specific procedures and tools for needs assessment.

The chapters that follow should provide some guidance for you respecting that aspect of the enterprise.

# CHAPTER 7

## THE PROCESS OF NEEDS ASSESSMENT

In this chapter we shall examine some of the major aspects of the needs assessment process. Included in the chapter are discussions on delimiting the undertaking to manageable dimensions, the planning for needs assessment, a needs assessment model, and methods of data collection. The next chapter will offer examples of needs assessment instruments.

### DELIMITING NEEDS ASSESSMENT

The question naturally arises, "Where do I begin?"

It has to be assumed that the person or people leading a needs assessment process knows something about the district or schools being studied and, therefore, has some at least intuitive notions of where to begin based either on personal exposure over some period of time or from discussions with those who have requested that the needs assessment take place.

For example, we might ask if the perceived problems or areas of prime concern are of an administrative, supervisory, or instructional nature or some combination of these? Are the perceived problems arising from some other complex of the school system? Is it a superintendent–school board problem? Are there decision-making difficulties, suspect hiring practices, poor discipline, inadequate communications, or ineffective supervisory and evaluative practices? Is the district or school rife with rumor? Is morale low? Are parents hostile? Are students misplaced? Is student achievement low? Usually some felt discrepancy exists; a difference between what you perceived to be and what you feel ought to be.

In the absence of some confidence that you know where to begin, a multiphase process of needs assessment will likely be required to delimit the current effort to manageable proportions. That is, you cannot address all problems at once. Even if a comprehensive needs assessment is undertaken, some priority ranking will have to take place. You will have to determine which areas of need can be addressed by the inservice staff development of the nature and extent that can be provided by the human and material resources at your disposal.

If you attempt to undertake more than the human energies and material resources at your disposal can sustain, then the effort is likely to end in failure and frustration for you and for the teachers who are the intended beneficiaries. If you have not undertaken needs assessment before, it might be wise to undertake initial experiences at one subject and grade level or about one topic. More extensive needs assessment efforts can be undertaken as you experience the kinds of problems and frustrations that these efforts can throw your way. For example, if you undertake an extensive needs assessment that involves considerable quantification and statistical analysis, you will have to determine whether your data can be validly manipulated statistically and whether you have the expertise at your command to undertake the statistical analysis. It is frequently assumed that any numerical data can be statistically analyzed. This is not the case. Consider, for example, the following question from an actual needs assessment instrument:

Was the degree of teacher involvement

1. Too little?
2. About right?
3. Too much?

It may appear that you might add all the responses to each category and then find some sort of average as an aggregate description of all the responses. We might want to say, for example, that the response on this item "averaged" 2.25. But that statement has no meaning. The numbers are names of categories only, and have no quantifiable value. We could have asked the question this way, for example:

Was the degree of teacher involvement

a. Too little?
b. About right?
c. Too much?

This example is almost identical to the first, with the exception that the letters a, b, and c are used to designate the categories. We wouldn't think of averaging a, b, and c, would we? Since the numerals 1, 2, 3 in the first example are ordinal (i.e., rank-ordered) and are not cardinal (i.e., quantities), then it follows that 1, 2, and 3 cannot be averaged in this case. Before averaging could occur, we would have to know that the relative value difference from "too little" to "about right" is the same as the value difference from "about right" to "too much." In the present example, we have no way of knowing that. Any averaging based on such ordinal data would be meaningless.

It should be obvious, now, why the data derived from such questions have to be analyzed by processes appropriate to the type of data. If you feel that you do not have the statistical capability to manipulate various types of data, it would be wise to undertake initial needs assessment experiences whose data can be "eyeballed" or analyzed by very simple statistical tools. Otherwise, it may be wise to seek help in the construction of instruments and in the analysis of the data resulting from your collection efforts.

Once it has been determined which need areas can be addressed by the staff development methods and resources at the disposal of your school or district, then you can direct attention to determining which of several categories of needs can be addressed. Bishop,[1] for example, has identified seven categories of educational needs, which are utilized here with permission:

1. *Informational.* Some needs can be met if desired information has been made available. The frequently voiced complaints that "we don't know what is going on" or "nobody told me" illustrate this category of need. Methods of interpersonal communication might be the subject of the needs assessment.

2. *Content/skills.* This refers to the learning outcomes desired for the students. The philosophy of education and philosophy of instruction of the district along with specific instructional objectives might constitute the subject of the needs assessment undertaken.

3. *Competencies.* Competencies are denoted in relationship to the ability of teachers and other faculty members to deliver instruction, leadership, and classroom or program management and to provide for pupil-personnel needs. If there were a general feeling that the function of the educational enterprise was not as effective or as efficient as it might otherwise be, it might be decided to focus needs assessment efforts toward this category of need.

4. *Resources and utilization.* This category refers to the quantity and quality of resources available to effect the instructional and experiential program of the school or district. Resources may range all the way from adequacy of textbooks to the availability of audiovisual hardware; from actual classroom or laboratory facilities to additional professional personnel.

5. *Organization.* This is a rather large category and might easily be subdivided. Reference is made to classroom organization, administrative functioning, utilization of personnel, committee structures, organization of the curriculum and curricular objectives, and other general service aspects of the school or district. Faults in organization may be made manifest by myriad felt needs.

6. *Attitudes.* The commitment and feelings of teachers, administrators, support personnel, students, parents, and the community are all included in this category. People such as Downey[2] feel that this category of possible needs is generally inadequately and unsystematically addressed. While it may be difficult to address this needs category, it has the potential to be the most pressing and influential category of unmet needs.

THE PROCESS OF NEEDS ASSESSMENT

7. *Process.* This category refers to the general modes of operation, the ways of working, the general flow of decision making, the approaches to the curriculum, and the transactional elements and organization.

Bishop's formulation can be conveniently illustrated with a diagram. (See Figure 7-1). It will be noted that each of the categories of need can have at least three dimensions: the human dimension, the task dimension, and the institutional dimension. This diagram may assist you in further delimiting your needs assessment.

**Figure 7-1**

**The Relationship Between Need Areas and Need Categories as Formulated by Bishop**

| | NEED CATEGORIES | |
|---|---|---|
| **Human** | **Task** | **Institutional** |

NEED AREAS

INFORMATION

CONTENT/SKILLS

COMPENTENCIES

RESOURCES&UTILIZATION

ORGANIZATION

ATTITUDES

PROCESSES

From L. J. Bishop, *Staff Development and Instructional Improvement Plans and Procedures* (Boston: Allyn & Bacon, 1976), pp. 29–31. Reprinted with permission.

## ERRORS IN NEEDS ASSESSMENT

The literature abounds with discussions of needs assessment and records of related case studies. Additionally, the literature is beginning to list needs assessment in practically every "guide to conducting inservice." Yet the literature still indicates that inservice education is not a very successful enterprise. It seems logical to assume that if the enterprise is faulty, then it must be because of one or more weak links in the chain of procedures from needs assessment to project completion. According to Kuh and his colleagues, "some procedures used by school personnel have inherent weaknesses that undermine the validity and usefulness of the results."[3] They claim that a number of conceptual and procedural errors are frequently made. A brief outline of these suggested errors is given here. (This condensation has been done with permission of the authors. You are referred to the original document for a detailed discussion.)

1. The real reason for the needs assessment is not apparent for some reason. The real reason for the needs assessment may even be deliberately concealed.

2. Needs assessment is planned by one person or by a small number of individuals representing only a few of the target groups. It is strongly recommended that one person should never plan, implement, or interpret findings from a needs assessment alone since a diversity of perspectives will reduce the possibility that important issues are overlooked.

3. The target audiences are inappropriately selected or inaccurately described. In other words, the people responsible for the planning don't know with sufficient clarity the audience for the ISSD.

4. A strength analysis is not performed. It is suggested that a strength analysis should be performed in addition to the needs analysis so that a perspective can be maintained and confidence will not be eroded while the needs or weaknesses are focused on. (The object of a strength analysis is to determine the relative strength of the various diagnosed needs. A particular need may indicate that action should be taken immediately to address it, while another diagnosed need may be such that it can wait awhile. A third identified need may require much more extensive and long-term effort than a fourth determined need, and so on.)

5. The needs assessment focuses exclusively on individuals rather than including an assessment of the organization within which they work. It must be recognized that the environment in which a teacher works may facilitate or inhibit performance. The physical facilities and resources as well as administrative processes, attitudes, and assumptions need to be taken into account. Of course, the possible weaknesses or needs of the teacher must be considered as well.

6. The definition of need is based entirely on discrepancy formulas, defining need as the distance between a desired or ideal state of functioning and present performance. It is important to measure the degree of importance

of the items being assessed as well as the discrepancy. Ideal states, the standards of measurement of the discrepancies, do not imply "necessity."[4] "Necessary states" or even "desirable states" would be better standard.

7. A single criterion or method is used to determine need.[5] Three criteria need to be addressed in particular: (a) Needs cannot be determined merely by asking people what their needs are. A standard rule seems to be that one should use a minimum of three needs assessment instruments. (b) Arbitrary criteria, such as national norms, political benchmarks, and so on, may be grossly inappropriate when applied to a specific situation. Needs must be determined in terms of relevant contextual criteria. (c) The majority is not always right. It may be highly injurious to the education of children to have parents "democratically" determine the content and processes of curriculum—simply because most parents do not have professional education backgrounds. Besides, voting on issues may restrict discussion or may even be used precisely to stifle discussion.

8. Political pressure alone is allowed to determine need. Lobby groups or special interest groups should not determine needs. Mob psychology is not known to be rational or consistent.

9. Needs are given priority by a rank ordering process. This means that the needs "on top" get completely satisfied before the next need is addressed. It may make more educational sense to give some attention to each of the first twenty needs or some attention to all needs in light of decisions about which of the needs cannot wait to be addressed. Rank ordering merely indicates order of importance, not how much more important.

10. Positive and negative side effects are overlooked. The needs assessment itself may have both positive and negative effects. One negative effect, for example, is that teachers may feel that a "witch hunt" is being conducted and may distrust and subvert future district thrusts.

11. Needs assessment must be completed before planning can begin. In a very real way, needs assessment is never completed because it is an ongoing process, a part of cyclical planning. Some needs may be addressed while others are being determined. You must begin to plan as soon as you are satisfied that you have adequate information to allow you to begin. If you wait until you have a "complete" needs assessment, you may never be able to begin!

12. Needs assessment viewed as an end in itself. There seems to be some natural propensity to closure. Because of the time and energy that can be expended on this activity, there may be some desire, even pressure, to produce a finished product. The completion or partial completion of a needs assessment merely defines a starting point for needs addressing; it is a way station, not a termination point.

It is obvious, therefore, that needs assessment is not a simplistic time-specific, task-specific activity. It is, rather, one feature of the totality of schools management, a feature that is continuous and ever changing. If you perceive it from this perspective, then needs assessment may become a means to keep your school or district responsive to the needs that now exist or that may emerge over time.

## PLANNING FOR NEEDS ASSESSMENT

I have emphasized throughout that staff development has to be conducted according to highly professional methods. One aspect of this professionalism is involvement of all people who will be affected by the proposed efforts. This criterion exists for needs assessment no less than for the other phases of staff development. It is imperative that teachers, in particular, be engaged in a participative and consultative manner. Otherwise, they may legitimately ask what you have to hide and, understandably, may distrust your efforts.

The opinions of experts in the field, consistent with research results, support the stance that success in any staff development effort is strongly and directly related to whether the people for whom the inservice activity was designed felt that they had genuinely participated in planning and expediting the activity. Research results strongly suggest that if planning for all phases of staff development does not involve the intended recipients, then the project lacks both validity and any strong defense.

It is important, even crucial,[6] that this involvement not be ignored or carried out in a superficial manner. The politics in this case have a strong base. Derr,[7] for example, points out that professional educators have high autonomy needs. If they are to feel a sense of ownership and if they are to exhibit attitudes of receptivity, then it is imperative that they perceive themselves as equal partners in a search for a common goal and as having an equal stake in the outcomes.[8] The implication is that all role groups with a stake in the activity should have an opportunity to be involved in all stages of the planning and execution of the effort. Ackoff[9] suggests that such planning must be flexible and interactive.

However, the basis for this "participative management" position is not only political but also pragmatic. Erly and Greenberg[10] point out that the perspective brought to bear on the data gathering and on its analysis may be severely limited by the nature of the insight (or its lack) of those undertaking the inquiry. If genuine needs are going to be permitted to emerge, then people have to be involved. The more people who are involved in the process, the more likely valid needs will not be ignored. But, anyway, you would want to conduct the process in an unbiased and fair manner.

How many people you should involve in the needs assessment process will depend on the locale and the scope of the intent. The process may include all the target group or a very small representative committee.

If you are principal of a small school, for example, you may decide to involve all faculty who wish to be involved in a series of after-school and lunch hour meetings, with released time for those whose responsibility it is to collate and prepare the data. A principal of a large school might choose some combination of appointed members and democratically elected faculty representatives. At the

*THE PROCESS OF NEEDS ASSESSMENT*

district level, the inservice personnel may ask for elected school representatives or, if the thrust is subject or grade specific, all teachers of the particular subject or grade who wish to be involved may be chosen.

The number of people involved must be manageable. The number selected will be determined by practical considerations such as the scope of the project, released time available, geographical distances, and district financial resources. Figure 7-2 is a general outline that might be used as a model in conducting needs assessment.

### Figure 7-2

### A Needs Assessment Model

**Stage I**

1. Make initial decisions respecting the scope of the needs assessment. Which aspects, grades, or subjects are to be the focus of the effort?
2. Decide on initial budgetary requirements (finances, personnel, and time).
3. Obtain appropriate permissions.
4. Make contact with all who might have a vested interest in the outcome.
5. Decide on a maximum representative number for the needs assessment committeee taking salient parameters into account (geography, finances, time, etc.).
6. Arrange the selection of committee members. As many as possible should be elected democratically. All role groups with a vested interest should be represented. Remember, at least in this context, you cannot appoint a true representative for someone else. A person is represented only if he or she has a say in the selection of his or her representative.

**Stage II**

1. Convene a meeting of committee.
2. Select secretary, statistician, communications person, treasurer, and others as needed. (Of course, none or all of these jobs may be necessary!)
3. Brainstorm. Give your initial intent and purpose and let the discussion take place.
4. Determine if the "problem" is a valid one, and if it can be addressed with the resources available.
5. Delimit the job to be undertaken to manageable proportions.
6. Appoint someone to determine if the effort is a duplicate. Maybe your efforts can be best expended in a slightly (or significantly) different area.
7. Decide on data collection procedures, the type of instruments and techniques, plans for distribution and collection of instrument, and directions for responding to the instruments.

*Continued*

**Figure 7-2 (continued)**

8. Prepare specific needs assessment instruments and techniques. This may mean the development of tools, or the selection and modification of those that may already be available.
9. Decide how the data will be collated and analyzed.
10. Determine which resources will be needed.
11. Make a time line and allocate specific duties and assignments to the various committee members.

**Stage III**

1. Undertake data collection.
2. Prepare collation and compilation of data.
3. Analyze data.
4. Make decisions respecting the need for further, refined, data collection.

   Stages II (Items 7–11) and III may have to be repeated several times, depending on the extent of the original data collection effort.

**Stage IV**

1. Attempt to determine the messages found in the analysis of data. What are the needs that have to be addressed? (This may not be easy; the messages from an initial assessment may be vague, indeed!)
2. Decide if the needs can be rank ordered according to priority. Should several needs be addressed concomitantly? These ranked needs become your *objectives*. Now prepare "outcomes statements"—statements about what you hope to achieve.
3. Communicate results to all role groups concerned.
4. Hand over jurisdiction to the people who have responsibility for the next phase of staff development.
5. Disband or pursue a new needs assessment thrust.

Some of these stages are going to be difficult. Getting the necessary permissions from the appropriate superordinate may be particularly difficult. If the particular administrator or supervisor feels threatened, then you may have to retreat. It would be wise to have some prior idea of the particular sensitivities of the person who has permission-granting authority. If your first request is denied, you must then decide if a second is advisable. Keep in mind that your administrator may not have sufficient self-assurance to allow any needs to surface that may reflect negatively on him or her. However, if needs are left until they surface by themselves, the problem may be of far-reaching and unmanageable proportions. A little bit of the wisdom of Solomon would sure be nice!

With respect to both data collection and the subsequent analysis, some consideration may be given to having both undertaken by people outside the school or district. These people should have no vested interest in the results. This probably means that all school district personnel are automatically ruled ineligible. The determining factors with respect to this decision may be the sensitivity of the issues being brought into focus, financial resources, degree of trust within the school or district, and availability of appropriate personnel and instrumentation.

It may be quite appropriate and advisable to include parent representatives as well as representatives of students on the needs assessment committee. This determination will probably be left to the individual initiating the needs assessment, superordinates, or the initial committee. Again, it will depend on the specifics of the issues and the situation.

## METHODS OF DATA COLLECTION FOR NEEDS ASSESSMENT

When the needs assessment committee has determined the general area and categories to be addressed and when it has delimited the task to manageable proportions, then decisions have to be made with respect to the methods to be used in collecting the needed data. There are many data collection methods, only some of which I will discuss here.

Before we begin to collect data, we must determine which sources of data are valid for our needs. There are several general sources:

1. Administrators
2. Supervisory people
3. Teachers
4. Students
5. Parents
6. Other publics
7. Outside "experts"

Data can be collected by and from these people by a number of methods. (The discussion, from this point is derived primarily from materials prepared by Martha Williams for the 1978 National Dissemination Forum, The NETWORK, Andover, Massachusetts, and from G. D. Kuh, T. Orbaugh, and K. Byers, *Designing and Conducting Needs Assessment in Education*. Bloomington: National Inservice Network, School of Education, Indiana University, 1981. These materials have been used with permission.)

**Personal Interviews**

The advantage of personal interviews include high probability of a response from all desired participants and small likelihood of response categories being misunderstood.

Among the disadvantages of personal interviews as a data collecting method are the enormous amounts of time required, the difficulty of categorizing and quantifying nonstandard responses, the need for highly skilled interviewers, and the difficulty of getting honest responses from teachers, say, when their anonymity cannot be guaranteed.

There are two major classifications of interviews, unstructured and structured:

1. *Active listening (unstructured interview).* In this approach, the workers in the system (or the clients or consumers) are approached and are invited and requested to expose their opinions and perceptions with the express purpose of assisting in the identification and clarifying of needs (system needs, individual needs, or both). The data collector makes no attempt to structure the responses and asks questions only to clarify any respondent statements. The discussion will probably be recorded by audio/video means. (However, it may be naive to expect personnel to respond honestly, knowing that they are being recorded.)

2. *Structured interview.* Structured interviews contain specific questions asked of all respondents. Usually the interview has an approximately fixed length; the data collector has the list of questions and may or may not share them with the respondent. The questions are presented in sequence; appropriate probing questions are often anticipated on the interview protocol sheet. If the respondent strays from the question, the data collector may disregard that information. If the questions are not relevant to the respondent, limited opportunity is provided for restructuring them. Data are usually recorded on a form; interviews may be audiotaped as a second source of information.

Use interviews when

1. It is necessary to observe not only what a respondent says but *how* (e.g., evasive, reluctant) it is said.
2. It is necessary to build up and maintain rapport to keep respondent interested and *motivated to finish questions.*
3. *High participation by target group* is needed.
4. *Population is accessible.*
5. Supplemental information may be needed for *respondent's understanding* and to prevent misinterpretation of the questions.
6. *Budget* will allow for expense of this method.
7. It is necessary for respondent to react to visual materials.

# THE PROCESS OF NEEDS ASSESSMENT

8. *Spontaneous reactions* are necessary, with sufficient time and probes to recall relevant information
9. Information about the respondent's personal characteristics and environment are needed to interpret results and evaluate the representativeness of the persons surveyed
10. There are *time and resources to train and supervise interviewers properly* (otherwise data recorded may be inaccurate or incomplete).

Major steps are to

1. Specify focus of interview—information to be gathered and target audience characteristics.
2. Establish a time frame and identify interviewers.
3. Develop questioning procedures to be included in interview.
    a. Motivate the respondent to answer.
    b. Give the respondent a "stake" in the interview (e.g., a chance to influence change).
    c. Establish rapport.
    d. Record responses using respondent's own words.
    e. Be prepared to probe for clarification, amplification, and so on.
    f. Summarize major points at end as a check.
4. Analyze and evaluate each interview as soon as it is completed.
5. Compile information from series of interviews using categories of response and write a summary.

For further information on interviewing techniques, see the following resources:

BINGHAM, W., AND B. MOORE, *How to Interview.* New York: Harper, 1959.
GORDON, R., *Interviewing Strategies, Techniques and Tactics.* Homewood, Ill.: Dorsey, 1969.
LOFLAN, J., *Analyzing Social Settings.* Belmont, Calif.: Wadsworth, 1971.
RICHARDSON, S. A., B. DOHRENWEND, AND D. KLEIN, *Interviewing: Its Forms and Functions.* New York: Basic Books, 1965.
WOLF, R., *Strategies for Conducting Naturalistic Evaluation in Socio-educational Settings.* Occasional Paper Series of the Evaluation Center, Western Michigan University, Kalamazoo, 1979.
MERTON, R., M. FISK, AND P. KENDALL, *The Focused Interview: A Manual of Problems and Procedures.* Glencoe, Ill.: Free Press, 1956.

## Response Forms

The advantage of response forms is that every person's voice counts. They are also fairly easy to distribute, collect, collate, quantify, and analyze. In addition, the mail-back form can provide anonymity.

Difficulties associated with response forms include receiving a high enough rate of return for the analysis to be valid and ambiguity of the response categories.

Probable, the two most common types of response forms are the questionnaire and the checklist. There are many styles of each.

*Questionnaire* The questionnaire can be relatively client centered or system centered, depending on its approach. It may include questions that address needs directly, such as "Do you need help with...?" or it may ask for information only indirectly related to the respondent's perception of need, such as "Do students in your class receive individualized assistance with reading?" In the latter case, the information-seeking question may be followed by a more open-ended question, such as a "why" question. These may require a forced choice response (selection of one response from four or five options).

The questionnaire can probe information, opinions, or attitudes. Because it is a paper-pencil technique, instructions are usually contained on the questionnaire form and little guidance or encouragement is given for expanding the boundaries of the instrument. It can be administered individually or in large groups, through the mail or in person.

Use a questionnaire when

1. Wide distribution is necessary (and budget will not permit telephone or other interview).
2. A sense of *privacy* is needed.
3. *Complete uniformity* in the manner in which questions are posed is necessary to avoid biasing responses.
4. *Presence of interviewers* are likely to affect responses.
5. Respondent needs to *secure or check information*.
6. Obtaining *unanticipated* definitions of situations and unquantifiable responses is *not* desired.
7. Self-administration and logistical ease *is* desired.
8. Cost must be kept at a minimum.

Major steps are

1. Specify information to be gathered.
2. Frame questions to be included.
   a. Make questions clear and understandable.
   b. Establish a logical sequence.
   c. Consider spacing and format, making type of response clear.
   d. Pretest questionnaire and modify if needed.
3. Determine to whom and how questionnaire will be distributed and how a high return rate will be effected.

a. Distribute and collect at meeting of respondents.
b. Provide self-addressed stamped envelope for return.

4. Compile results of questionnaire and summarize.

For further information about questionnaire and survey techniques, see

OPPENHEIM, A., *Questionnaire Design and Attitude Measurement.* New York: Basic Books, 1966.

HYMAN, H., *The Interivew in Social Research.* Chicago: University of Chicago Press, 1954.

*Checklist* A checklist, like a questionnaire and structured interview, can contain items directly related to need (such as a checklist of need areas) or items indirectly related to need (such as a checklist of characteristics of the respondent) or both. The respondent makes forced choices but generally within a fairly extensive group of alternatives. The choices are usually not forced down to one but contain provision for several responses to be checked, often for the priority ranking of the responses. Also checklists can be used to codify archival data (information routinely collected from various individuals in the system such as nurses, bus drivers, etc.) The method of use of the checklist is similar to that for the questionnaire.

## Observations

Teachers almost always claim that the presence of an observer in the classroom creates an artificial situation. A skilled observer is needed who is able to recognize and allow for the artificial aspects. Observation in the faculty lounge, principal's office, superintendent's office, and board room might also be considered. The "artificiality" argument may still apply. It has been my perception that artificiality, if it exists at all, may be a factor during a first visit, but not necessarily during subsequent visits, especially if the observer becomes a familiar presence.

Many authors recommend peer observation for a variety of purposes. It is suggested that teachers may perceive peer observation as being less threatening than observations by superordinates or consultants. However, this technique involves significant administration and possible disruption of the classes of the visiting peer. Also, it seems that many teachers are reluctant to observe in a colleague's classroom for a variety of reasons.

Observation is the most system-centered form of data collection because it involves no direct input from clients. Data collectors using observation guidelines go directly to the site of activity and record what they see and hear within coded or structured data collection formats. This technique is the most system centered because it dictates a perspective from which the client's reality is viewed—and because of the lack of interaction, the perspective cannot be challenged by the subjects.

Use observation when

1. Firsthand experience is required.
2. Respondents may not be able to relate needed information directly.

3. Budget allows for observers' time required for lengthy observations.
4. Sufficient time in the needs assessment plan is available to make reliable observations.

Major steps are to

1. Determine the format for observation including
   a. Extent to which observation guide is structured prior to observations.
   b. Extent to which observer is or is not a participant in the activity being observed.
   c. Extent to which the observational situation is natural or contrived.
   d. Extent to which subjects are aware of observer's role and purpose.
2. Identify site or observational situation.
3. Gain access or permission to observe—establish an agreement with administrators.
4. Take overt or covert role of observer.
5. Establish trust and rapport. (While this may not be necessary if observation is unobtrusive, any covert activity raises the question of ethics.)
6. Record observations using one or more of the following:
   a. Predetermined schedule or checklist.
   b. Notetaking in narrative form.
   c. Tape recording observations as they occur.
7. Analyze observations through focusing and categorizing process.
8. Write report summarizing observations.

For further information about observational techniques, see

BOGDAN, R., AND S. J. TAYLOR, *Introduction to Qualitative Research Methods*. New York: Wiley, 1975.

JAHODA, M., M. DEUTSCH, AND S. W. COOK, *Research Methods in Social Relations*. New York: Dryden, 1951.

MCCALL, J., AND J. L. SIMMONS, *Issues in Participant Observation*, Reading, Mass.: Addison-Wesley, 1969.

## Archival Research

Archival materials are those that exist in recorded, usually filed, form. It might be teacher employment and qualifications files, inservice records for teachers, supervisory records, or administrative records. The utility of this technique will depend on the variety and state of completeness of the records as well as on the selection and analysis skills of the participants.

Use archival material when

1. Appropriate records are easily and legally accessible.

2. Budget limits the use of more expensive data gathering methods.
3. Time and space restrictions do not permit direct access to target population.
4. Naturally occurring data from the target setting are desired as opposed to more contrived data from interviews, questionnaires, and the like. "Let the record speak for itself."
5. Information is needed to supplement and substantiate information obtained through interviews and other methods.
6. Potential errors in records can be recognized and dealt with through other needs assessment techniques.
7. Comparisons across record-keeping systems are feasible (similar formats, language, type of information).
8. Repeated measures of values, attitudes, and so on are desired over time.

Major steps are to

1. Determine data desired from records.
2. Determine appropriate sources of data. Which of random, stratified, or purposive sampling of available documents is preferable?
3. Contact persons in charge of appropriate records and gain access to records.
4. Review records for desired information using document analysis techniques. More than one judge is desirable for subsets of documents.
5. Summarize information obtained from each record or document with attention given to issues of completeness and accuracy.
6. Collapse information across records using emergent categories to gain more general picture.

Some possible sources of archival material include

1. *Official reports and documents.* Student achievement records, teacher evaluation records, building administrators' reports, central administration reports on particular programs, school board meeting minutes, grant applications and proposals, library checkout records, bus driver reports.
2. *Unofficial and personal records.* Teacher lesson plans and diaries, student written materials, and the like.

For further information about archival material, see

ANDERSON, D., AND P. BENJAMINSON, *Investigative Reporting.* Bloomington: Indiana University Press, 1976.

GUBA, E., "TOWARD A METHODOLOGY OF NATURALISTIC INQUIRY FOR EDUCATIONAL EVALUATION," *CSE Monograph Series No. 8.* Los Angeles: UCLA, Center for the Study of Evaluation, 1978.

Holsti, O. R., *Content Analysis for the Social Sciences and Humanities.* Reading, Mass.: Addison-Wesley, 1969.

Williams, P. N., *Investigative Reporting and Editing.* Englewood Cliffs, N.J.: Prentice-Hall, 1978.

**Small-Group Meetings**

Small-group meetings may be useful for an initial survey designed to determine the parameters of the scope of the problem. Meetings of any kind will require skilled direction. Response statements and questions have to be very carefully, sensitively, and unambiguously phrased, yet open-ended enough to encourage creative responses. It is difficult to categorize and quantify the results of such meetings.

**Committees**

If an administrator or supervisor is not present, this may be a good forum in which to raise needs. It can be a "griping session." However, it will need a skilled chairperson to keep the meeting on track.

**Case Studies**

The validity and usefulness of case studies will depend on the kind of materials selected (e.g., anecdotal records), the specific selection procedure, and the participant skills.

## A FINAL WORD

While some of this chapter may appear "textbookish," bear in mind that it is the lack of attention to such details that has earned inservice efforts the indictment "the slums of education." The point has to be emphasized that desired or needed information has to be gathered by appropriate means. If we gather information by inappropriate means, what confidence can we have that we can rely on decisions based on that information?

We are professional people, highly trained (and some would claim highly paid) and occupying positions of considerable power, responsibility, and trust. Our obligation is to provide the most competent management with the resources at our disposal. Data-gathering methodologies constitute one such resource.

# CHAPTER 8

# NEEDS ASSESSMENT INSTRUMENTS

This chapter is devoted exclusively to the presentation of sample needs assessment instruments to help you in your efforts to design your own. Whatever your educational situation and purpose, you should be able to find something here that will be useful to you.

The following instruments address school life at several levels and also provide initial overall assessments.

## SCHOOL SOCIAL CLIMATE QUESTIONNAIRE

The first instruments presented result from the research efforts of several people at Simon Fraser University. Figure 8-1* is for completion by teachers; Figure 8-2, by parents. Their objective is the determination of certain aspects of school social climate, with an emphasis on elementary schools.

Dr. Peter Coleman, the supervisor of the project, is prepared to assist anyone wishing to use these instruments by providing data from a sample of British Columbia schools. Write to Dr. Peter Coleman, associate professor, Faculty of Education, Simon Fraser University, Burnaby, British Columbia, Canada V5A 1S6.

## MICHIGAN SCHOOL IMPROVEMENT PROJECT

The state of Michigan has undertaken a massive program of school improvement. Figures 8-3 and 8-4 were used in that effort. Figure 8-3 is designed to survey all

*All figures for Chapter 8 appear at the end of the chapter.

teaching and nonteaching staff; Figure 8-4 is of a discrepancy design and can be utilized in the creation of a school profile along several dimensions. With some modification and selection, instruments modeled after these could be utilized for obtaining student response as well.

## A TELEPHONE SURVEY

Figure 8-5, interesting because of its design, addresses a number of staff development issues. It is worth noting the standardized introduction and the technique utilized to obtain the cooperation of the respondent.

This instrument is taken from *Designing and Conducting Needs Assessment in Education* by G. D. Kuh, T. Orbaugh, and K. Byers (Bloomington: National Inservice Network, Indiana University, School of Education).

## NEEDS ASSESSMENT SURVEY FOR INSTRUCTIONAL STAFF

Figure 8-6 is a "quicky" survey designed to obtain an initial picture of the inservice interests of teaching staff. The document is taken from *Inservice Education: Current Trends in School Policies and Programs* (Arlington, Va.: National School Public Relations Association).

## INSTRUMENTS FROM THE KOLL AND COZAD COLLECTION

Figures 8-7 and 8-8 are wide ranging. They were utilized by individual Wisconsin school districts in their ISSD needs assessment efforts.

These instruments were taken from *Staff Development: A Process Approach* by P. J. Koll and L. Cozad (Oshkosh: University of Wisconsin Extension, 1981).

## PORTLAND CONSORTIUM TRAINING COMPLEX: TEACHER SURVEY INSTRUMENT

Figure 8-9 is another wide-ranging instrument. The focus is the teaching environment and methodologies. It is not subject or topic specific.

This instrument is taken from *Inservice Education: Criteria for and Examples of Local Programs*, edited by R. A. Edelfelt (Bellingham: Western Washington State College, 1977).

NEEDS ASSESSMENT INSTRUMENTS 79

## STAFF DEVELOPMENT SURVEY

Figure 8-10 was used in a research effort at the University of Maryland. The original instrument was designed for possible computer collation adaption.

This instrument is taken from *Customizing a Needs Assessment Process for Planning Staff Development: A Model of Collaboration* by M. C. Erly and J. D. Greenberg, a paper presented at the Fourth International Seminar for Teacher Education in the 1980s and 1990s, hosted by North East London Polytechnic at Digby Stuart College, Roshampton, Surrey, England, April 13–19, 1984.

## A SPECIFIC NEED INSTRUMENT

Figure 8-11 was utilized at Littleton, Colorado, in an effort to determine specific needs respecting reaching handicapped children. This instrument has been included as an example of the level of specificity that can be addressed by needs assessment procedures.

This document is taken from *Designing and Conducting Needs Assessment in Education* by G. D. Kuh, T. Orbaugh, and K. Byers (Bloomington: National Inservice Network, Indiana University, School of Education).

## STAFF ASSESSMENT OF PRINCIPAL

Evaluation instruments can be ideal for needs assessment. There are many such evaluation instruments available. Figure 8-12 has been selected because it is designed for teacher-rating of principals, the outcome of which can be very valuable.

Figure 8-13 is designed to rate principal-teacher interviews. Note, again, the degree of specificity.

**Figure 8-1**

**Teacher's Form—Social Climate Scale**

---

**ELEMENTARY SCHOOL SOCIAL CLIMATE SCALE**

**Teacher Form**

*Please respond to all items with reference to the school in which you received the survey.*

*Directions*

To respond to each item, please insert the number representing the *most accurate* response, in your opinion, in the box at the right-hand margin.

Select your response from the following alternatives:

      (1) Strongly agree
      (2) Agree
      (3) Disagree
      (4) Strongly disagree
      (5) Cannot answer—no knowledge

*Please respond to all items.*

1. Students are grouped in classrooms in a way that helps with instruction. ☐
2. The principal in this school spends a lot of time helping teachers with problems. ☐
3. The principal in our school keeps interruptions of classroom activities to a minimum. ☐
4. Teachers plan the instructional program cooperatively in this school. ☐
5. Teachers in the school feel free to disagree with the principal in meetings. ☐
6. Teachers are usually able to achieve consensus on educational goals and values at this school. ☐
7. The principal encourages teachers to try alternative ways of solving instructional problems. ☐
8. The principal in this school facilitates the professional development of teachers. ☐
9. Teachers can participate in decision making in this school if they wish to. ☐
10. Teachers in this school feel free to try out their own ideas. ☐
11. Teachers support school policies on supervision and discipline in our school. ☐
12. Staff meetings serve a useful purpose. ☐
13. The principal makes opportunities for teachers to plan together in this school. ☐
14. Teaching assignments in this school are as appropriate as possible. ☐
15. Generally, how would you rate the social climate of this school as a place for students to learn in? ☐
    (*Enter one response from the scale.*)

   10    9    8    7    6    5    4    3    2    1

COPYRIGHT PEAC Consultants, 15055 Royal Avenue, White Rock, B.C., V4B 1M1

(604) 531-6209

---

Reprinted with permission of Peter Coleman and Linda LaRocque, Faculty of Education, Simon Fraser University.

**Figure 8-2**

Parent Form—Social Climate Scale

## ELEMENTARY SCHOOL SOCIAL CLIMATE SCALE

### Parent Form

*Please respond to all items with reference to the school from which you received the survey.*

*Directions*

To respond to each item, please insert the number representing the *most accurate* response, in your opinion, in the box at the right-hand margin.

Select your response from the following alternatives:

        (1) Strongly agree
        (2) Agree
        (3) Disagree
        (4) Strongly disagree
        (5) Cannot answer—no knowledge

*Please respond to all items.*

1. Our school makes visitors feel welcome.
2. The principal in our school is very knowledgeable about elementary school programs.
3. Students in our school have the necessary ability to achieve well in basic skills.
4. Students in this school have the necessary motivation to achieve well in basic skills.
5. The principal spends a lot of time looking for ways to improve our school.
6. The academic emphasis in our school is challenging to students.
7. The principal sets a good example for staff.
8. Our school day is full of challenging activities for students.
9. The principal provides opportunities for open discussion of problems in the school.
10. The principal is "open" and approachable.
11. The principal deals firmly and rapidly with problems in the school.
12. The principal in our school knows most of the students by name.
13. The principal frequently talks with students around the school.
14. The principal is available in the school most of the time.
15. Parents in this school set high standards of achievement for their children.
16. Discipline policies are applied consistently to all children in this school.
17. The instructional program in our school helps to motivate students.
18. Students are proud of our school.
19. The principal in this school treats parent opinions with respect.
20. Students believe that the school respects their opinions.
21. In this school, information about students is treated as confidential.
22. Parents are supportive of school discipline policies.

*Continued*

### Figure 8-2 (Continued)

23. Students in this school respect the principal. ☐
24. Students are excited about learning in this school. ☐
25. This school has a comfortable feeling about it. ☐
26. Teachers in this school feel they are responsible to parents. ☐
27. Punishment for misbehavior of students is fair in this school. ☐
28. Students are always the main concern in this school. ☐
29. Parents and teachers respect each other at this school. ☐
30. Children feel safe at this school. ☐
31. Students are good ambassadors for the school. ☐
32. Teachers and parents at this school want the same things for students. ☐
33. Students like the teachers in this school. ☐
34. This school reflects the values of the community in which it is located. ☐
35. Teachers in our school are consistent in their expectations of students. ☐
36. My child(ren) is (are) happy to go to school. ☐
37. Parents are given information in advance on any changes in the school. ☐
38. Parents find teachers easily approachable at this school. ☐
39. This school is an important part of the community. ☐
40. Generally, how would you rate the social climate of this school as a place for students to learn in? ☐
    (*Enter one response from the scale.*)

```
 10    9    8    7    6    5    4    3    2    1
  |    |    |    |    |    |    |    |    |    |
```

COPYRIGHT PEAC Consultants, 15055 Royal Avenue, White Rock, B.C., V4B 1M1
(604) 531-6209

---

Reprinted with permission of Peter Coleman and Linda LaRocque, Faculty of Education, Simon Fraser University.

Figure 8-3
Staff Survey

**STAFF SURVEY**

This survey is designed to let you express your feelings about our school district.

It asks about your job...the people you work with...and your impressions about our schools.

There are no right or wrong answers. We are only interested in what you think.

The resulting information will be used to make your work environment better and to improve our educational program.

Individual answers to this questionnaire will remain confidential. All questionnaires will be averaged to provide a general picture of the school district.

*Instructions*

Most of the survey consists of statements.
After reading each statement, decide if you

      (1) Agree
      (2) Are unsure, but probably agree
      (3) Are unsure, but probably disagree
      (4) Disagree

*Example*

| | Agree | Unsure, Probably Agree | Unsure, Probably Disagree | Disagree |
|---|---|---|---|---|
| Our school district is in the United States. | ① | 2 | 3 | 4 |

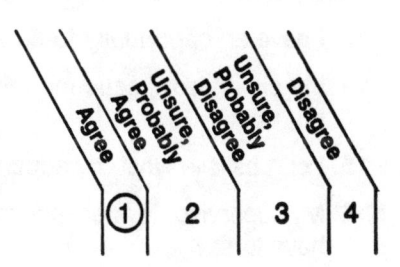

If you agree with the example statement, circle the number in the "Agree" column.

If you feel you cannot answer a question, don't mark anything in the column following that question.

When you have completed the survey, staple this booklet closed and return it to the address on the back cover.

*Continued*

**Figure 8-3 (Continued)**

| | Agree | Unsure, Probably Agree | Unsure, Probably Disagree | Disagree |
|---|---|---|---|---|
| 1. Generally speaking, working conditions in this school district are good. | 1 | 2 | 3 | 4 |
| 2. I am satisfied with my work assignment. | 1 | 2 | 3 | 4 |
| 3. I consider my job interesting. | 1 | 2 | 3 | 4 |
| 4. Most people have respect for the kind of work I do. | 1 | 2 | 3 | 4 |
| 5. My job gives me a chance to learn new skills. | 1 | 2 | 3 | 4 |
| 6. As long as I do good work, I'll have a job. | 1 | 2 | 3 | 4 |
| 7. You can state your honest opinions in this school district without worrying that someone will "get back at you." | 1 | 2 | 3 | 4 |
| 8. If I have a complaint or suggestion, I feel free to express it. | 1 | 2 | 3 | 4 |
| 9. My supervisor has a real interest in the personal welfare and happiness of his or her staff. | 1 | 2 | 3 | 4 |
| 10. My supervisor cares about me as an individual. | 1 | 2 | 3 | 4 |
| 11. I consider my job challenging. | 1 | 2 | 3 | 4 |
| 12. My work provides me with a sense of accomplishment. | 1 | 2 | 3 | 4 |
| 13. I have an opportunity to develop friendships at work. | 1 | 2 | 3 | 4 |
| 14. My supervisor keeps me informed on matters important to my work. | 1 | 2 | 3 | 4 |
| 15. I can believe what my supervisor says. | 1 | 2 | 3 | 4 |
| 16. My supervisor is interested in what his or her staff members have to say. | 1 | 2 | 3 | 4 |
| 17. I feel free to discuss job problems with my supervisor. | 1 | 2 | 3 | 4 |
| 18. Most employees in this school district do a good job. | 1 | 2 | 3 | 4 |
| 19. Differences of opinion in my department/school are usually resolved without conflict. | 1 | 2 | 3 | 4 |
| 20. The possibility of being laid off doesn't concern me. | 1 | 2 | 3 | 4 |
| 21. My work environment permits free and open exchanges of ideas and information. | 1 | 2 | 3 | 4 |
| 22. Most of the people I work with work hard. | 1 | 2 | 3 | 4 |
| 23. In my opinion, most of the people I work with are well qualified for their jobs. | 1 | 2 | 3 | 4 |
| 24. I get along well with the people with whom I work. | 1 | 2 | 3 | 4 |
| 25. Most employees here are loyal to the organization. | 1 | 2 | 3 | 4 |
| 26. Most employees here are willing to "go the extra mile" to get a job done. | 1 | 2 | 3 | 4 |

### Figure 8-3 (Continued)

| | Agree | Unsure, Probably Agree | Unsure, Probably Disagree | Disagree |
|---|---|---|---|---|
| 27. My supervisor usually gives me "a pat on the back" when I do a good job. | 1 | 2 | 3 | 4 |
| 28. I have sufficient materials and supplies to do my job. | 1 | 2 | 3 | 4 |
| 29. My salary is fair in relation to my job responsibilities. | 1 | 2 | 3 | 4 |
| 30. I can count on my supervisor for support in the performance of my job. | 1 | 2 | 3 | 4 |
| 31. I believe staff members like me can bring about change in my department/school. | 1 | 2 | 3 | 4 |
| 32. I believe my efforts here are appreciated. | 1 | 2 | 3 | 4 |
| 33. People in my department/school seem to care about one another. | 1 | 2 | 3 | 4 |
| 34. I am concerned about losing my job. | 1 | 2 | 3 | 4 |
| 35. I am concerned about being reassigned to another job responsibility area. | 1 | 2 | 3 | 4 |
| 36. My supervisor likes to try new things. | 1 | 2 | 3 | 4 |
| 37. I believe my department/school operates as a team. | 1 | 2 | 3 | 4 |
| 38. My job provides me rewards that can't be measured in dollars. | 1 | 2 | 3 | 4 |
| 39. My work provides me with opportunities for professional growth. | 1 | 2 | 3 | 4 |
| 40. My work provides me with opportunities for promotion. | 1 | 2 | 3 | 4 |
| 41. My supervisor listens when I have an idea. | 1 | 2 | 3 | 4 |
| 42. Communication between my supervisor and me is adequate. | 1 | 2 | 3 | 4 |
| 43. My supervisor has a sense of humor. | 1 | 2 | 3 | 4 |
| 44. Some of the people I work with have a poor attitude toward their jobs. | 1 | 2 | 3 | 4 |
| 45. My supervisor gives me the support I need to get my job done. | 1 | 2 | 3 | 4 |
| 46. I could work harder than I do. | 1 | 2 | 3 | 4 |
| 47. If I could start my working career over again, I would probably do something different. | 1 | 2 | 3 | 4 |
| 48. I used to care more about my work than I do now. | 1 | 2 | 3 | 4 |
| 49. I think my supervisor is generally effective. | 1 | 2 | 3 | 4 |
| 50. Most of the people I work with care about doing a good job. | 1 | 2 | 3 | 4 |
| 51. I would be more effective if I had more on-the-job freedom. | 1 | 2 | 3 | 4 |

*Continued*

### Figure 8-3 (Continued)

|   | Agree | Unsure, Probably Agree | Unsure, Probably Disagree | Disagree |
|---|---|---|---|---|
| 52. I need more training to do my job better. | 1 | 2 | 3 | 4 |
| 53. My department/school is better this year than it was last year. | 1 | 2 | 3 | 4 |
| 54. My supervisor helps people grow in their jobs. | 1 | 2 | 3 | 4 |
| 55. I am a better employee this year than I was last year. | 1 | 2 | 3 | 4 |
| 56. I can influence what goes on in my department/school. | 1 | 2 | 3 | 4 |
| 57. I often go home frustrated because of my job. | 1 | 2 | 3 | 4 |
| 58. If I had a personal problem, I'd feel free to talk about it with my supervisor. | 1 | 2 | 3 | 4 |
| 59. My most recent evaluation helped me perform better in my job. | 1 | 2 | 3 | 4 |
| 60. Compared to people who have similar jobs, my fringe benefits are adequate. | 1 | 2 | 3 | 4 |
| 61. I believe my job is important. | 1 | 2 | 3 | 4 |
| 62. The people I work with believe my job is important. | 1 | 2 | 3 | 4 |
| 63. My department/school does "quality work." | 1 | 2 | 3 | 4 |
| 64. Most people in my department/school have the freedom they need to do their job well. | 1 | 2 | 3 | 4 |
| 65. I have to go through a lot of "red tape" to get things done at work. | 1 | 2 | 3 | 4 |
| 66. I feel like I am making a contribution to my department/school. | 1 | 2 | 3 | 4 |
| 67. I usually feel good about my job. | 1 | 2 | 3 | 4 |
| 68. Staff morale in my department/school is good. | 1 | 2 | 3 | 4 |
| 69. Sometimes I feel like I am "fighting the system." | 1 | 2 | 3 | 4 |
| 70. When I do a good job I know it's appreciated. | 1 | 2 | 3 | 4 |
| 71. Employee ideas and suggestions get a fair hearing in this school district. | 1 | 2 | 3 | 4 |
| 72. Employees here are encouraged to share work-related ideas and suggestions. | 1 | 2 | 3 | 4 |
| 73. I receive enough recognition for the work I do. | 1 | 2 | 3 | 4 |
| 74. My chances for advancement in this school district are good. | 1 | 2 | 3 | 4 |
| 75. Some of the people I work with get jealous when I get credit for doing a good job. | 1 | 2 | 3 | 4 |
| 76. All things considered, this is a good place to work. | 1 | 2 | 3 | 4 |
| 77. Students in this school district are assigned enough homework. | 1 | 2 | 3 | 4 |

### Figure 8-3 (Continued)

| | Agree | Unsure, Probably Agree | Unsure, Probably Disagree | Disagree |
|---|---|---|---|---|
| 78. Most students here like school. | 1 | 2 | 3 | 4 |
| 79. Student progress in our school is closely related. | 1 | 2 | 3 | 4 |
| 80. Our schools emphasize reading, writing, and arithmetic. | 1 | 2 | 3 | 4 |
| 81. Our schools can be described as "a good place to learn." | 1 | 2 | 3 | 4 |
| 82. Our schools are orderly and conducive to learning. | 1 | 2 | 3 | 4 |
| 83. Our students have enough supplies and materials. | 1 | 2 | 3 | 4 |
| 84. The teaching staff here expects all students to do well. | 1 | 2 | 3 | 4 |
| 85. Teachers here are involved in setting learning goals for students. | 1 | 2 | 3 | 4 |
| 86. My principal expects the best from staff and students. | 1 | 2 | 3 | 4 |
| 87. Administrators here won't tolerate poor staff performance. | 1 | 2 | 3 | 4 |
| 88. Students who have learning problems can get extra help in our school district. | 1 | 2 | 3 | 4 |
| 89. When students graduate from this school district, most of them will know how to read, write, and do arithmetic. | 1 | 2 | 3 | 4 |
| 90. Class sizes in this school district are too large. | 1 | 2 | 3 | 4 |
| 91. Students in our schools are encouraged to do the best they can. | 1 | 2 | 3 | 4 |
| 92. Students here believe the staff is "warm" and cares about them. | 1 | 2 | 3 | 4 |
| 93. Our schools should involve more parents in the instructional program. | 1 | 2 | 3 | 4 |
| 94. Most classrooms in our school district are well disciplined. | 1 | 2 | 3 | 4 |
| 95. Our schools have learning goals for students. | 1 | 2 | 3 | 4 |
| 96. Most parents believe our schools are doing a good job. | 1 | 2 | 3 | 4 |
| 97. I believe our schools are doing a good job. | 1 | 2 | 3 | 4 |
| 98. This community expects a good educational program. | 1 | 2 | 3 | 4 |
| 99. The goals of my department/school are "on target." | 1 | 2 | 3 | 4 |
| 100. I am proud to work in this school district. | 1 | 2 | 3 | 4 |

PLEASE CONTINUE ON TO THE NEXT PAGE.

*Continued*

**Figure 8-3 (Continued)**

The survey concludes with a few questions about you. Your response will enable us to classify the answers so the survey results will be more meaningful to you.

A. Which of the following best describes your job?

| | |
|---|---|
| (1) Classroom teacher | 1 |
| (2) Special education teacher | 2 |
| (3) Counselor | 3 |
| (4) Principal | 4 |
| (5) Custodian (skip to question E) | 5 |
| (6) Secretary (skip to question E) | 6 |
| (7) Bus driver (skip to question E) | 7 |
| (8) Cafeteria personnel (skip to question E) | 8 |
| (9) Aide (skip to question E) | 9 |
| (10) Central office administrator (skip to question E) | 10 |
| (11) Other _____ (skip to question E) | 11 |

B. What is the grade level to which you are assigned?

| | |
|---|---|
| (1) Preschool | 1 |
| (2) Grades kindergarten through 6 | 2 |
| (3) Grades 7, 8, or 9 | 3 |
| (4) Grades 10, 11, or 12 | 4 |
| (5) Other _____ | 5 |

C. What subject area are you assigned to a majority of the time?

| | |
|---|---|
| (1) Art | 1 |
| (2) Business | 2 |
| (3) English/language arts | 3 |
| (4) Foreign language | 4 |
| (5) Physical education/health | 5 |
| (6) Home economics | 6 |
| (7) Industrial arts/vocational education | 7 |
| (8) Mathematics | 8 |
| (9) Music | 9 |
| (10) Science | 10 |
| (11) Social studies | 11 |
| (12) Special education | 12 |
| (13) Other | 13 |

D. How many years of full-time teaching experience did you have prior to this year?

| | |
|---|---|
| (1) Less than 3 years | 1 |
| (2) 3–6 years | 2 |
| (3) 7–10 years | 3 |
| (4) 11–20 years | 4 |
| (5) 21–30 years | 5 |
| (6) 31 years or more | 6 |

E. What was the last grade in school you completed?

| | |
|---|---|
| (1) Did not graduate from high school | 1 |
| (2) High school graduate | 2 |
| (3) Some college | 3 |
| (4) Associate degree | 4 |

### Figure 8-3 (Continued)

| | |
|---|---|
| (5) Bachelor's degree | 5 |
| (6) Master's degree | 6 |
| (7) Specialist's degree | 7 |
| (8) Doctorate | 8 |

F. What is your age?

| | |
|---|---|
| (1) Under 25 years of age | 1 |
| (2) 25–30 | 2 |
| (3) 31–40 | 3 |
| (4) 41–50 | 4 |
| (5) 51–60 | 5 |
| (6) 61 or older | 6 |

G. How long have you worked here?

| | |
|---|---|
| (1) Less than one year | 1 |
| (2) 1–5 years | 2 |
| (3) 6–10 years | 3 |
| (4) 11–20 years | 4 |
| (5) 21 years or more | 5 |

H. Are you?

| | |
|---|---|
| (1) Male | 1 |
| (2) Female | 2 |

Thank you for helping make this a better place to learn...and work. Please staple your survey booklet closed and return it to:

**WILLIAM J. BANACH ASSOCIATES, INC.**
21969 Cimarron
Romeo, Michigan 48065
313/784-9888

*Return Completed Survey to:*

Copyright 1982. William J. Banach Associates, Inc., 21969 Cimarron, Romeo, Mich. 48065. All rights reserved. This survey document may be reproduced in its entirety for use by public educational agencies. No changes in the material are permitted. Reproduction must be by photocopy or offset printing and must carry this copyright notice. Agencies using this survey are required to send one copy of the results to the copyright holder.

These documents are components of the Michigan School Improvement Project. Reproduced with the permission of the Michigan State Board of Education, Lansing, Mich.

**Figure 8-4**

## School Improvement Survey

### THE SCHOOL IMPROVEMENT SURVEY

Within any school, a variety of characteristics influence to a greater or lesser degree the effectiveness and professional satisfaction of those who work there. Four of these characteristics are particularly worth examining because to a considerable degree, they can be controlled or influenced by staff members.

When viewed as a composite, these characteristics provide a "picture" or profile of life in that school as seen by those who work there. This picture or profile provides information that school staff can use to make decisions about areas for school improvement that are most important to them.

Below is a series of statements concerning these four sets of effectiveness/satisfaction characteristics. On the scale to the LEFT of each statement place an "X" at the point that represents your estimate of the *present situation* in your school. On the scale to the RIGHT of each statement place an "X" at the point that represents where you believe your school *should be and could be*.

### I. TEAMWORK AND COMMUNICATION

| The present situation in my school | | How my school Should be and could be |
|---|---|---|
| very rarely  occasion-  more   almost<br>              ally     often than always<br>                       not<br>1   2   3   4   5   6   7   8 | a. Communication among teachers about school matters is open and candid... | very rarely  occasion-  more   almost<br>              ally     often than always<br>                       not<br>1   2   3   4   5   6   7   8 |
| very rarely  occasion-  more   almost<br>              ally     often than always<br>                       not<br>1   2   3   4   5   6   7   8 | b. Communication between the principal and teachers is open and candid... | very rarely  occasion-  more   almost<br>              ally     often than always<br>                       not<br>1   2   3   4   5   6   7   8 |
| very little  sometimes quite a bit  a very<br>                                great deal<br>1   2   3   4   5   6   7   8 | c. We use cooperation and teamwork in our efforts to accomplish our goals... | very little  sometimes quite a bit  a very<br>                                great deal<br>1   2   3   4   5   6   7   8 |

90

d. Staff members plan together and coordinate their efforts...

| seldom | once in awhile | frequently | almost always |
|---|---|---|---|
| 1  2 | 3  4 | 5  6 | 7  8 |

e. Conflicts among teachers are...

| usually ignored or suppressed | raised but seldom resolved | resolved by all those affected | |
|---|---|---|---|
| 1  2 | 3  4 | 5  6 | 7  8 |

## II. ADMINISTRATOR-TEACHER RELATIONS

f. The principal knows the problems faced by teachers...

| not at all | somewhat | quite a bit | very well |
|---|---|---|---|
| 1  2 | 3  4 | 5  6 | 7  8 |

g. The principal tries to help me with my problems...

| very rarely | occasionally | more often than not | almost always |
|---|---|---|---|
| 1  2 | 3  4 | 5  6 | 7  8 |

h. The principal gives me useful ideas and information...

| rarely | once in awhile | often | very frequently |
|---|---|---|---|
| 1  2 | 3  4 | 5  6 | 7  8 |

i. I feel free to talk with the principal about school matters...

| almost never | depends on the topic | | yes, almost always |
|---|---|---|---|
| 1  2 | 3  4 | 5  6 | 7  8 |

j. The level of trust between teachers and the principal is...

| very low | low | moderate | very high |
|---|---|---|---|
| 1  2 | 3  4 | 5  6 | 7  8 |

*Continued*

91

## Figure 8-4 (Continued)

**The present situation in my school** / **How my school Should be and could be**

k. Conflicts between teachers and principal are...

| usually ignored or suppressed | resolved by principal | resolved by all those affected |
|---|---|---|
| 1  2  3 | 4  5 | 6  7  8 |

### III. SCHOOL EFFECTIVENESS

l. The acquisition of basic skills by students takes precedence over other school activities...

| not at all | to some extent | quite a bit | completely |
|---|---|---|---|
| 1  2  3 | 4 | 5  6 | 7  8 |

m. This school's goals/expectations for students' educational performance are...

| very low | below average | above average | very high |
|---|---|---|---|
| 1  2  3 | 4 | 5  6 | 7  8 |

n. The day-to-day climate in our building is...

n–1
| disorderly | | orderly |
|---|---|---|
| 1  2  3 | 4  5 | 6  7  8 |

n–2
| noisy | | quiet |
|---|---|---|
| 1  2  3 | 4  5 | 6  7  8 |

n–3
| oppressive | | comfortable |
|---|---|---|
| 1  2  3 | 4  5 | 6  7  8 |

rigid — — — — — — — — flexible
1 2 3 4 5 6 7 8

rarely — occasion- — consider- — almost
         ally        ably       always
1 2 3 4 5 6 7 8

rarely — occasion- — consider- — almost
         ally        ably       always
1 2 3 4 5 6 7 8

very little — depends on — widespread
              the teacher   through school
1 2 3 4 5 6 7 8

1 2 3 4 5 6 7 8

very little — depends on — widespread
              the teacher   throughout school
1 2 3 4 5 6 7 8

1 2 3 4 5 6 7 8

*n – 4*

o. The principal helps the staff focus on accomplishing the schools' goals for students…

p. The teachers help each other stay focused on accomplishing the schools' goals for students…

## IV. INSTRUCTIONAL EFFECTIVENESS

q. The staff works to maximize time spent on instruction…

For example,
—Teachers reinforce students when they attend to instructional tasks.
—Staff minimizes time spent on non-instructional activities.
—Teachers spend most of their time in direct instructional contact with students.

r. Staff gives accurate feedback to students in a positive manner…

For example,
—The staff praises students often, but only for correct responses.
—Staff specifies the particular behavior or accomplishment being praised.
—Staff informs students of behaviors that are desirable and worthy of reinforcement.

rigid — — — — — — — — flexible
1 2 3 4 5 6 7 8

rarely — occasion- — consider- — almost
         ally        ably       always
1 2 3 4 5 6 7 8

rarely — occasion- — consider- — almost
         ally        ably       always
1 2 3 4 5 6 7 8

very little — depends on — widespread
              the teacher   throughout school
1 2 3 4 5 6 7 8

1 2 3 4 5 6 7 8

very little — depends on — widespread
              the teacher   throughout school
1 2 3 4 5 6 7 8

1 2 3 4 5 6 7 8

*Continued*

## Figure 8-4 (Continued)

**The present situation in my school**

very little — depends on the teacher — widespread throughout school

1 2 3 4 5 6 7 8

**How my school Should be and could be**

very little — depends on the teacher — widespread throughout school

1 2 3 4 5 6 7 8

s. Tutoring on a one-on-one basis is used in my school...

For example,
— Older students work with younger students to improve their academic performance.
— Students needing help are often paired with classmates who are able to provide assistance.
— Adults, such as aides and volunteers, often work with students needing assistance.

very little — depends on the teacher — widespread throughout school

1 2 3 4 5 6 7 8

very little — depends on the teacher — widespread throughout school

1 2 3 4 5 6 7 8

t. Teachers ask questions and elicit student responses...

For example,
— Teachers call on all students—not just the best prepared or most verbal.
— Teachers ask questions that require students to build on small discrete "links" in a "chain" of learning.
— Teachers monitor student responses and adjust their lesson plans accordingly.

rarely — occasionally — consistently

1 2 3 4 5 6 7 8

rarely — occasionally — consistently

1 2 3 4 5 6 7 8

u. The principal sets high, but achievable, goals for students...

For example,
— The principal assumes responsibility for setting and meeting goals in this school.

— The principal expresses commitment to goal attainment; for example he or she observes classrooms frequently, provides useful inservice, and/or monitors teacher performance.
— Teachers and the principal explicitly communicate about student progress toward goals.
— The principal expects that even low-achieving students can be brought to grade level.

v. Teachers set high, but achievable goals for students...

| rarely | | depends on the teacher | | widespread throughout school |
|---|---|---|---|---|
| 1  2 | 3  4 | 5 | 6  7 | 8 |

For example,
— Teachers assume responsibility for setting and meeting goals in their classrooms....
— Teachers expect that even low-achieving students can be brought to grade level.
— Teachers in this school believe that they have an impact on student performance.

w. The staff in this school monitor student progress toward the achievement of instructional goals...

| rarely | | depends on the teacher | | widespread throughout school |
|---|---|---|---|---|
| 1  2 | 3  4 | 5 | 6  7 | 8 |

For example,
— The principal and teachers have a system for communicating with each other about the progress of students.
— Teachers have a well-defined method of checking pupil progress; for example, criterion-referenced tests, homework, checklists, unit or textbook quizzes, or tests.

*Continued*

## Figure 8-4 (Continued)

**The present situation in my school**

rarely — depends on the teacher — widespread throughout school

1  2  3  4  5  6  7  8

**How my school Should be and could be**

rarely — depends on the teacher — widespread throughout school

1  2  3  4  5  6  7  8

x. Teachers in this school manage classrooms effectively....

For example,
— Teachers monitor simultaneous student activities in their classrooms.
— Teachers organize classroom "housekeeping" activities so as to maximize time for instructional activities so that goals are clear and can be accomplished.
— Teachers combine task orientation with warmth and encouragement.

rarely — depends on the teacher — widespread throughout school

1  2  3  4  5  6  7  8

rarely — depends on the teacher — widespread throughout school

1  2  3  4  5  6  7  8

y. Parents are actively involved in the education of their children...

For example,
— Parents volunteer to serve as aides or paraprofessionals in my school.
— The staff suggests specific educational activities for parents to use with their children.
— Parents are informed of their children's progress on a regular basis.

These documents are components of the Michigan School Improvement Project. Reproduced with the permission of the Michigan State Board of Education, Lansing, Mich.

## Figure 8-5
### Telephone Survey

**TELEPHONE SURVEY**

Name _____
Level: Elementary _____ Jr. High _____ Sr. High _____
School _____ Grade/Subject _____

    The NIN Task Force is now developing our proposal for our staff development plans for next year. Our charge is to develop activities to aid classroom teachers in dealing more effectively with their students, especially those with handicaps. We hope you will provide specific information that will help us to design our program.
    We have a questionnaire that will take a maximum of 10 minutes to complete. Do you have time to answer now, or when may I call you back?
    These items will relate to the questions that ranked highest on our needs assessment survey. Which of these areas would you like to see included in our staff development program? Answer yes or no.

|  | Yes | No |
|---|---|---|
| 1. Help in materials development | ___ | ___ |
| 2. Assistance in curriculum modification | ___ | ___ |
| 3. Consultation at time of need | ___ | ___ |
| 4. Demonstration lessons | ___ | ___ |
| 5. Joint planning time with Special Services personnel | ___ | ___ |
| 6. Aide time for tutoring | ___ | ___ |
| 7. Aide time for materials development | ___ | ___ |
| 8. Technique for motivation | ___ | ___ |
| 9. Behavior management | ___ | ___ |
| 10. Classroom management (grouping, individualizing, use of centers, games, etc.) | ___ | ___ |
| 11. Scheduling | ___ | ___ |
| 12. Informal diagnostic techniques | ___ | ___ |
| 13. Methods and materials to aid peers in acceptance of handicapped children | ___ | ___ |
| 14. Techniques for effective use of aides and/or volunteers in working with handicapped students | ___ | ___ |
| 15. Application of district standards to the evaluation of the mainstreamed children's progress in the classroom | ___ | ___ |
| 16. Other _____ | ___ | ___ |

*Continued*

**Figure 8-5 (Continued)**

For mainstreamed students in your classroom, would you like help in providing instruction in any of these areas:

____ Developmental reading      ____ Physical education
____ Content area reading      ____ Music
____ Language arts      ____ Art
____ Math      ____ Practical arts (home economics, typing, etc.)
____ Science
____ Other _____

One of the major concerns indicated on our needs assessment was the develpoment of our effective communication system between regular and special education. Some of the items just discussed may help to alleviate the problems on an individual basis.

Do you feel a more encompassing communication problem exists?
____ Yes ____ No

If yes, do you feel a more effective communication system *should* be developed?
____ Yes ____ No

Another concern indicated was the procedures for identification, referral, and placement of handicapped students. Do you feel these district procedures need to be improved?
____ Yes ____ No

In planning our program, there are many formats that might be used. Which of these options would be attractive to you?

**INCENTIVE**
____ College credit
____ District inservice credit
____ Personal growth

**TIME**
____ After school
____ Weekends
____ Released time
____ Summer

**FORMATS**
____ Speaker/lecture
____ College courses
____ Material production workshop
____ Consultive services
____ Simulated classroom
____ Idea sharing seminar
____ Hands-on workshop
____ Demonstration lessons
____ Building-level workshops
____ Small-group discussions
____ Workshop/class with follow-up consultation
____ Individualized instruction (learning packets)
____ Diagnostic-prescriptive teams as consultants
____ Establishment of professional development center
____ Miniworkshops (short, single topics)
____ Other _____

Thank you for your time.

Reproduced with permission of the National Inservice Network.

Figure 8-6

Needs Assessment Survey for Instructional Staff

## LINCOLN INTERMEDIATE UNIT #12

### New Oxford, Pennsylvania

NEEDS ASSESSMENT SURVEY FOR INSTRUCTIONAL STAFF

*(Directions:* Please check all items according to your degree of interest. Return this completed form to the administrative office.)

|  | Degree of Interest |||
| --- | --- | --- | --- |
|  | None | Some | Much |
| 1. Method of motivating students | ___ | ___ | ___ |
| 2. Behavioral objectives | ___ | ___ | ___ |
| 3. Dealing with individual differences | ___ | ___ | ___ |
| 4. New grouping patterns (nongraded school team teaching) | ___ | ___ | ___ |
| 5. Teaching critical thinking skills | ___ | ___ | ___ |
| 6. Programmed learning | ___ | ___ | ___ |
| 7. Designing independent study projects | ___ | ___ | ___ |
| 8. Work-study programs | ___ | ___ | ___ |
| 9. Career education | ___ | ___ | ___ |
| 10. Using performance objectives | ___ | ___ | ___ |
| 11. Advanced placement | ___ | ___ | ___ |
| 12. Linguistics | ___ | ___ | ___ |
| 13. Teacher-made tests and mechanical scoring | ___ | ___ | ___ |
| 14. Modern math workshop | ___ | ___ | ___ |
| 15. Elementary science (experiment and demonstration) | ___ | ___ | ___ |
| 16. Seminar on literature | ___ | ___ | ___ |
| 17. Computer programming (course of study) | ___ | ___ | ___ |
| 18. Oral communication | ___ | ___ | ___ |
| 19. Education for economic competencies | ___ | ___ | ___ |
| 20. Developmental reading | ___ | ___ | ___ |
| 21. English for junior and senior high teachers (develop a course of study) | ___ | ___ | ___ |
| 22. Audiovisual aids workshops (teachers) | ___ | ___ | ___ |
| 23. Audiovisual aids workshops (teachers' aides) | ___ | ___ | ___ |
| 24. Negro history workshop | ___ | ___ | ___ |
| 25. Consumer education in the secondary curriculum | ___ | ___ | ___ |
| 26. New directions in social studies | ___ | ___ | ___ |
| 27. Outdoor education workshop | ___ | ___ | ___ |
| 28. Ecology workshop | ___ | ___ | ___ |
| 29. Minicourses (in your field) | ___ | ___ | ___ |
| 30. Music for elementary teachers | ___ | ___ | ___ |

*Continued*

**Figure 8-6 (Continued)**

|  | Degree of Interest |  |  |
|---|---|---|---|
|  | None | Some | Much |

31. Seasonal art projects for elementary classrooms ___ ___ ___
32. Public library resources ___ ___ ___
33. Selection and evaluation of audiovisual and other instructional media ___ ___ ___
34. Spanish for teachers ___ ___ ___
35. Math for first and second grade teachers ___ ___ ___
36. Learning disabilities (identification and remediation) ___ ___ ___
37. Social studies for fifth and sixth grade teachers ___ ___ ___
38. Art workshop ___ ___ ___
39. Field trips ___ ___ ___
40. Physical education specialties ___ ___ ___
41. School library ___ ___ ___
42. Industrial arts (all purpose) ___ ___ ___
43. Pupil services ___ ___ ___
44. Speech therapy ___ ___ ___
45. Driver training (rap sessions) ___ ___ ___
46. Learning center (elementary) ___ ___ ___
47. Teaching English composition ___ ___ ___
48. Modern economics ___ ___ ___
49. Medical seminar (nurses) ___ ___ ___
50. Math enrichment (elementary) ___ ___ ___
51. Retirement and Social Security (teachers of retirement age) ___ ___ ___
52. New elementary math adoptions (primary) ___ ___ ___
53. New elementary math adoptions (intermediate) ___ ___ ___
54. Early childhood (kindergarten curriculum) ___ ___ ___
55. Teachers' legal limitations and liabilities in the school ___ ___ ___
56. Learning and behavior ___ ___ ___
57. Behavior and discipline in the elementary school ___ ___ ___
58. The open space school ___ ___ ___
59. Language arts (elementary) ___ ___ ___
60. Elementary library facilities ___ ___ ___
61. Parent-teacher relations ___ ___ ___
62. Involving the child in social studies (elementary) ___ ___ ___
63. Involving the child in science (elementary) ___ ___ ___
64. Personalizing math (elementary) ___ ___ ___
65. Music for secondary teachers ___ ___ ___
66. Orientation for new teachers ___ ___ ___
67. The psychology of the disadvantaged child ___ ___ ___
68. Classroom management ___ ___ ___
69. Behavior modification ___ ___ ___
70. Parliamentary procedure ___ ___ ___

### Figure 8-6 (Continued)

|    | | Degree of Interest | |
|---|:---:|:---:|:---:|
| | None | Some | Much |
| 71. Home economics | ___ | ___ | ___ |
| 72. Special education on elementary level | ___ | ___ | ___ |
| 73. Special education on secondary level | ___ | ___ | ___ |
| 74. Guidance workshop | ___ | ___ | ___ |
| 75. Seminar in your subject area | ___ | ___ | ___ |
| 76. Adolescent psychology in the modern world | ___ | ___ | ___ |
| 77. General trends in education | ___ | ___ | ___ |
| 78. Newspaper in the classroom | ___ | ___ | ___ |
| 79. Data processing seminar (student attendance and grade reporting) | ___ | ___ | ___ |
| 80. Teacher-made training aids | ___ | ___ | ___ |
| 81. Rap sessions in your subject area | ___ | ___ | ___ |
| 82. Creative classroom (display and bulletin boards) | ___ | ___ | ___ |
| 83. Individualized reading | ___ | ___ | ___ |
| 84. Techniques of teaching slow children | ___ | ___ | ___ |
| 85. Instructional materials | ___ | ___ | ___ |
| 86. Instructional games | ___ | ___ | ___ |
| 87. Physical education (elementary) | ___ | ___ | ___ |
| 88. Constructive seat work | ___ | ___ | ___ |
| 89. Individualized teaching and learning (elementary) | ___ | ___ | ___ |
| 90. Involving the child in language arts (elementary) | ___ | ___ | ___ |
| 91. Updating courses of study (in your field) | ___ | ___ | ___ |
| 92. Community resources | ___ | ___ | ___ |
| 93. Effective questioning | ___ | ___ | ___ |
| 94. Interaction analysis | ___ | ___ | ___ |
| 95. Metric measurement (international system) | ___ | ___ | ___ |
| 96. Communications and drug abuse seminar | ___ | ___ | ___ |
| 97. Other suggestions | ___ | ___ | ___ |

Reprinted by permission by National School Public Relations Association, from the publication *Inservice Education: Current Trends of School Policies and Programs,* Copyright 1975, NSPRA.

**Figure 8-7**

Staff Inservice Education Needs Assessment

## FOND DU LAC SCHOOL DISTRICT
## STAFF INSERVICE EDUCATION NEEDS ASSESSMENT

This survey is designed to gather information for the purpose of providing you with a more effective inservice education program. The results will be analyzed and summarized by the District Inservice Education Council in their planning of programs for the coming school year.
Please fill out the survey and return it to your building principal. The Council appreciates your cooperation and participation!

*Part I*
On the grid in the upper right corner of the answer sheet, with columns numbers 1 to 4, identification of grade, subject area, and building information will be obtained. Darken the number corresponding to your position as appropriate. Column 2 should be completed by secondary staff members only. Please use a No. 2 pencil.

*Column 1: Grade*
0 K
1 1–3
2 4–6
3 7–9
4 10–12
5 Elementary specialist MAPE
6 Special education
7 Pupil services
8 Administration
9 Other

*Column 2: Subject*
0 English and foreign languages
1 Social studies
2 Mathematics
3 Science
4 Physical education and health
5 Home economics and industrial arts
6 Library/media
7 Business education
8 Art, music
9 Others, special education, etc.

*Column 3: Elementary School*
0 Chegwin
1 Evans
2 4th St./La An
3 Franklin
4 Lakeside
5 Parkside
6 Pier
7 Roberts
8 Rosenow
9 Waters

*Column 4: Secondary School and Other*
0 Sabish
1 Theisen
2 Woodworth
3 Goodrich
4 Administration Office

*Part II*
You are asked to respond to the need items on the next page to share your perceptions of the relative importance of each item and the "kind of need" that each is. The "kind of need" is generally viewed in one of three (3) ways:

A knowledge need = a need for more information and/or understanding
A skill need = a need for developing a particular teaching competency or practice in implementing a particular strategy
An attitude need = a need for changing one's feelings toward something

For example, if you feel that you have adequate knowledge about drug and alcohol abuse, you may feel that you need to develop skills in implementing and practicing drug abuse education in your classroom. This, therefore, would be a *skill* need.

**Figure 8-7 (Continued)**

If you have the knowledge and skill in working with special learners in your classroom, but you resent having to work with them, then this would be an *attitude* need.

For each of the following items, please use the following coding to indicate your perceptions of the importance of the item as an inservice education need:

A. Highest importance
B. Very important
C. Important
D. Limited importance
E. No importance

After indicating the level of importance, please indicate the kind of need the item represents using the following coding:

A. Knowledge need
B. Skill need
C. Attitude need

Use a No. 2 pencil to fill in the appropriate rectangles on your answer sheet.

| | Importance as an Inservice Education Need | Kind of Need |
|---|---|---|
| Legal problems in education | 1. A B C D E | 2. A B C |
| Child abuse | 3. A B C D E | 4. A B C |
| Copyright laws | 5. A B C D E | 6. A B C |
| Drug and alcohol abuse | 7. A B C D E | 8. A B C |
| Competency-based education | 9. A B C D E | 10. A B C |
| Reading comprehension | 11. A B C D E | 12. A B C |
| Alternative education | 13. A B C D E | 14. A B C |
| Values education | 15. A B C D E | 16. A B C |
| Stress management | 17. A B C D E | 18. A B C |
| Nonsexist education | 19. A B C D E | 20. A B C |
| Classroom discipline | 21. A B C D E | 22. A B C |
| Special education | 23. A B C D E | 24. A B C |
| Federal title programs | 25. A B C D E | 26. A B C |
| Chapter 90 reading programs | 27. A B C D E | 28. A B C |
| Student motivation | 29. A B C D E | 30. A B C |
| Special learner in the regular classroom | 31. A B C D E | 32. A B C |
| Continuous progress | 33. A B C D E | 34. A B C |
| The emotionally disturbed child | 35. A B C D E | 36. A B C |
| Vocabulary development | 37. A B C D E | 38. A B C |
| Gifted and talented in the regular classroom | 39. A B C D E | 40. A B C |
| Manageable ways of individualizing learning | 41. A B C D E | 42. A B C |
| Development of basic skills in the content areas | 43. A B C D E | 44. A B C |
| Teaching for thinking: questioning skills | 45. A B C D E | 46. A B C |
| Developing student self-esteem | 47. A B C D E | 48. A B C |
| Improving communication skills | 49. A B C D E | 50. A B C |
| Improving time management | 51. A B C D E | 52. A B C |
| Evaluating the curriculum | 53. A B C D E | 54. A B C |
| Problem-solving process skills | 55. A B C D E | 56. A B C |
| Grading and reporting pupil progress | 57. A B C D E | 58. A B C |
| Educational uses of computers | 59. A B C D E | 60. A B C |
| Better utilization of school library/media centers | 61. A B C D E | 62. A B C |

*Continued*

**Figure 8-7 (Continued)**

| | | |
|---|---|---|
| Helping English teachers handle the paper load | 63. A B C D E | 64. A B C |
| Improving social studies in grades 5–12 | 65. A B C D E | 66. A B C |
| Nutrition education | 67. A B C D E | 68. A B C |
| Maintaining reading/writing skills in other subject areas | 69. A B C D E | 70. A B C |
| Coordinating K–12 science instruction | 71. A B C D E | 72. A B C |
| Helping limited-English-speaking students | 73. A B C D E | 74. A B C |
| The importance of second language instruction | 75. A B C D E | 76. A B C |
| Energy conservation education | 77. A B C D E | 78. A B C |
| Career education activities for each subject area | 79. A B C D E | 80. A B C |
| _____ | 81. A B C D E | 82. A B C |
| _____ | 83. A B C D E | 84. A B C |

Please indicate any additional need areas on the blanks above. Thank you for your assistance!

## INSERVICE STUDY

Please indicate your interest in the topics below. Your responses will be utilized in planning inservice programs.

### General Concerns
____ Teacher effectiveness and classroom management
____ Values clarification for classroom use
____ Parent-teacher partnership
____ Writing behavior/learning objectives
____ Student evaluations: alternatives
____ Mastery learning
____ Options for alternative education
____ Creating learning stations
____ Games, activities, packets K–6
____ Socialization of the school-age child

### Interdisciplinary
____ Teaching the gifted
____ Child abuse
____ Consumer education and the law
____ Co-ed family life education
____ Safety and first aid
____ Home management
____ Moral education: building belief systems
____ Futurism: tomorrow now
____ Teaching for decision making
____ Basic photography and darkroom techniques
____ Movement and music K–9
____ American society and the arts

**Figure 8-7 (Continued)**

*Art*
____ Studio approaches: print making
____ Visual education K–9
____ Art appreciation 10–12
____ Learning stations for art K–6
____ New approaches to textiles and weaving

*Foreign Languages*
____ Ethnic songs, dances, forklore crafts
____ Career opportunities in foreign language
____ New development in foreign language methods
____ Teacher-developed materials
____ Use of media for foreign language instruction

*Homemaking*
____ New sewing methods and materials
____ Housing and interior design
____ Nutrition and today's food
____ Microwave cooking updated
____ Co-ed home management

*Language Arts*
____ Motivation and activities for creative writing
____ Reading in the content areas
____ Response-centered curriculum in writing
____ Skills in diagnosing reading
____ Activity approaches to language arts 10–12
____ Developing language arts units
____ Adolescent literature revisited

*Industrial Arts*
____ Graphics and photo reproduction
____ Co-ed industrial arts
____ Electronics instruction 10–12
____ Working metals: welding bending lathe
____ New trends in home construction

*Media*
____ Buying equipment what to believe
____ Individualizing library skills
____ Using films for active learning
____ Learning activities for the media center

*Math*
____ Approaches to algebra 1 and 2
____ How to teach the basics 6–12
____ Metric education K–8
____ Strategies for teaching intermediate math
____ How to K–12 math articulation
____ Improving the teaching of problem solving
____ Strategies for the disenchanted

*Music*
____ Instrumental workshop woodwinds
____ Instrumental workshop brass
____ Instrumental workshop strings
____ Vocal repertoire selection
____ Minor instrument repair

*Continued*

**Figure 8-7 (Continued)**

***Physical Education***
\_\_\_\_ Prevention and care of injuries
\_\_\_\_ Co-ed strategies 9–12
\_\_\_\_ Individual fitness programs
\_\_\_\_ Individual sports, tennis, and archery
\_\_\_\_ Team sports, volleyball, and basketball

***Science***
\_\_\_\_ New ideas in elementary science
\_\_\_\_ New ideas in secondary science
\_\_\_\_ Astronomy and telescope making
\_\_\_\_ Total human environment
\_\_\_\_ Supplies and materials

***Social Science***
\_\_\_\_ Inquiry and development skills for environment issues
\_\_\_\_ Selection of instructional materials
\_\_\_\_ Teacher development programs for topical issues
\_\_\_\_ Equal rights: students, women, minorities
\_\_\_\_ New ideas for map and globe skills

(Adapted from computerized survey of Grant Wood Education Agency, Cedar Rapids, Iowa. Date not known.)

---

From P. J. Koll and L. Cozad *Staff Development: A Process Approach,* University of Wisconsin Extension, 1981. Reprinted with permission of the Fond du Lac School District, 72 S. Portland Street, Fond du Lac, Wisc. 54935.

**Figure 8-8**

**Continuing Education Needs Assessment**

---

Name _____

Building _____

Grade Level or Department _____

Prairie du Chien School District "Continuing Education" Needs Assessment

The Inservice Council of the Prairie du Chien School District solicits your opinions as to needs to be addressed in Inservice Planning for the future. Continuing education has been identified as a major area of focus for 1981–1982, and possibly beyond, for inservice programming. At the end of the one-hour discussion relating to these needs, please complete the assessment and return to the leader of your session. The Inservice Council will tabulate the results and develop an inservice plan for at least the 1981–1982 year.

In the first blank, please indicate the importance this topic, idea, skill, or problem is to you for being a basis for some type of inservice programming. To rank the importance, use 5, 4, 3, 2, 1 (with 5 = highly important to 1 = not important).

In the second blank please indicate the type of inservice programming you would choose for each topic you have rated 3 or higher:

A. A three-hour or less inservice program which provides information and an awareness of the topic. (Example: Teaching the Process of Creative Problem Solving—What is it and what is the rationale for teaching it.)

B. Several inservice sessions—up to six to nine hours, total. (Example: Teaching the Process of Creative Problem Solving—practicing in a group setting the five step process so that you would have a minimal skill in teaching it to your students.)

C. An inservice program with fifteen or more hours—several sessions (could be for college credit, C.E.U.s, or no credit). (Example: Teaching the Process of Creative Problem Solving—having an awareness of creativity, learning the five-step process, practicing it with two different problems, learning how to incorporate the topic into your subject area, providing definite ideas as to the utilization of such).

**Rate   Type**

_____  _____   1. Teaching the study of the future

_____  _____   2. Teaching How to Use Creative Problem Solving

_____  _____   3. Effective Management of Your Non-Teaching Hours (Time Management)

_____  _____   4. Strategies for Motivating Students

_____  _____   5. Acting Skills for Teachers

_____  _____   6. Reducing the Stress of Teaching

_____  _____   7. How to Eliminate "Job Burnout"

_____  _____   8. The Reality Therapy Discipline Approach

_____  _____   9. The Reality Therapy One-to-One Communication Approach

*Continued*

**Figure 8-8 (Continued)**

**Rate  Type**

___  ___  10. The Reality Therapy Approach to Conducting Open Classroom Meetings
___  ___  11. Teaching Reading Skills in the Content Area
___  ___  12. Teaching Writing Skills in the Content Area
___  ___  13. Teaching Listening Skills in the Content Area
___  ___  14. Nutrition Education Curriculum Ideas
___  ___  15. "Make and Take" Ideas for Language Arts
___  ___  16. "Make and Take" Ideas for Mathematics
___  ___  17. Using Learning Centers in Your Classroom
___  ___  18. Using the Newspaper as a Teaching Tool
___  ___  19. Special Education
___  ___      a. How to Write I.E.P.s
___  ___      b. How to Conduct M Team Meetings
___  ___      c. Rights of Parents, Students, Teacher, and PL 94-142
___  ___      d. Mainstreaming and the Least Restrictive Alternative
___  ___      e. Parent Communication and Counseling
___  ___      f. Concepts of Exceptionality
___  ___  20. Teaching Strategies for the Gifted
___  ___  21. Curriculum Concepts for the Gifted
___  ___  22. Child Abuse Laws and School Responsibilities
___  ___  23. Copyright Laws and Requirements for Schools
___  ___  24. Assertiveness as a Discipline Strategy
___  ___  25. Effective Questioning Techniques
___  ___  26. Advising Skills for Teachers
___  ___  27. Using Creativity Teaching Techniques in the Classroom
___  ___  28. Skills for Conducting Parent-Student Conferences
___  ___  29. Goal-Setting Teaching Techniques
___  ___  30. Values Education Curriculum Ideas
___  ___  31. Student Rights and Teacher Liability
___  ___  32. Use of Humor as a Teaching Technique
___  ___  33. Use of the Computer in Your Subject Area or Grade Level
___  ___  34. Techniques of Teaching Basic Skills in Elementary Grades
___  ___  35. Teaching Leadership Skills to Potential Student Teachers
___  ___  36. Incorporating the Use of the Library into the Individualization of Classroom Assignments

## Figure 8-8 (Continued)

| Rate | Type | Agriculture |
|------|------|-------------|
| ____ | ____ | _____ |
| ____ | ____ | _____ |
| ____ | ____ | _____ |
| ____ | ____ | _____ |
| ____ | ____ | _____ |

**Art**
| | | |
|---|---|---|
| ____ | ____ | Visual Education K–6 |
| ____ | ____ | Art Appreciation 9–12 |
| ____ | ____ | New Approaches to Textiles and Weaving |
| ____ | ____ | Learning Stations for Art K–6 |
| ____ | ____ | _____ |
| ____ | ____ | _____ |
| ____ | ____ | _____ |

**Business Education**
| | | |
|---|---|---|
| ____ | ____ | Affective Education Curriculum |
| ____ | ____ | New Wisconsin Business Education Curriculum |
| ____ | ____ | _____ |
| ____ | ____ | _____ |
| ____ | ____ | _____ |

**Counseling**
| | | |
|---|---|---|
| ____ | ____ | Adviser-Advisee System |
| ____ | ____ | _____ |
| ____ | ____ | _____ |
| ____ | ____ | _____ |

**Elementary Education**
| | | |
|---|---|---|
| ____ | ____ | Creative Dramatics |
| ____ | ____ | Mathematics—The DMF Approach (Developing Mathematical Foundations) |
| ____ | ____ | Puppetry as a Teaching Tool |
| ____ | ____ | _____ |
| ____ | ____ | _____ |
| ____ | ____ | _____ |

*Continued*

## Figure 8-8 (Continued)

| Rate | Type | |
|---|---|---|
| | | **Social Studies** |
| ____ | ____ | Citizenship Education |
| ____ | ____ | Map and Globe Skills |
| ____ | ____ | Teaching Inquiry Skills |
| ____ | ____ | Law-Related Education |
| | | **English Language Arts** |
| ____ | ____ | New Writing Curriculum Projects |
| ____ | ____ | Diagnosing Reading Skills |
| ____ | ____ | Motivating Students to Write |
| ____ | ____ | Teaching with the Use of Film |
| ____ | ____ | Teaching Listening Skills |
| ____ | ____ | _____ |
| ____ | ____ | _____ |
| ____ | ____ | _____ |
| | | **Foreign Language** |
| ____ | ____ | Career Opportunities |
| ____ | ____ | Methods of Drill |
| ____ | ____ | _____ |
| ____ | ____ | _____ |
| ____ | ____ | _____ |
| | | **Health** |
| ____ | ____ | Wellness |
| ____ | ____ | Chemical Dependence |
| ____ | ____ | Stress Control |
| ____ | ____ | Death and Aging |
| ____ | ____ | _____ |
| ____ | ____ | _____ |
| ____ | ____ | _____ |
| | | **Homemaking—Home Economics** |
| ____ | ____ | Nutrition and Education |
| ____ | ____ | Family Life—Problem Solving |
| ____ | ____ | _____ |
| ____ | ____ | _____ |
| ____ | ____ | _____ |

## Figure 8-8 (Continued)

| Rate | Type | Industrial Arts |
|---|---|---|
| ___ | ___ | _____ |
| ___ | ___ | _____ |
| ___ | ___ | _____ |
| ___ | ___ | _____ |

**Mathematics**

| | | |
|---|---|---|
| ___ | ___ | Teaching Metrics |
| ___ | ___ | Problem Solving |
| ___ | ___ | Use of Learning Stations |
| ___ | ___ | Minicomputers |
| ___ | ___ | _____ |
| ___ | ___ | _____ |
| ___ | ___ | _____ |

**Media**

| | | |
|---|---|---|
| ___ | ___ | Censorship Trends |
| ___ | ___ | _____ |
| ___ | ___ | _____ |
| ___ | ___ | _____ |

**Music**

| | | |
|---|---|---|
| ___ | ___ | Computer Utilization |
| ___ | ___ | _____ |
| ___ | ___ | _____ |
| ___ | ___ | _____ |

**Physical Education**

| | | |
|---|---|---|
| ___ | ___ | Movement Education |
| ___ | ___ | Title IX Regulations |
| ___ | ___ | Initiative Tasks |
| ___ | ___ | Curriculum Ideas (example: Co-ed Activities) |
| ___ | ___ | Fitness and Fitness Testing |
| ___ | ___ | _____ |
| ___ | ___ | _____ |
| ___ | ___ | _____ |

*Continued*

**Figure 8-8 (Continued)**

| Rate | Type | Reading |
|------|------|---------|
| ____ | ____ | Diagnosis Ideas |
| ____ | ____ | Improving Comprehension |
| ____ | ____ | _____ |
| ____ | ____ | _____ |
| ____ | ____ | _____ |

**Science**

| Rate | Type | |
|------|------|---|
| ____ | ____ | Energy Conservation Curriculum |
| ____ | ____ | Genetic Manipulation |
| ____ | ____ | _____ |
| ____ | ____ | _____ |
| ____ | ____ | _____ |

Reprinted with permission of Prairie du Chien Area School District, Prairie du Chien, Wisc.

**Figure 8-9**

Teacher Survey Instrument

**TEACHER SURVEY INSTRUMENT**

This survey is designed to gather information for the purpose of planning the inservice programs. The results will be summarized and analyzed by your Inservice Committee. It will recommend what programs would best meet the needs of the teachers and staff in your school. To the extent possible, the inservice program will reflect the recommendations made by the School Inservice Committee. REMEMBER, YOUR RESPONSES WILL REMAIN ANONYMOUS.

*Directions:* Review the instrument. There are thirty-one statements on the instrument that are related to teacher effectiveness. Each item is accompanied by a rating scale from 0 to 10, with 0 representing "never" and 10 representing "always." Rate each item by placing a vertical mark ( I ) across the scale at the place you feel best represents your perception of the situation at your school. For example, if you felt that teachers seldom provided individualized instruction for students (item #18), you might place your mark as follows:

```
               |
0     1     2     3     4     5     6     7     8     9     10
Never       Seldom         Sometimes         Often         Always
```

Remember, it is your best perception that counts.

1. Teachers and staff exhibit characteristics of self-awareness, self-acceptance, self-evaluation, and personal esteem.

```
0     1     2     3     4     5     6     7     8     9     10
Never       Seldom         Sometimes         Often         Always
```

2. Teachers and staff are open to change, receptive to feedback, and willing to experiment with different behaviors and roles.

```
0     1     2     3     4     5     6     7     8     9     10
Never       Seldom         Sometimes         Often         Always
```

3. Teachers and staff use effective interpersonal and group process skills in working with others.

```
0     1     2     3     4     5     6     7     8     9     10
Never       Seldom         Sometimes         Often         Always
```

4. Teachers play an active role in planning, evaluating, and making decisions regarding the school.

```
0     1     2     3     4     5     6     7     8     9     10
Never       Seldom         Sometimes         Often         Always
```

5. The school environment encourages a problem-solving approach to conflicts that occur.

```
0     1     2     3     4     5     6     7     8     9     10
Never       Seldom         Sometimes         Often         Always
```

*Continued*

## Figure 8-9 (Continued)

6. The school environment facilitates open communication.

| 0 | 1 | 2 | 3 | 4 | 5 | 6 | 7 | 8 | 9 | 10 |
|---|---|---|---|---|---|---|---|---|---|----|
| Never | | Seldom | | | Sometimes | | Often | | | Always |

7. The school environment encourages parent and community involvement.

| 0 | 1 | 2 | 3 | 4 | 5 | 6 | 7 | 8 | 9 | 10 |
|---|---|---|---|---|---|---|---|---|---|----|
| Never | | Seldom | | | Sometimes | | Often | | | Always |

8. The school climate is conducive to learning.

| 0 | 1 | 2 | 3 | 4 | 5 | 6 | 7 | 8 | 9 | 10 |
|---|---|---|---|---|---|---|---|---|---|----|
| Never | | Seldom | | | Sometimes | | Often | | | Always |

9. The clasroom climate is conducive to learning.

| 0 | 1 | 2 | 3 | 4 | 5 | 6 | 7 | 8 | 9 | 10 |
|---|---|---|---|---|---|---|---|---|---|----|
| Never | | Seldom | | | Sometimes | | Often | | | Always |

10. Each student's performance is interpreted in relation to his or her individual capability.

| 0 | 1 | 2 | 3 | 4 | 5 | 6 | 7 | 8 | 9 | 10 |
|---|---|---|---|---|---|---|---|---|---|----|
| Never | | Seldom | | | Sometimes | | Often | | | Always |

11. Students help to plan and identify instructional goals for classroom activities.

| 0 | 1 | 2 | 3 | 4 | 5 | 6 | 7 | 8 | 9 | 10 |
|---|---|---|---|---|---|---|---|---|---|----|
| Never | | Seldom | | | Sometimes | | Often | | | Always |

12. Students help to plan learning activities related to instructional goals.

| 0 | 1 | 2 | 3 | 4 | 5 | 6 | 7 | 8 | 9 | 10 |
|---|---|---|---|---|---|---|---|---|---|----|
| Never | | Seldom | | | Sometimes | | Often | | | Always |

13. Students help to organize materials and the physical environment of the classroom to fit learning activities.

| 0 | 1 | 2 | 3 | 4 | 5 | 6 | 7 | 8 | 9 | 10 |
|---|---|---|---|---|---|---|---|---|---|----|
| Never | | Seldom | | | Sometimes | | Often | | | Always |

14. The classroom is organized to respond positively to the needs of the "disruptive child."

| 0 | 1 | 2 | 3 | 4 | 5 | 6 | 7 | 8 | 9 | 10 |
|---|---|---|---|---|---|---|---|---|---|----|
| Never | | Seldom | | | Sometimes | | Often | | | Always |

15. The classroom environment encourages a problem-solving approach to conflicts that occur.

| 0 | 1 | 2 | 3 | 4 | 5 | 6 | 7 | 8 | 9 | 10 |
|---|---|---|---|---|---|---|---|---|---|----|
| Never | | Seldom | | | Sometimes | | Often | | | Always |

**Figure 8-9 (Continued)**

16. The classroom environment encourages open communication.

| 0 | 1 | 2 | 3 | 4 | 5 | 6 | 7 | 8 | 9 | 10 |
|---|---|---|---|---|---|---|---|---|---|---|
| Never | | Seldom | | | Sometimes | | Often | | | Always |

17. The classroom environment encourages parent and community involvement.

| 0 | 1 | 2 | 3 | 4 | 5 | 6 | 7 | 8 | 9 | 10 |
|---|---|---|---|---|---|---|---|---|---|---|
| Never | | Seldom | | | Sometimes | | Often | | | Always |

18. Teachers provide individualized instruction for students.

| 0 | 1 | 2 | 3 | 4 | 5 | 6 | 7 | 8 | 9 | 10 |
|---|---|---|---|---|---|---|---|---|---|---|
| Never | | Seldom | | | Sometimes | | Often | | | Always |

19. Teachers use a diagnostic-prescriptive teaching model.

| 0 | 1 | 2 | 3 | 4 | 5 | 6 | 7 | 8 | 9 | 10 |
|---|---|---|---|---|---|---|---|---|---|---|
| Never | | Seldom | | | Sometimes | | Often | | | Always |

20. Teachers provide for the special needs of exceptional children.

| 0 | 1 | 2 | 3 | 4 | 5 | 6 | 7 | 8 | 9 | 10 |
|---|---|---|---|---|---|---|---|---|---|---|
| Never | | Seldom | | | Sometimes | | Often | | | Always |

21. Teachers provide for needs of students from diverse cultures.

| 0 | 1 | 2 | 3 | 4 | 5 | 6 | 7 | 8 | 9 | 10 |
|---|---|---|---|---|---|---|---|---|---|---|
| Never | | Seldom | | | Sometimes | | Often | | | Always |

22. Teachers provide for matching teaching styles with student learning styles.

| 0 | 1 | 2 | 3 | 4 | 5 | 6 | 7 | 8 | 9 | 10 |
|---|---|---|---|---|---|---|---|---|---|---|
| Never | | Seldom | | | Sometimes | | Often | | | Always |

23. Teachers provide alternative learning activities for different students.

| 0 | 1 | 2 | 3 | 4 | 5 | 6 | 7 | 8 | 9 | 10 |
|---|---|---|---|---|---|---|---|---|---|---|
| Never | | Seldom | | | Sometimes | | Often | | | Always |

24. Teachers use methods that promote independent, responsible, and capable learners.

| 0 | 1 | 2 | 3 | 4 | 5 | 6 | 7 | 8 | 9 | 10 |
|---|---|---|---|---|---|---|---|---|---|---|
| Never | | Seldom | | | Sometimes | | Often | | | Always |

25. Teachers use methods that reflect an understanding of the different curriculum areas.

| 0 | 1 | 2 | 3 | 4 | 5 | 6 | 7 | 8 | 9 | 10 |
|---|---|---|---|---|---|---|---|---|---|---|
| Never | | Seldom | | | Sometimes | | Often | | | Always |

*Continued*

### Figure 8-9 (Continued)

26. Teachers use parents and other community members as community resources in planning and implementing learning activities.

| 0 | 1 | 2 | 3 | 4 | 5 | 6 | 7 | 8 | 9 | 10 |
|---|---|---|---|---|---|---|---|---|---|---|
| Never | | Seldom | | | Sometimes | | Often | | | Always |

27. Teachers plan learning activities that deal effectively with cultural and racial stereotypes.

| 0 | 1 | 2 | 3 | 4 | 5 | 6 | 7 | 8 | 9 | 10 |
|---|---|---|---|---|---|---|---|---|---|---|
| Never | | Seldom | | | Sometimes | | Often | | | Always |

28. Teachers plan learning activities that deal effectively with the psychological and socioeconomic impact of prejudices.

| 0 | 1 | 2 | 3 | 4 | 5 | 6 | 7 | 8 | 9 | 10 |
|---|---|---|---|---|---|---|---|---|---|---|
| Never | | Seldom | | | Sometimes | | Often | | | Always |

29. Teachers help students to confront and understand the feelings of students from other cultural, racial, and ethnic groups.

| 0 | 1 | 2 | 3 | 4 | 5 | 6 | 7 | 8 | 9 | 10 |
|---|---|---|---|---|---|---|---|---|---|---|
| Never | | Seldom | | | Sometimes | | Often | | | Always |

30. Teachers use techniques for building and enhancing the self-concept of *all* students.

| 0 | 1 | 2 | 3 | 4 | 5 | 6 | 7 | 8 | 9 | 10 |
|---|---|---|---|---|---|---|---|---|---|---|
| Never | | Seldom | | | Sometimes | | Often | | | Always |

31. Identify and briefly describe the three most important concerns or needs the inservice program might legitimately address in your school. Be as specific as you can at this time.

(a) _____

_____

_____

(b) _____

_____

_____

(c) _____

_____

_____

Reproduced with the permission of Dr. R. Edelfelt.

## Figure 8-10
## Staff Development Survey

### STAFF DEVELOPMENT SURVEY

| Sex | Age | Years of experience in present role | Role | Highest level of education |
|---|---|---|---|---|
| Male ___ <br> Female ___ <br><br> Level <br> Elementary ___ <br> Middle school or Junior High ___ <br> Senior High ___ <br> Central Office ___ | 20-29 ___ <br> 30-39 ___ <br> 40-49 ___ <br> 50-59 ___ <br> 60-69 ___ <br><br> Have you earned any workshop credits? <br> Yes ___ <br> No ___ | 1-2 ___ <br> 3-8 ___ <br> 9-15 ___ <br> 16 or More ___ <br><br> Are you currently in an advanced degree program at a college or university? <br> Yes ___ <br> No ___ | Special Education Teacher ___ <br> Regular Teacher ___ <br> Administrator or Supervisor ___ <br> Pupil Services ___ <br><br> Total years of experience in education <br> 1-2 ___ <br> 3-8 ___ <br> 9-15 ___ <br> 16 or More ___ | Bachelor's Degree ___ <br> Master's Degree ___ <br> Master's—30 ___ <br> Master's—60 ___ <br> Doctorate ___ <br><br> Which certificate do you presently hold? <br> Provisional ___ <br> Standard ___ <br> Advanced Professional ___ |

*Directions:* Step 1: Rate by gridding the appropriate response

| Not Applicable | Applicable But Not a Problem | Minor Problem | Major Problem |
|---|---|---|---|
| 1 | 2 | 345 | 67 |

Step 2: If a problem, select the best approach (complete step 2 only if a response of 3 through 7 was indicated in step 1)

A. Highly individualized    B. School based
C. Cross-school    D. Cannot be dealt with by staff development activity

Permission to reproduce granted by Dr. J. D. Greenberg, Office of Laboratory Experiences and Outreach Programs, Division of Human and Community Resources, University of Maryland, College Park, Md. 20742.

*Continued*

**Figure 8-10 (Continued)**

|  | Step 1 Problem? | | | | | | | Step 2 Best Approach (select one) |
|---|---|---|---|---|---|---|---|---|
|  | N/A | A/NP | MINOR | PROBLEM | | | MAJOR | |
| 1. Learning how to create change in a school | 1 | 2 | 3 | 4 | 5 | 6 | 7 | A B C D |
| 2. Dealing with a teacher who does not "pull his or her own weight" | 1 | 2 | 3 | 4 | 5 | 6 | 7 | A B C D |
| 3. Teaching culturally different students | 1 | 2 | 3 | 4 | 5 | 6 | 7 | A B C D |
| 4. Teaching handicapped students | 1 | 2 | 3 | 4 | 5 | 6 | 7 | A B C D |
| 5. Building positive professional self-image | 1 | 2 | 3 | 4 | 5 | 6 | 7 | A B C D |
| 6. Dealing with job-related stress | 1 | 2 | 3 | 4 | 5 | 6 | 7 | A B C D |
| 7. Motivating teachers to excel | 1 | 2 | 3 | 4 | 5 | 6 | 7 | A B C D |
| 8. Training for staff members "set in their ways" | 1 | 2 | 3 | 4 | 5 | 6 | 7 | A B C D |
| 9. Spreading tasks equally over the entire staff as a result of staff reductions | 1 | 2 | 3 | 4 | 5 | 6 | 7 | A B C D |
| 10. Improving teacher morale | 1 | 2 | 3 | 4 | 5 | 6 | 7 | A B C D |
| 11. Developing self-assertiveness skills | 1 | 2 | 3 | 4 | 5 | 6 | 7 | A B C D |
| 12. Developing skills to conference successfully with parents | 1 | 2 | 3 | 4 | 5 | 6 | 7 | A B C D |
| 13. Developing skills to conference successfully with teachers | 1 | 2 | 3 | 4 | 5 | 6 | 7 | A B C D |
| 14. Developing interdisciplinary cooperation on the School Instructional Team (SIT) | 1 | 2 | 3 | 4 | 5 | 6 | 7 | A B C D |
| 15. Developing interdisciplinary cooperation on Supplemental Services Team (SST) | 1 | 2 | 3 | 4 | 5 | 6 | 7 | A B C D |
| 16. Understanding legal mandates (e.g., federal, state rulings) | 1 | 2 | 3 | 4 | 5 | 6 | 7 | A B C D |
| 17. Complying with legal mandates | 1 | 2 | 3 | 4 | 5 | 6 | 7 | A B C D |
| 18. Dealing with class size | 1 | 2 | 3 | 4 | 5 | 6 | 7 | A B C D |
| 19. Finding the time to conference with parents | 1 | 2 | 3 | 4 | 5 | 6 | 7 | A B C D |
| 20. Finding the time to conference with teachers | 1 | 2 | 3 | 4 | 5 | 6 | 7 | A B C D |
| 21. Handling extra school duties (e.g., bus duty, lunch duty) | 1 | 2 | 3 | 4 | 5 | 6 | 7 | A B C D |
| 22. Finding the time to grade papers | 1 | 2 | 3 | 4 | 5 | 6 | 7 | A B C D |
| 23. Understanding county policies | 1 | 2 | 3 | 4 | 5 | 6 | 7 | A B C D |
| 24. Complying with county policies | 1 | 2 | 3 | 4 | 5 | 6 | 7 | A B C D |
| 25. Handling classroom clerical duties (e.g., collecting money for field trips) | 1 | 2 | 3 | 4 | 5 | 6 | 7 | A B C D |
| 26. Continuing professional growth activities | 1 | 2 | 3 | 4 | 5 | 6 | 7 | A B C D |
| 27. Relating to large numbers of students on a more individualized basis | 1 | 2 | 3 | 4 | 5 | 6 | 7 | A B C D |
| 28. Preparing classroom instructional materials | 1 | 2 | 3 | 4 | 5 | 6 | 7 | A B C D |
| 29. Motivating students | 1 | 2 | 3 | 4 | 5 | 6 | 7 | A B C D |
| 30. Preventing problems (i.e., early intervention) | 1 | 2 | 3 | 4 | 5 | 6 | 7 | A B C D |

|  | Step 1<br>Problem? |  |  | Step 2 |
|---|---|---|---|---|
|  | N/A  A/NP | MINOR<br>PROBLEM | MAJOR | Best Approach<br>(select one) |
| 31. Dealing with disruptive students | 1  2 | 3  4  5 | 6  7 | A  B  C  D |
| 32. Managing classroom organization effectively | 1  2 | 3  4  5 | 6  7 | A  B  C  D |
| 33. Dealing with absenteeism and truancy | 1  2 | 3  4  5 | 6  7 | A  B  C  D |
| 34. Using the student conduct code | 1  2 | 3  4  5 | 6  7 | A  B  C  D |
| 35. Being aware of various discipline techniques | 1  2 | 3  4  5 | 6  7 | A  B  C  D |
| 36. Working with parents who have special needs | 1  2 | 3  4  5 | 6  7 | A  B  C  D |
| 37. Counseling with students in general | 1  2 | 3  4  5 | 6  7 | A  B  C  D |
| 38. Using ability grouping within classrooms | 1  2 | 3  4  5 | 6  7 | A  B  C  D |
| 39. Adapting materials for students with special needs | 1  2 | 3  4  5 | 6  7 | A  B  C  D |
| 40. Assessing special needs of students | 1  2 | 3  4  5 | 6  7 | A  B  C  D |
| 41. Counseling with students who have special needs | 1  2 | 3  4  5 | 6  7 | A  B  C  D |
| 42. Developing career education programs | 1  2 | 3  4  5 | 6  7 | A  B  C  D |
| 43. Using the School Instructional Team (SIT) as a referral process | 1  2 | 3  4  5 | 6  7 | A  B  C  D |
| 44. Using the Supplemental Services Team (SST) as a referral process | 1  2 | 3  4  5 | 6  7 | A  B  C  D |
| 45. Having available instructional materials for slow learners | 1  2 | 3  4  5 | 6  7 | A  B  C  D |
| 46. Using curriculum for slow learners | 1  2 | 3  4  5 | 6  7 | A  B  C  D |
| 47. Working with mainstreamed students in the regular classroom | 1  2 | 3  4  5 | 6  7 | A  B  C  D |
| 48. Preparing for working in the middle school | 1  2 | 3  4  5 | 6  7 | A  B  C  D |
| 49. Being aware of the Talented and Gifted (TAG) Program | 1  2 | 3  4  5 | 6  7 | A  B  C  D |
| 50. Using the Talented and Gifted curriculum | 1  2 | 3  4  5 | 6  7 | A  B  C  D |
| 51. Utilizing human and material resources effectively in programming for students | 1  2 | 3  4  5 | 6  7 | A  B  C  D |
| 52. Being aware of available resources to program effectively for students | 1  2 | 3  4  5 | 6  7 | A  B  C  D |
| 53. Understanding the SLRD Program | 1  2 | 3  4  5 | 6  7 | A  B  C  D |
| 54. Using the SLRD curriculum | 1  2 | 3  4  5 | 6  7 | A  B  C  D |
| 55. Evaluating the effectiveness of classroom materials. | 1  2 | 3  4  5 | 6  7 | A  B  C  D |
| 56. Evaluating the effectiveness of classroom teaching strategies | 1  2 | 3  4  5 | 6  7 | A  B  C  D |
| 57. Dealing with out of field assignments/certification | 1  2 | 3  4  5 | 6  7 | A  B  C  D |

### Figure 8-11
### NIN General Needs Assessment

You are being asked to compete a needs assessment survey designed to help us determine the staff's areas of concern regarding participation in the special services procedures. It is important that we have a large response to this instrument.

This survey is designed to indicate general areas of concern. In order to obtain more specific data, it will be necessary for the NIN Task Force to collect additional information. If you are willing to express your more specific views on this matter, please write your name and phone number in the space provided on the survey.

**NIN GENERAL NEEDS ASSESSMENT**

*Circle Responses:*

Level of Position:   Elementary       Jr. High       Sr. High       Other

Responses indicate degree of interest, need to receive additional information, or affect change regarding the following topics:

Interest/Need
None/Little/Much/Great

|  | | | | |
|---|---|---|---|---|
| 1. Recent federal and state legislation regarding handicapped students | 1 | 2 | 3 | 4 |
| 2. Clarification of district policy for educating handicapped students | 1 | 2 | 3 | 4 |
| 3. Roles and responsibilities at the building, district, and state levels | 1 | 2 | 3 | 4 |
| 4. Coordination and administration of special services programs | 1 | 2 | 3 | 4 |
| 5. Due process in special services procedures | 1 | 2 | 3 | 4 |
| 6. Effective procedures for identification, referral, and placement of handicapped students | 1 | 2 | 3 | 4 |
| 7. Case discussion, staffing and other diagnostic procedures: what must be done, why, how, when | 1 | 2 | 3 | 4 |
| 8. Rationale and philosophy for mainstreaming handicapped students | 1 | 2 | 3 | 4 |
| 9. Effective techniques for integrating handicapped students into regular classrooms | 1 | 2 | 3 | 4 |
| 10. Clarification of the meaning of "least restrictive environment" | 1 | 2 | 3 | 4 |
| 11. Development of an effective communication system among regular education, special services, and administration | 1 | 2 | 3 | 4 |
| 12. Alternative environments for providing services to handicapped students | 1 | 2 | 3 | 4 |
| 13. Making effective use of districtwide support personnel | 1 | 2 | 3 | 4 |
| 14. Developing an Individual Educational Program (IEP) for each handicapped students | 1 | 2 | 3 | 4 |
| 15. Assisting regular classroom teachers to improve the education of handicapped students | 1 | 2 | 3 | 4 |

## Figure 8-11 (Continued)

                                                           **Interest/Need**
                                          **None/Little/Much/Great**

16. Curriculum refinement responsive to student needs and classroom management     1    2    3    4

17. Understanding the criteria for each of the handicapping conditions     1    2    3    4

18. Correlation between class size and the programming of handicapped students     1    2    3    4

19. Techniques for improving active parental involvement and support in the education of the handicapped student     1    2    3    4

20. Within the last five years have you had or do you now have an identified handicapped student in your classroom?     Yes / No

21. Are there any other topics or concerns you would like to see addressed? Please specify

_____

*Optional:*
Name _____    School Phone _____
                                                                       Home Phone _____

Permission to reprint has been granted by the National Inservice Network.

**Figure 8-12**

Administrative Evaluation—Staff Interview

## ADMINISTRATIVE EVALUATION—
## STAFF INTERVIEW

**Interview Process**

1. The administrator can opt into the interview process conducted by the superintendent on the following basis:
   a. The interview questions are reviewed with the administrator.
   b. All teachers will be interviewed in groups of five to eight teachers.
   c. The administrator can participate in the interview if he or she wishes.
   d. Teacher participation is voluntary.

**Interview Results**

1. The conclusions from the interview will be reviewed with the teacher group.
2. A positive report will be prepared. Any concerns identified during the interview activity will be discussed with the administrator. No concerns will be recorded in writing. If major concerns are identified, the interview will conclude immediately, and an additional evaluation process will be established and implemented.
3. If no major concerns are identified, the interview conclusions will become part of an evaluation report, and the teacher will receive a copy of the report.

## ADMINISTRATIVE APPRAISAL
## STAFF GROUP INTERVIEW DISCUSSION QUESTIONS

A. *Beliefs*—What does he or she believe?
   1. What do you think are his or her major goals and priorities as a school principal?
   2. What seems to bring him or her the greatest satisfaction in his or her role as a school principal?
   3. Upon what basis or criterion are school priorities established?

B. *Relationships*—How does he or she relate to others?
   4. Does he or she conscientiously strive to build rapport with teachers? if so, how?
   5. As a school principal, in what ways does he or she find out what students and parents are thinking?
   6. What does he or she do as a school principal to establish, maintain, and improve staff morale?

C. *Action*—How does he or she help others be productive?
   7. Upon what basis or criterion does he or she delegate or assign responsibilities to teachers?
   8. How does he or she go about getting an idea accepted and implemented in the school?
   9. How does he or she get teachers excited about trying new ideas?
   10. How does he or she determine if, or to what extent, the school is achieving what it hopes to achieve?
   11. When he or she has an important decision to make, how is it made?

D. *Self-Initiation*—How does he or she remain productive?
   12. What do you see as his or her foremost topic of preoccupation and conservation?
   13. Does he or she appear to be a well-organized administrator? What observations lead you to this conclusion?
   14. Does he or she enjoy being a leader? On what observations do you base your answer?

---

Reprinted with permission of the Red Deer Public School District, Red Deer, Alberta, Canada.

Figure 8-13

Principal-Teacher Interviews

**PRINCIPAL—TEACHER INTERVIEWS**

|     | Yes | No |
|---|---|---|

A. Does the principal ensure that
  1. The school goals and objectives for the year are clearly stated?
  2. Consensus is developed among staff around school goals and behavior expectations?
  3. Progress toward school goals is closely monitored?
  4. Teacher performance is frequently monitored and performance feedback is provided teachers regularly?
  5. The building environment is orderly and quiet without being repressive?
  6. Support is provided for staff inservice programs?
  7. Time is available for teachers to plan together?

B. 8. Does the principal establish high expectancies for teacher and student performance?
  9. Does the principal become strongly involved with the instructional program?
  10. Does the principal know what is happening in the classrooms?
  11. Does the principal assume personal responsibility for the school's achieving its objectives?
  12. I feel that my ideas are listened to and used in this school.
  13. When important decisions are made about the programs in this school, I, personally, have heard about the plan beforehand and have been involved in some of the discussions.
  14. When all is said and done, I feel that I *count* in this school.
  15. Administration and teachers collaborate toward making the school run effectively, there is little administrator-teacher tension.
  16. The principal really cares about students.
  17. School is a nice place to be because I feel wanted and needed there.
  18. The administration is supportive of teachers.
  19. The school operates under a set of rules that were worked out with students, teachers, parents, and administration all participating.
  20. The principal is aware of and lets staff members and students know when they have done something particularly well.
  21. Problems in this school are recognized and worked upon openly; they are not allowed to slide.
  22. If I have a school-related problem, I feel there are channels open to me to get the problem worked on.
  23. People in this school solve problems; they don't just talk about them.
  24. There are procedures open to me for going to a higher authority if a decision has been made that seems unfair.
  25. In this school the principal tries to deal with conflict constructively, not just "keep the lid on."
  26. When we have conflicts in this school, the result is constructive, not destructive.
  27. Teachers feel free to communicate with the principal.
  28. The principal talks with us frankly and openly.
  29. The principal encourages experimentation in teaching.
  30. Does the principal conscientiously strive to build rapport with teachers?
  31. Does the principal appear to be a well-organized administrator?
  32. Does the principal enjoy being a leader?

Reprinted with permission of the Red Deer Public School District, Red Deer, Alberta, Canada.

# CHAPTER 9

## IMPLEMENTING INSERVICE STAFF DEVELOPMENT

This chapter provides a brief survey of some relevant research into certain crucial aspects of ISSD. It will provide a basis for decision-making respecting the actual implementation of inservice. Although the myriad positions taken by various people and agencies are sometimes conflicting and confusing, this chapter will provide you with some reference points with which to evaluate pronouncements on the topic and to assess conflicting opinion.

### SETTING THE STAGE

The implementation phase of staff development is, without doubt, the most crucial aspect of the enterprise. But before staff development is "delivered," decisions have to be made concerning a number of issues. The following are some questions that have to be answered:

1. What learnings are teachers expected to acquire from the effort?
2. What level of response is expected with respect to
    a. Knowledge?
    b. Change in attitude?
    c. Change in individual behavior?
    d. Change in group behavior?

e. Change in student outcomes:
   (1) Knowledge
   (2) Attitudes
   (3) Behavior

3. Where will the sessions be held?
4. How will the sessions be scheduled?
5. Who, specifically, will participate? How will participants be chosen?
6. Who will conduct the sessions?
7. What techniques and procedures will be used?
8. Which materials will be used?
9. What long-term provisions will be made?
10. When will the staff development have been "delivered"?
11. How will you know if the objectives have been achieved?
12. Which methods seem to produce the best results?
13. How much should teachers be involved?
14. What do teachers prefer?
15. What kind of groups seem to work best?
16. What is the best content for the activities?

These and other issues will be addressed in this and the next several chapters.

## Preliminary Notions

From a survey of the literature, it is not at all difficult to find opinions on all the questions just listed and a fair degree of consistency among many of them. However, the degree of consistency between the stated opinions and the reported research is somewhat lower. As a matter of fact, there is relatively little hard research reported in the literature, and what is reported tends to be vague. Respecting this matter, Nicholson and Joyce[1] believe that the research that does exist is not very useful. They charge that existing research "fails to throw light on the basic question: Which methods of inservice teacher education work better than others?"[2] They further state that little hard research is being done in the area of inservice staff development for teachers and that "what there is is rather sketchy."[3]

There are a number of reviews of research in the area to which one might wish to refer.[4] However Nicholson and Joyce dismiss existing research reviews as "a hodgepodge, unorganized collection of unrelated findings and suggestions with no unifying framework."[5] Unfortunately, these authors seemed unable to outline what a unifying framework might contain. But let's not lose heart just yet.

Based on a brief survey of generally more recent research (1978 and later), I will try to spell out what I see as a unifying structure. However, the fact remains that there is not a great deal to survey, and what does exist is frequently not strongly related. It is, therefore, difficult to classify or unify. (I must, however, acknowledge that several authors would disagree with my perception.) Some of the structural components of this review are timing, organization, content, technique, planning, scheduling, participants, trainers, and various combinations of these.

It is appropriate to begin the survey by summarizing a survey of the research in the field up to the late 1970s. In 1981, Hartenbach[6] reviewed the literature and the research and concluded that successful development and refinement of staff development programs depended on the following elements:

1. Power and decision making with respect to staff development activities is shared within the organization through collaborative processes between administration and faculty.
2. ISSD is school based.
3. ISSD grows out of the needs of teachers.
4. The type and number of changes expected of participants in a staff development program is predetermined to prevent task overload and to allow for installation and stabilization of new knowledge and skills.
5. Concrete demonstration, guided practice, and performance feedback are vital components.
6. Systematically planned interventions are responses to expressed concerns of participants.

Hartenbach's review suggests five stages in the delivery of staff development: diagnosis, design, development, diffusion, and evaluation.

Many researchers in the post-1977 period tended to focus on teacher desire with respect to inservice staff development, and through a variety of instruments they attempted to determine the effectiveness of staff development efforts on three factors: teacher knowledge, teacher attitudes, and teaching behavior. Bieber,[7] for example, concluded from a study in Washington State that teachers preferred individualized staff develolpment and inservice in small groups. They preferred to take part in inservice during released time from regular instructional duties, and during the period in the autumn or late summer immediately before school started. He further concluded that the following criteria were important to staff development efforts:

1. Flexibility in design
2. Teacher involvement
3. Cooperative effort
4. Coordination and planning
5. Operation guided by objectives
6. Relevance to the participant
7. Released time for the sessions

## Scheduling Inservice

It is not unusual to find, still, many inservice activities being essentially one-day, one-shot affairs. These efforts enjoy very little support in the literature. Bunday,[8] for example, concluded from a study of about a thousand teachers in Colorado that the one-day inservice was not effective. Morrison's[9] research on the questioning behavior of teachers and students in secondary social studies classes in Virginia supports Bunday's conclusion. Morrison inferred that the one-day workshop had no effect on teachers' patterns of questioning (i.e., in the sense of more higher-level and fewer lower-level questions). The patterns of questioning by the teachers continued as they were before the inservice sessions. There were no sex, experience, or age differences among the teachers. Also, there were no measurable differences in the level of student questioning.

Other researchers, however, do not dismiss one-day inservice sessions as having no merit at all. Atkins,[10] for example, concluded that one-day workshops are effective in some aspects of practice, and Meadows[11] inferred from a study of 188 teachers that half-day and one-day lengths of inservice instruction were able to produce effective rating scores.

This latter, more positive, view of inservice received support from the earlier research of Lawrence[12] who concluded that programming aimed at improvement of teacher knowledge tends to be more successful than those directed toward performance, which in turn fare better than programs trying to modify teacher attitudes. The notion that knowledge is more easily transmitted than attitudinal changes seems to be well supported in other research. Doyle[13] concluded that brief (four one-hour sessions) inservice was effective in transmitting knowledge, a conclusion supported by the research of Hess.[14]

This research supports the notions of theorists who use an effort-time model to illustrate the difficulty in achieving substantive and fundamental change. That is, as attention is focused on changes in knowledge, attitudes, individual behavior, and group behavior, respectively, much more effort is required over a much longer period of time. Change in knowledge is relatively easy to achieve in terms of effort and time. Changes in attitude require more effort over a much longer period of time. Changes in behavior is still more difficult. Research results provide strong support for this theoretical model.

The research finding that there is difficulty in achieving attitudinal changes on the part of teachers receives considerable support. Cox,[15] for example, concluded from his research in Virginia that there were no changes in attitude or self-concept on the part of teachers or students. He does acknowledge, however, that there could be instrumentation difficulties. The inservice sessions may have resulted in changes that might manifest themselves after internalization. Such changes might be very difficult to measure, especially in the short term.

Attitudinal and more fundamental changes were also addressed by Longobardi[16] in a study of the effect of staff development on the moral development of teachers and their students. He concluded that there was no statistically significant growth in moral development on the part of either teachers or students. It must be noted, however, that moral development is a value-laden concept and would be very difficult to measure.

Research findings in this aspect of inservice staff development are not consistent. Moore's[17] work with twenty-six fourth, fifth, and sixth grade teachers seemed to indicate a more positive outcome of ISSD. He concluded that there was a great deal of evidence to indicate that teachers who had received a specific training session were more effective in creating an affective atmosphere in the classroom than were control groups of teachers.

There is some evidence to support the contention that as more global or comprehensive approaches are taken to the preparation and presentation of staff development, results become more encouraging. The research of Rodriguez[18] is a case in point. He used two individual days of videocassette sessions one week apart and concluded that this procedure was effective for changing self-perceptions, changing reactions to school climate, creating more flexibility in reactions to situations, creating more self-acceptance, and enabling a higher ability to transcend dichotomies. Surprisingly, from the same research and almost in contradiction of his first conclusions, he also determined that his procedures were not effective in helping teachers to respond to their own needs and feelings, freedom to act spontaneously, acceptance of aggression, or ability to develop meaningful relations.

The research literature does support the notion that more long-term inservice can be effective. Friederwitzer,[19] for example, concluded that four full-day workshops, spaced over seven months and aimed at teaching measurement concepts to third, fifth, and sixth grade teachers, resulted in not only knowledge, but also in changes in teachers' instructional modes.

## ADDRESSING THE ISSUES

When we arrive at the point where we are ready to begin planning inservice experiences, we can be guided by some of the inservice staff development experiences of teachers. This section addresses some of the questions that naturally arise.

### Relative Effectiveness of Inservice Staff Development Methods

A natural question, one of pressing importance to staff development personnel, is that respecting the relative effectiveness of various methods of presenting inservice staff development to teachers. It is very difficult to make definitive statements from the research available. Respecting this question, Nicholson and Joyce[20] indicate that the means of instruction in staff development efforts does not seem to be an important variable in the effectiveness of the program with the exception of videotaped minicourses and programs that employ books, both of which seem to give a high degree of success. Other research tends to support this conclusion. Hess,[21] for example, researched three methods of delivering inservice training: expository (lecture, films, audiotape, duplicated materials), modular (commercially prepared), and gaming (commercial board games). He concluded that none of these three was more effective than the others.

More recent research might lead one to come to different conclusions. Garmston,[22] for example, found that students of teachers receiving inservice training by observation did better than those of teachers receiving inservice by workshops or by workshops and observations. However, there was no measurable difference between the achievement of students of the inserviced teachers and students of teachers receiving no inservice whatever.

It is very difficult to accommodate such seemingly contradictory research inferences. It would appear from the inferences of this last researcher that students would be better off if their teachers did no inservice at all, a most disconcerting realization, if valid. Maybe it points out the necessity not to give too much importance to the findings from a small number of unreplicated research efforts.

In a vein similar to that of the researchers mentioned, Doyle[23] tried to determine the relative effectiveness of the lecture, guided discussion, and demonstration methods of delivering inservice. He concluded only that multimedia methods were more effective than just cassette and that printed materials alone were more effective than cassette alone.

The remainder of the reported research of the period under consideration tends to support the view that inservice is a complex enterprise, requiring emphasis being given to a number of supporting factors. Young,[24] for example, utilized long-term (fifteen sessions) laboratory-type, small-group sessions with one-to-one attention and independent study after school to present his staff development program. He concluded that his efforts produced positive effects at the local school level when teachers were involved in the development of personalized objectives. Research by Kearnes[25] also supports this notion. He utilized a model characterized by a building-based grade-level team approach, a school-specific program-design component, and continuous activity after the scheduled inservice days. The model focused on specific instructional problems and provided continuous administrative support. He concluded that his program led to positive changes in teacher behavior, attitudes, and motivations. However, it was not clear if teachers were successful in transferring whatever was learned to their classroom situations as there was no clear evidence of any change in pupil performance.

Since it is better classroom performance and higher student achievement that are the foci of inservice staff development for teachers, this last research finding can be a source of considerable consternation. However, the situation may not be as serious as it at first appears. Mandelbaum,[26] concluded from an examination of his research findings that teachers could change their classroom techniques through participation in ISSD programs that provide problem-solving experiences for the participants and that offer support in the teachers' classrooms. This latter view is supported by the research of Roberson[27] who, using Flander's[28] Interaction Analysis and Roberson's Self-Appraisal (a teacher self-appraisal inservice program), concluded that there was an increase in reading achievement of those students whose teachers participated in the staff development program. Such increases were attributed, rightly or wrongly, to the program. Roberson also concluded that teacher engagement in writing behavioral objectives at all cognitive and affective levels seem to bring about more changes in teacher methods than does training in classroom observation methods.

### Teacher Involvement in Planning for Inservice Staff Development

A considerable amount of research in staff development has been devoted to the issue of teacher involvement in planning and preparing staff development programs. Generally, the research supports the notion that when teachers are involved in the planning stages of inservice, they receive more benefit from the inservice sessions.

Kelly and Dillon[29] studied extensive teacher involvement in designing, implementing, and evaluating their own inservice, as well as participating as trainers in several Lincoln, Nebraska, junior high schools. The following conclusions are, for us, most significant:

1. There was voluntary participation of 70 percent of the staff.
2. There were increased positive attitudes about building administrators.
3. There was a feeling that the focus was on the achievement of students.
4. There was increased identification with the goals, purposes, and objectives of the school district.
5. There was an increased spirit of administrator-teacher cooperation.

Jensen, Betz, and Zigarmi, based on research in South Dakota, concluded that teachers perceive staff development that is planned and executed by teachers in cooperation with their administrators as being more useful than that planned by administrators without teachers. They state "when teachers participate in the determination, initiation, and organization of their own inservice programs, the incentive to succeed is greatly strengthened,"[30] They also state that, "Because teachers have had unsatisfactory experiences with inservice activities in the past, it seems essential that they become involved in identifying needs and planning programs in response to these needs."[31]

In other words, it seems that a planning group consisting of teachers and administrators is desirable, as opposed to total teacher or administrative control. This sort of planning group would depend on past teacher experiences, on the administrative leadership style, and on feelings of mutual trust.

Cheatly[32] studied the professional development of teachers in urban school divisions of metropolitan Winnipeg, Canada, and concluded that teacher involvement leads to increased receptivity of inservice. Based on his study of approximately sixty-five hundred teachers, he concluded that

1. Many inservice programs appear not to be based on needs assessment but rather on who or what is available.
2. Teachers wish to become more involved in inservice planning.
3. Teachers want opportunity to individualize their inservice.
4. Frequent duplication, repetition, and overlap exist in the staff development available to teachers.

Schroedinger[33] reached similar conclusions from his research based at the

University of Idaho. From his study of 289 secondary school teachers, he reports four major conclusions:

1. Teacher attitudes and perceptions toward staff development seem not to differ with respect to school size, subject and grade taught, teaching experience, sex, or age.
2. Teacher attitudes toward staff development efforts are generally negative.
3. Teachers perceived staff development to be most effective when they were active participants in small-group meetings and when the programs were designed to meet their specific, individual professional needs.
4. Staff development efforts were perceived to be least effective when teachers were not involved in the planning and implementation, and when the activities were too theory oriented or too general to meet individual needs.

Lawrence's[34] research also suggested the importance of teacher involvement in planning inservice activities. He reviewed ninety-seven studies and concluded that staff development efforts have a greater chance of success if teachers are involved in planning, managing, and goal setting for staff development programs.

It must be noted that the research does not provide unanimous or unqualified support for the notion of all teachers wanting equal amounts of involvement. Curran,[35] for example, did a study of teacher self-concept as a predictor of inservice needs and concluded that male and female teachers perceive themselves as having different needs, and self-concept measures were neither associated with nor predictive of teacher inservice needs.

This latter finding may indicate that male and female teachers desire different amounts of involvement, with all teachers probably wanting some. Joyce and his colleagues deplore the fact that teachers are generally not consulted enough. They state that "For some reason, the system does not allow for the adequate assessment of the needs of teachers and is not always able to help them receive the training they request, when and how they request it. This appears to be a generic problem [of ISSD]."[36] They further state that almost everyone seems to agree that there is a serious problem in relating staff development to teachers' jobs and to what teachers feel they need and when they need it.

Some authors use the phrase "incentive to succeed" as an argument for teacher involvement in planning for inservice. The phenomenon at work might be called "psychological ownership." If teachers are involved in the planning, they "possess" the staff development activity, and they are anxious that it succeed because their egos are involved; their self-concepts are at stake. This is an important aspect of staff development. Its utilization will allow staff development people to insert other elements into the total activity. The whole is still owned by the teachers, and they will be committed to its success.

**Teacher Preferences in Staff Development**

Since there seems to be some kind of consensus that teachers should be involved in all phases of inservice staff development that is supposed to benefit them, it seems to follow that it would be desirable to determine the nature of the inservice that teachers prefer. A number of studies have isolated several relevant factors in this regard. The research findings of Jensen, Betz, and Zigarmi[37] will provide a good summary. From their research in South Dakota, they arrived at a number of conclusions:

1. Teachers prefer, in this order,
    a. Assistance from other teachers.
    b. Workshops on college campuses.
    c. Observation of other teachers.
    d. Special courses at the local level.
    e. Summer workshops.
2. A variety of resource persons should participate.
3. A variety of presentation methods should be used.
4. Inclusion of administrators in inservice activities.
5. Leadership should come from administrators.
6. There should be some staff development activity every year.
7. Inservice should be continuous and ongoing, with continuous and ongoing follow-up and evaluation.
8. Inservice sessions should be scheduled during the school day, primarily, for at least half of the inservice.
9. Incentives should be provided (for example, credit for credentials, released time, college credit, advancement on salary schedule).

Monahan,[38] working out of the Iowa University Center for School Administration, studied teachers in five states and concluded that teachers perceive the improvement of their teaching skills as their chief inservice requirement. He also concluded that five major conditions have to be addressed in the development of any inservice staff development for teachers:

1. The nature of the purposes that the program must serve
2. The appropriate organizational structure for program development
3. Well-planned, appropriate activities
4. Competence and skills of the resource people, staff, planners, and participants
5. Evaluation

Related to these findings are the data from Joyce's team, which indicate that 43 percent of teachers interviewed felt that the primary function of staff development activities should be the promotion of more effective professional development for teachers on a continuing basis.[39]

Ainsworth[40] also investigated teacher perception of staff development

## IMPLEMENTING INSERVICE STAFF DEVELOPMENT

priorities by surveying seventy-three teachers in Maine. According to his results, the five qualities of ISSD most highly regarded by teachers are

1. Practicality (79.5 percent).
2. Product development for use in classroom (58 percent).
3. Support and encouragement (56.2 percent).
4. Variety (45.9 percent).
5. Teacher sharing (42.5 percent).

Those staff development features least mentioned by teachers in this study were choice (20 percent) and self-direction (24 percent).

In a similar study, Brim and Tollet[41] surveyed 646 teachers in Tennessee and found that 94 percent of them agreed that the real test of effectiveness of ISSD programs is whether they help the teacher cope more successfully with professional tasks.

The studies of Burrello and Orbaugh[42] echo this finding. They determined that for ISSD to be of value to a professional, it must be in tune with the participants' perceived needs, it must have immediate application features, and it must build on participants' past experiences. This seems to indicate that if ISSD is going to facilitate change then trainers must include participants in making decisions about the content to be learned and about the most appropriate methods to facilitate these learnings.

### Preferred Composition of Inservice Staff Development Groups

Some research has also been conducted in an effort to determine optimum group composition for staff development activities. The research of Sireno, Devlin, and Stephens,[43] for example, focused on preferences with respect to group size. They concluded that greater enthusiasm was exhibited for small-group work sessions where participants worked together to prepare individual lesson plans and supplementary activities. They determined that little interest was exhibited for large-group activities except where participants felt it was addressing their personal and individual needs.

These findings are consistent with those reported by Davis,[44] based on his research with elementary teachers at Knoxville, Tennessee. He concluded that the staff development activities favored by teachers were demonstrations by other teachers, grade-level discussion groups, workshops, and conferences with the principal, all of which are small-group activities. He also found that teachers perceive as least effective those meetings for all teachers from kindergarten to grade 12.

### Preferred ISSD Trainers

There seems to be some degree of consensus regarding teachers perceiving other practicing teachers as the most desired inservice trainers. Rubin, for example, says that "a practicing teacher is the best possible trainer of teachers."[45]

Related to this finding are the conclusions of Nicholson and Joyce to the effect that teachers perceive as most effective and successful, in descending order, the teacher himself, other practicing teachers, supervisors or administrators, and university professors. They state that "A teacher... may very well be his own change agent in properly designed [inservice] programs."[46] The catch phrase here, of course, is "properly designed." "Properly designed" staff devlopment can work miracles. Unfortunately, to say "properly designed" may be to say nothing unless we are able to know the determining characteristics of that desirable state of affairs. The authors do not provide the needed information.

Joyce[47] was involved in another related study. This time he and his colleagues found that 20 prcent of the teachers surveyed preferred university personnel as trainers, 20 percent preferred other teachers, 15 percent preferred outside (paid) consultants, and only 2 percent preferred the administrators and supervisory personnel of their own districts. They state "In no category of persons interviewed were local education agency administrators strongly considered as appropriate trainers"[49] and suggested that it may be because administrators represent the same establishment that evaluates teachers. I would suggest it is because administrators traditionally have not been trained in supervisory and staff development techniques.

Another conclusion also supporting teacher participation was reached by Wilson.[49] He showed that teacher involvement in professional growth activity had a significant effect on the level of teacher commitment and improvement in teaching. He also concluded that school districts should provide motivation and time for teachers to participate.

**Preferred Content for Inservice Staff Development Activities**

A number of research efforts have been directed at determining which activities teachers would prefer to have as inservice content. These research efforts have been based on the premise that teachers are capable of identifying their professional needs and of ranking them so that they can concentrate on those that are most relevant to their current professional endeavors. As was noted earlier,[50] this assumption is not necessarily well founded. The research of Davis[51] supports this assessment. She found that not only was there an incongruence between what teachers said they were doing when teaching reading and what the observer saw, but also that teachers were unaware of any discrepancies. However, it does seem reasonable to assume that teachers are capable of determining at least some of their real professional needs.

With respect to this issue, Henson[52] concluded from his research that teachers perceive workshops structured around their own professional development requests to be superior to district-developed inservice programs in which teachers did not participate in the planning. In a related vein, Ingersoll[53] developed and used the Teacher Needs Assessment Survey and concluded that the following issues were perceived by teachers as being most important to them:

1. Interpersonal communication and administration

2. Development of pupil self
3. Individualizing instruction
4. Student assessment
5. Student discipline
6. Developing personal self
7. Classroom management

Using Ingersoll's research instrument, Evans, Byrd, and Coleman[54] replicated the research and concluded that the following factors were most descriptive of teacher inservice needs:

1. Pupil interpersonal skills and teacher self-improvement
2. Implementing instruction
3. Instructional planning
4. Classroom management skills
5. Individualizing instruction
6. Diagnosing student needs

Similarly Clark,[55] focusing on the views of 169 teachers at all grade levels, inferred that professional growth is an individual activity that cannot be accommodated by group-administered experiences.

## A FINAL WORD

In this chapter we have looked at some of the results coming out of the research into topics related to inservice staff development for teachers. In the next chapter, we shall pursue the matter further, but, there, we shall examine some information that is able to help us prevent many of the factors that seem to cause inservice failure.

# CHAPTER 10

## PREVENTING FAILURE

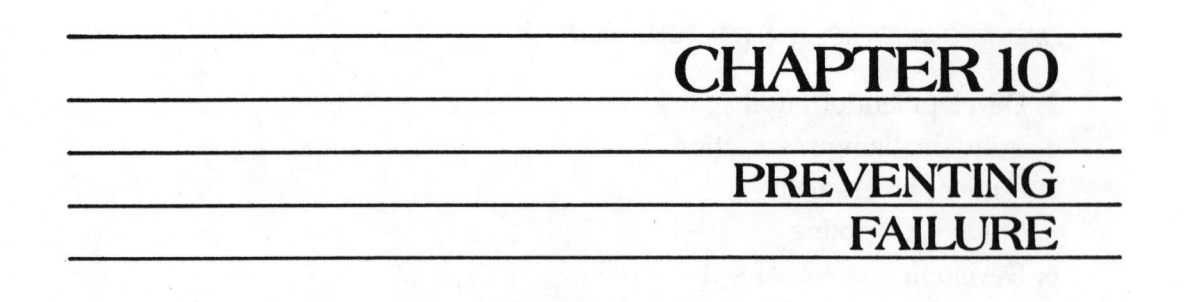

This chapter's purpose is, first, to encourage a healthy skepticism respecting statements that are made about ISSD issues. Second, some of the causes of failure of ISSD efforts will be listed and briefly examined. Several studies have resulted in the identification of factors that prevent ISSD from being successful and indicate to us practices that can be utilized to create conditions more conducive to successful ISSD experiences. Some of these practices are suggested in the form of sets of guidelines for successful inservice.

### A CRITICAL PERSPECTIVE

I have included in this chapter inferences and guidelines suggested by various authors. These "conclusions" have some degree of consistency, but there is a degree of inconsistency as well. Some of the guidelines are firmly supported by research findings; others are at variance with the research. Some of the guidelines seem to be based more on gut feelings or intuition, which may be as reliable as anything else in the absence of more substantive bases; others are based on considerable experience "in the field." While I might issue a caution against generalizing from personal experience, given the state of the craft and the state of knowledge of ISSD for teachers at the present time, experience "on the firing line of teaching and delivering inservice" is probably as valid as any of the other data bases. The validity will increase, of course, as the number of experiences and the number of people having them increase and as these experiences are reported in the literature and are synthesized.

You might argue that it is not necessary to give all the guidelines, conflicting or otherwise, as they may very well be. Why not simply summarize? Summaries may be elegantly stated and pat answers to pressing problems may be neatly put. But as is the case with most pat answers, they would probably conceal more than they reveal. To give a neat package of guidelines would be to practice a deception. The impression given would be that someone, "they," "the experts," have it all figured out. This is not the case! While some of the "experts," self-styled or otherwise, have indeed given elegant guidelines, the fact is that some of these guidelines are not necessarily based on research findings. As a matter of fact, the research may indicate that some of the guidelines are on shaky ground, if not downright naive and (unintentionally) false.

We are talking about major interventions into the lives of numerous fellow human beings. We should participate in the enterprise with our eyes open to the fact that more seems to be unknown than is known.

Furthermore, as we have already noted, what you perceive as ISSD will influence your selection of data, your analysis of the evidence, and your resulting conclusions and recommendations. Your values and even your political views, especially as they relate to union-management affairs, say, will color what you see. While I accept the truth of the cliché, "You believe what you see," it is also true that "You see what you believe." That is, you tend to see what you are predispositioned to see. For example, the notion of "teacher involvement" seems to be based as much on the ideology (dare I say propaganda?) of democracy as on objective findings. "Administrative" decisions smack of "foreign" influence and may be rejected on ideological grounds.

The danger is that, if I were to summarize, those bothersome bits of data that conflicted with my political, philosophical, social, religious, economic, or sexual reality would be dismissed—maybe unconsciously. Furthermore, summaries tend to be generalizations, averages, and aggregates that drown isolated bits of possible truth. Meta analysis is one such technique that does precisely that. Just as "the average person is (man + woman)/2 = homosexual" is false, so might generalizations here be false. A wise man has said that if fifty thousand people say a stupid thing, it is still a stupid thing, the ideology of democracy to the contrary, maybe. Besides, by my presenting you with a variety of views on the subject, I will not provide closure and thereby encourage you to stop thinking, but by leaving the inconsistencies and contradictions dangling and open ended, your synthesizing capabilities will continue to operate, maybe unconsciously, and you may make additional contributions to this field by your own unique and creative extrapolating and synthesizing abilities. While some summaries, elegant or otherwise, will be provided, it will be left to you to determine if the summaries are faithful to the data base or if they complement or conflict with your own experiences, also a valid component of that data base.

## Assumptions, Beliefs, and Premises

Much that has been written about inservice has been characterized by unexamined assumptions, personal beliefs, and invalid premises, all of which may be unacknowledged, and maybe even unrecognized, as being such. As we have noted, few or none of these premises are founded on research, although they may be based on some generalizations from selective memory of personal experience. I am not claiming, here, that such documents don't have value. There is so little hard research in this field that staff development is still dependent on intuitive notions, generalizations from other professional fields, and theorizing based on the little research findings that do exist.

It is also important, I think, to be aware that many statements about ISSD are as much platitudinous as stereotyped. There is a danger that cliché statements may be accepted without question or analysis. One can frequently feel a defiance that statements not be challenged. Who, for example, would dare challenge the notion that "teachers know what is good for them," or would dare to ask the meaning of the statement that "inservice has to be based on teacher strengths"? It does sound good, even sensible. But, what does it mean in operational terms?

It is from that perspective that we will probably profit most from Hruska's[1] conclusions about inservice staff development. Her statements are representative of a great deal of the literature on the topic. She espouses six basic beliefs about staff development for teachers.

1. Participants should be actively involved in solving real problems. People learn to do what they do. Learning takes place when people receive data and have opportunity to interact with these data.
2. Participants respond positively to the opportunity to work from their strengths. People are more effective when they feel good about themselves. Success is built upon success.
3. Participants seem better able to apply new learnings, refine their skills, and continue growing as they get feedback and support from others. Human support systems encourage movement toward renewal.
4. Participants should be involved in decision making about the design, implementation, and evaluation of their own programs. Shared decision-making increases involvement.
5. Participants' needs must be met. To deal with higher-order needs (cognitive, self-actualizing), lower-order needs (physiological, security, belongingness) must be met.
6. Participants will benefit from self-initiated and self-directed inservice. People are their own instruments for growth; they do not sabotage their own projects.

Hruska's statements are not atypical. However, as with many statements to follow, some from eminent "authorities" in the field, it is not to be supposed that all the statements are based on solid research. Some of the statements are of the nature of political rhetoric; some sound significant, but may tend to be trite or so vague as to be of little use as, for example, "Participants will benefit from self-initiated inservice...."

**Putting Theory into Practice**

Another problem exists in the propensity of some people in this field to attempt to apply certain theory directly to inservice practice. For example, consider Maslow's hierarchy of needs formulation. While the theory is intuitively sound, and while it is substantially supported by research,[2] it would be erroneous to presume that all lower-order needs have to be met before higher-order needs can be addressed. Maslow's hierarchy is perceived as having only a vertical dimension. It is my perception that there is at least one other dimension as well. The implication is that certain higher-order needs may be addressed even though certain noncritical lower-order needs may not be satisfied. This implies that a person's nature and behavior are not simply mechanistic or animalistic, but are complex and multifaceted, with the potential and inclination to rise above even his or her own needs. This is exemplified by the fact that many teachers are excellent, even outstanding, in spite of the fact that they are grossly underpaid in some jurisdictions; and by the fact that teachers are able to devote attention and concern to their students even when they have significant unsolved personal problems. I think that by avoiding simplistic procedures based on oversimplified interpretations of theory and research, we will increase success rates of our ISSD efforts.

## WHY DO STAFF DEVELOPMENT EFFORTS FAIL?

As has been demonstrated in an earlier chapter, it is not difficult to find opinions and conclusions regarding the failure of staff development efforts for teachers. This component of the literature is valuable to us since if we can determine why inservice efforts are unsuccessful, then maybe we can make corrections in our procedures and thereby give our efforts a greater chance of success.

Joyce and his colleagues charge that staff development activities are not efficient, not effective, and not popular and are often irrelevant to the needs of teachers.[3] This conclusion came from an examination of data collected in forty-two states that showed that two-thirds of the teachers interviewed indicated dissatisfaction with their inservice education. The authors go on to say that many of the people interviewed condemned the inservice enterprise as a disaster. The overall impression was negative.

It is important to note that even though teachers feel that much present inservice staff development is much less than successful, they still believe such professional development activities to be important. Joyce and his colleagues report that "nearly everyone... expressed the conviction that [staff development] was very important and that it should be continued and improved. No one stated that inservice education should be eliminated."[4]

A number of authors have identified specific reasons why inservice education is weaker than it should be. Nicholson and Joyce,[5] for example, have stated that the literature on the topic has been overly concerned with asking questions respecting the content of staff development programs to the virtual exclusion of asking why and how programs succeed or fail and that, in the research literature, content has been addressed to the exclusion of process. They charge that traditional staff development programs have consisted almost entirely of information gathering activities, such as attending workshops and college courses, reading professional journals, and so on, and that the utilization of that information or the opportunity to practice new techniques with appropriate feedback have been in the distinct minority.

The recognition that inservice education for teachers is relatively ineffective is not a new phenomenon. Beery and Murfin,[6] as early as 1960, listed a number of defects that they identified through their research efforts. They indicated the following as relevant factors:

1. *Time.* Inservice activities are frequently scheduled after school and at other times inconvenient for teachers.
2. *Attitude.* These authors state "Indifference, negativism, resistance, lack of interest, complacency or inertia have been identified as factors which sometimes limit efforts at growth through inservice techniques."[7]
3. *Stamina.* Teachers are frequently expected to implement innovations without any reduction in regular duties.
4. *Budget.* Some teachers still have to pay a substantial proportion of the cost of their inservice.

Because of its concern about the difficulties being experienced by "inservice," the Ohio Education Association and the National Education Association[8] undertook a study to determine why inservice efforts were unsuccessful. It was concluded that there were six major pitfalls of inservice staff development:

1. Inappropriate topic.
2. Long, drawn-out lectures that fail to hold attention.
3. Lack of knowledge by consultant.
4. Lack of involvement by participants. Time should be provided for questions, small-group discussions, and contributions from participants.
5. Poor leadership modeling by program organizers. Leaders should be punctual and involved and should become acquainted with participants.
6. Lack of understanding by consultant expert as to the educational, environmental, societal, and cultural background of the group.

Another author, Sobol,[9] also provided a number of reasons for the failure of staff development efforts. He concluded from his research that

1. Teachers lack a clear understanding about the new roles they were to play in the instructional process. They do not have any clear idea of the performances expected of them.
2. Teachers lack the necessary skills and knowledge to carry out the new learnings. Respecting this, Wood and Thompson[10] suggest that inservice activities should contain a practice component so that participants have an opportunity to try out the near learnings in simulated and real work settings.
3. Lack of required materials and equipment to implement the new methods.

4. Administrative arrangements in the teachers' schools were incompatible with the new methods.

Adding weight to the validity of these statements of shortcomings is James's[11] conclusion that teachers have difficulty applying the new principles presented in ISSD sessions, without extensive practice in incorporating the new teaching principles into their ongoing instructional program.

Bruce Joyce[12] and his colleagues also questioned teachers with respect to the shortcomings they perceived in the ISSD activities in which they had participated. The teachers indicated that some of the major weaknesses of inservice activities were

1. No provision for released time.
2. Inadequate monetary compensation. Apparently some teachers feel that they should receive supplementary pay for attending inservice activities. These authors indicate, however, that the issue of incentives is confused.[13]
3. Poor program organization.
4. Irrelevance of content. Jefferson says that there has been a failure to relate inservice programming to the genuine needs of the participants,[14] and Burrello and Orbaugh feel that staff development activities have been shaped by outside mandates and initiatives without any collaboration between the participants and those who provide the activities.[15]
5. Inconvenient location.

These authors concluded that poor planning and organization were probably the most obvious defects of inservice attempts.[16]

Jefferson[17] suggests additional factors contributing to the weakness of staff development efforts. She suggests

1. Lack of support from the administration and teacher unions during planning and implementation of district-level programs.
2. Failure to build upon or use existing resources in the school system.
3. Failure to implement inservice program activities with sufficient staff and other resources to assure effectiveness.
4. Failure to provide choices and alternatives that accommodate the differences among participants.
5. Focus of activity tends to be on information assimilation rather than on practical models. In other words, inservice education fails to do what teachers are expected to do in their role as educators.

You will remember that the notion of the necessity of choice in item 4 is not supported by research. It was the least important of the concerns expressed by teachers in Ainsworth's[18] study, for example. That is not to suggest that it is not valid. As a matter of fact, I believe it is of significant importance and should be kept in mind when planning ISSD activities. I think alternatives and choices should be provided for, at least to some degree, when feasible.

Different reasons for the failure of staff development activities have been isolated by Jensen and his colleagues.[19] They concluded that the following three stumbling blocks were most significant:

1. A lack of skill in group decision-making processes
2. Inadequacy and lack of skill in establishing and maintaining time lines
3. Inadequate evaluation and follow-up

This group of researchers emphasizes that the process can break down at any of the following steps of the inservice process: administrative commitment, planning for teacher involvement, needs assessment, goal setting, establishing specific objectives, implementation, evaluation, and follow-up.

The Ohio Education Association and the National Education Association argue strongly for inservice education that is teacher specific and situation specific. These organizations criticize the dominant form of inservice education efforts being part-day or one-day affairs. They state "We need to examine both 'why' we have inservice and 'how' our program is structured. To have all staff attend a program only because it was scheduled... is as absurd as teaching all our students the same reading assignment."[20]

These associations advocate that inservice education for teachers be perceived on a continuum consisting of six stages: attending, awareness, interest, commitment, skill development, and implementation.

They further advise that the dominant practice of all-day, all-staff meetings is ineffective since not all staff are ready to participate at the same time and because these kinds of meetings do not lend themselves to activity-oriented (e.g., "hands-on") sessions. Such meetings are seen as conducive to only low levels of commitment and interest. As teachers move through the continuum, their experiences must be more highly structured and individualized, according to their perceptions.

## RESEARCH IMPLICATIONS FOR IMPROVING INSERVICE STAFF DEVELOPMENT

We have, by now, reviewed a considerable amount of the research related to a number of aspects of inservice staff development. It is important for us at this juncture to examine some of the recommendations that researchers give, based on reflection on and interpretation of their research efforts. After that, we shall probe into some aspects of staff development implementation that are based on research findings, interpretation of these findings, learnings from related fields, and creative extrapolation.

We now turn to specific research implications for inservice staff development for teachers. This chapter will end on that note, and it will be picked up and carried by subsequent chapters. I wish to caution you that some of the generalizations may be based on rather limited evidence and also that the authors quoted are human, with the human propensity to extrapolate creatively. It is also possible that they have "seen" or "discovered" certain notions because they wanted to, or expected to, or couldn't conceive that it might be otherwise, thereby rejecting valid conclusions that didn't fit preconceived expectations.

Westby-Gibson,[21] associated with the Far West Laboratory for Education Research and Development, centered at Berkley, offers seven implications of research for inservice staff development:

1. Teachers themselves should determine to a much greater degree their inservice needs. Teachers should be encouraged to analyze their individual inservice requirements, and they should be involved in planning their inservice.
2. If changes in school programs are to be made, the reasons for the changes should be made clear to the teachers.
3. Whenever possible, new programs should be coordinated with old; they should be remodels rather than new models.
4. Some programs of inservice should differentiate between new and experienced teachers; teachers having differing needs for inservice education at different points in their careers.
5. Teachers need help in developing more realistic goal expectations and in understanding the consequences of role conflict and the ways to resolve it.
6. Inservice education should provide a variety of growth opportunities; ways should be found to assess teacher readiness for various kinds of programs.
7. The role of the teacher in [staff development planning] should be strengthened.

The National Education Association[22] has also provided recommendations for improving staff development programs:

1. Teachers should have an integral part in the planning and administration of the program.
2. There should be opportunity for promoting teacher improvement.
3. Curricular planning should be carried on cooperatively.
4. Research and experimentation by teachers and teacher groups should be encouraged.
5. New teachers should be well oriented to their positions.
6. There should be teacher-parent cooperation.
7. Sufficient time should be available to carry on group activities without injury to teachers' health and morale.
8. Teachers, administrators, and supervisors should work as a team.
9. The atmosphere should facilitate efforts to grow and change.
10. There should be cooperative appraisal and evaluation of the goals of the school system and of the means for achieving these goals.

Another set of six guidelines for effective staff development have been provided by Wood and Thompson.[23] They are printed with permission of the Association for Supervision and Curriculum Development, copyright 1980 by the Association for Supervision and Curriculum Development, all rights reserved.

1. The inservice sessions should include more participant control over the "what" and the "how" of learning.
2. There should be a focus on job-related tasks that the participants consider real and important.
3. There should be provision for choices and alternatives that accommodate the differences among participants.
4. Opportunities should be included for participants in staff development activities to practice what they are to learn in simulated and real work settings as part of their training.
5. There should be encouragement for the learners to work in small groups and to learn from each other.
6. The use of threat of external judgment from one's superordinates should be reduced by allowing peer participation to give each other feedback concerning performance and areas of needed improvement.

These authors point out that however attractive an inservice activity might be to the staff development planners, if teachers don't desire it, then it has little value. This raises the issue respecting the extent that teachers should be accountable to self-assessment that he or she needs training of a certain sort and the extent to which teachers have to be responsive to diagnosis by supervisors, principals, or other personnel. A related issue is to what extent teachers should be required to participate in inservice programs. With respect to this issue, the authors feel that it is probably not unreasonable to expect that a portion of the inservice activity should be optional according to personal feelings, a portion being determined by a diagnosis of a teacher's personal competence with respect to his or her professional responsibilities, and a portion that might be determined by district or system needs, goals, objectives, or thrusts.

Joyce and his colleagues also indicate that teachers would like to be included as inservice trainers, resource people, and discussion leaders much more than has been the case. They also state that staff development should be more responsive to teachers' job needs and more relevant to their emergent roles. There seems to be a strong feeling that collaborative methods should be utilized to guide inservice education, but "the more collaboration was specifically probed, the more vague the responses became,"[24] they state.

These authors also indicate two major structural problems in creating staff development programs to meet the desired conditions. They say that there are problems in "interfacing" the vast variety of possible training options with teacher needs and district thrusts. For example, theory-based approaches need to be followed up with clinical training. They also indicate that the vast problems of time needed for training, and training close to the work site, have not been solved.

This also has to be reconciled with the consistent finding that teachers prefer inservice activities that can be completed at school during school hours.[25]

## A FINAL WORD

This chapter has concentrated on the research on the implementation of staff development. The chapters that follow will focus on utilizing this research base in planning for implementation attempts.

# CHAPTER 11

## PRESESSION CONSIDERATIONS

Thus far, we have reviewed the research associated with inservice staff development for teachers. We have looked at some of the interpretations of that research and some of the implications for inservice staff development that researchers have synthesized. Now the discussion will turn to approaches to teacher inservice education that are based on a synthesis of many items of research and of theories proposed by a number of authors. This stage of the discussion is important because it is several stages beyond the research. A researcher must, to maintain his or her integrity, report his or her research findings honestly even though they may conflict with the research findings of other researchers. Interpreting the results of the individual research effort is the normal next step and is usually followed by attempts to extrapolate to implications for various aspects of education, inservice staff development for teachers, in this case. It is important to note that this is the normal process, based on *one* piece of research.

It is quite another thing to examine a number of pieces of research and a number of theories and then, by extrapolating—sometimes creatively, to describe conditions that may provide for more successful inservice. Many authors may be accused of looking at a narrow range of theory or of examining too few items of research. On the other hand, the logistics of the matter make it virtually impossible for any one author to examine the great bulk of the literature so that his or her synthesis would be on an exhaustive study basis. Even when reviewing those studies that purport to be exhaustive, as is sometimes the case with theses and dissertations, you must remember that the author-researchers are usually selecting literature related to a very narrowly delimited research question.

Therefore, this present analysis could be viewed as the fifth stage of a multistage process that, up to the present, might be viewed as follows:

Stage 1: Statements of research results.

Stage 2: Interpretation of research results.

Stage 3: Implications (i.e., extrapolations based on one research study).

Stage 4: Delimited synthesis—synthesis derived from an examination of a portion of the research and theory, as is the case with most dissertations, and with most individual items of literature such as journal articles and many books.

Stage 5: Second-stage synthesis—synthesis derived from the results of the efforts of researchers and other authors at stages 1 to 4.

The conclusions of the various researchers provided in previous sections were derived, in the main, from primary research, whereas the conclusions presented in the next several sections will be based on inferences drawn from a variety of research synthesis and theory, although primary research will still be utilized in a supporting role. In other words, I am attempting to bring us to stage 5 of the process of making decisions respecting inservice staff development.

## INSERVICE PREREQUISITES

Various authors have isolated and commented on quite a variety of concepts that need to be considered prior to the actual inservice sessions. Urick, Pendergast, and Hillman,[1] for example, advocate that consideration be given to three "preconditions" for inservice that they believe they have isolated from the research. They see the three prerequisite conditions as being awareness, readiness, and commitment. The authors describe these concepts somewhat as follows, which are reprinted with permission of the Association for Supervision and Curriculum Development, copyright 1981 by the Association for Supervision and Curriculum Development, all rights reserved.

### Awareness

Awareness includes two sets or clusters of factors: those characterized by the shared understanding among the staff of a school regarding the range of alternatives in school and district policies, curriculum, and instructional practice and those factors that influence student learning, that are responsive to control attempts by teachers, and that may be manipulated to produce or enhance learning.

### Readiness

This cluster of factors refers to the internal state of a school and the characteristic manner in which a school operates. Some authors[2] refer to these factors as characteristic of school climate. Included are such things as feelings, opinions, beliefs, and attitudes that a faculty has about the school and about their roles in the school operation.

Based on the work of Alexander,[3] these authors have identified seven characteristics of school life that, taken together, may provide a profile of those school aspects upon which change efforts likely depend. These seven identified characteristics are

1. *Organizational/personal pride.* The feelings of identity with the school and the satisfaction of the school staff relative to their roles in the school.
2. *Performance/excellence.* The attitudes and reactions of teachers relative to the perceived degree of improvement over past school and individual performance.
3. *Colleague/associate relations.* The nature of the interaction between members of the school staff.
4. *Leadership and supervision.* The perceptions of staff members with respect to the degree of trust and support manifested by school administration.
5. *Creativity/innovation.* The reaction and attitudes of the school's faculty toward new ideas and practices.
6. *Teamwork/cooperation.* The characteristic patterns at the school respecting how staff members share goals, collaborate in problem solving, and share information.
7. *Training/development.* The prevailing perceptions of the school staff with respect to efforts that have been directed at bringing about positive change at the school.

## Commitment

This precondition refers to the degree of willingness or agreement among school staff members to participate in curriculum change, or staff development. Locke[4] provides two components of commitment:

1. The level of intensity of involvement that is acceptable to the school's staff
2. The degree and nature of the participation of a school's staff in defining and specifying plans for curriculum change or staff development

This "precondition" has implications for our willingness to involve teachers in decision making respecting their continuing education.

## Delivery Systems Prerequisites

Joyce and his colleagues[5] have taken an approach somewhat different from the Urik group. They have commented to some extent on what they call delivery systems, which appear to be outgrowths of their conclusion that higher education institutions as well as school district supervisory staffs have tended to offer mere basic instruction to groups of teachers when, in reality, they have been ready for more advanced instruction. They feel that before staff development programs can be improved, both the professional and personal needs of teachers will have to be taken into account. Also, the inservice itself will have to be presented in modes that are appropriate to the subject matter and are acceptable to the teachers who are the intended participants. They see three major factors as having significance for the delivery of inservice education: incentives, interfaces, and staff. While all three of these notions have been addressed in some fashion previously, I think it is appropriate to summarize the notions of these authors because of the comprehensive nature of their supporting research.

**Incentives**

Joyce and his colleagues believe that incentives are needed to provide motivation for teachers to participate in inservice activities. Traditionally, credentials and salary increments have been contingent on the accumulation of college courses (relevant or not). These authors feel that teachers perceive university courses as being relatively distant from their actual work needs, a position supported by Crocker,[6] and that teachers have to be enticed to participate in inservice activities. These authors are concerned that many staff development activities are located some distance from teachers' job sites, some are held after school and on weekends, and some are irrelevant to teachers' needs. No wonder teachers have to be enticed to participate!

Arguments have been made for supplementary payments for attending inservice sessions, but these authors feel that money is not as important as time. They support the call of teacher organizations for inservice during "prime time," that is, during regular working hours with released, paid, time.

**Interfaces**

The Joyce group sees the matter of interfacing as the bringing together of the teacher and the needed inservice training. They claim that the greater the distance between the teacher's work site and the staff development activity, the more difficult it is to have a continuous interface between all aspects of training and the job functions of the teacher. They believe that the organization for inservice should include efforts to provide for a smooth meshing of the roles of the teacher in the classroom, the thrusts of the district, the individual needs of the teachers, and the demands that arise from colleagueship. The organization should provide for the teacher the incentives that make training seem reasonable in terms of teacher personal lifespace, contact with training in settings that are appropriate to the substance of the training, and staff development personnel who can help the teacher act on what is being taught. It is insufficient to expect transfer of training to be the sole responsibility of the teacher alone. Teachers need assistance in the form of feedback, and they need collegiality in the process of incorporating new elements received from staff development activities into their teaching repertoire.

**Staff**

These authors state that "Nearly all...groups agree...current inservice trainers are somewhat irrelevant to the training process...teachers are favored as the appropriate staff for at least part of the training."[7] The authors feel that the key words respecting trainers in inservice sessions are relevance and continuity. There seems to be a general suspicion by teachers about anyone who does not relate fully to their teaching situation. Teachers need trainers who are able to provide an integrated complex of activities. In addition to being able to introduce teachers to new approaches or ideas and being able to make relevant demonstrations, the trainers must also be able to give classroom followthrough that permits personal exploration for the teacher and provides the teacher with assistance in trying out the new approaches or ideas. This notion is addressed in more detail later in the book.

Joyce and his colleagues feel that the best delivery system will be one characterized by a collegial atmosphere at the school such that teachers continuously reflect on the products of their study. Furthermore, continuous follow-up to the inservice activity is made available in the teachers' in-classroom teaching situations.

In addition to these issues, these authors have also considered what might be called the substantive dimension of inservice. This refers to the actual content of the staff development sessions and the specific methods that are used in the process of delivery since, as they state, "What is learned in any education setting is what is taught and how it is taught."[8]

There is also the concern that inservice tends to be too general rather than being subject and grade specific. There needs to be a focusing, in the inservice activities, on the substance of the specific teaching methods appropriate to, and maybe peculiar to, each specific subject area and grade level.

The Joyce group feels that there is a need to provide inservice experiences that focus on teachers' organizational and professional self-management needs, as well as on their personal and interpersonal needs.

With respect to this latter notion of addressing personal and interpersonal needs, some people advocate the type of inservice practiced by Carl Rogers,[9] which he called "self-directed change." These inservice activities place an emphasis on process rather than on content. The goal is to help participants to be more open and flexible, more able to cope with change. The focus is not on cognitive learnings but on the process of becoming a self-directed learner. There is also considerable emphasis on such things as T-groups, sensitivity training, transactional analysis, and on other similar interpersonal awareness foci.

Joyce and his colleagues describe four general types of staff development having a process rather than a content focus:

1. *Social interaction.* The improvement of an individual's ability to relate to others and the development of an integrated functioning self.
2. *Information processing.* Problem solving, creativity, general intellectual ability, thinking strategies, and the like.
3. *Personalistic.* The process by which an individual constructs and organizes his or her reality; a person's internal organization as it affects relationships, particularly the human capacity to reach out, make contact with others, and venture where one has not been before; helping the individual develop

an authentic, reality-oriented view of himself or herself and his or her society.

4. *Behavior Modification.* B. F. Skinner–style operant conditioning is the central procedure. These efforts are designed to assist people in changing their external behaviors.

## DETERMINING THE NATURE OF THE INSERVICE EXPERIENCES

There are a number of conceptual designs that are helpful in planning for actual staff development activities, some of which will be discussed here.

### CBAM: Stages of Concern

The most useful of the designs is the one arising out of the Concerns-Based Adoption Model project (CBAM, pronounced "C-BAM") at the Research and Development Center for Teacher Education at the Austin campus of the University of Texas. This model has grown out of initial conceptualization by Francis Fuller[10] (and further developed and first described in the literature in 1973 by Hall, Wallace, and Dossett[11]).

The model has been subject to considerable empirical rigor and has undergone continued refinement. It is claimed that the utilization of this model can assist in the provision of staff development to teachers (and to other learners) with an optimum of timing and relevance. In particular, the diagnostic potential of the model lends itself to clinically oriented staff development activity.

The CBAM model is based on four major assumptions."[12]

1. Change is a process, not an event. Change takes time and involves a process of development through a sequence of phases and stages.
2. Change occurs in individuals before it occurs in institutions. The focus is change in individual teacher behavior. A school cannot be said to have changed unless the individuals within it have changed.
3. Change is a personal experience. The focus is not on the superficial, the trappings, the media, but on the perceptions and feelings of satisfaction, frustration, concern, and motivation of the individuals involved in any attempted change.
4. Behavioral change cannot be said to have occurred until there is change in feelings about and expertise in the relevant behaviors of the change effort.

The fundamental concept of the CBAM model is the concept of Stages of Concern (SoC), which describes representative feelings, perspectives, and attitudes of individual teachers as they experience the evolution of a change from a situation where they experience no concern to one where they are willingly and substantially involved in change articulation.

The seven stages of concern proposed by the CBAM model is shown in Figure 11-1 along with definitions of the various stage designations and typical expressions of concern that teachers might voice at each level.

This model proposes that, when individuals are involved with an innovation or change, they generally progress through three major phases in their concerns about the new approaches:

1. Self-concerns that are manifest during introductory stages and during which time the individual will typically be concerned about those aspects of the new development that will affect them personally.
2. Management concerns characterize initial use of the new ideas when the individual will typically be concerned about getting everything done in order, correctly, and on time.
3. After these prior concerns are resolved, then concerns about impact on learners dominate. That is, the teacher will typically then ask whether the students are learning what they are supposed to be learning.

It is worth noting that individual development through these stages of concern is consistent with the theory of a developmental hierarchy as proposed by Maslow:[13]

*First level:* Physiological needs (self-preservation).
*Second level:* Management (ego status, "Can I do it?").
*Top level:* Self-actualization. (The focus is now away from the self and on the students who constitute the teacher's responsibility.)

At the level of "awareness" (refer to Figure 11-1), the individual does not exhibit any concern at all about the innovation, maybe because it is perceived as having no relevance or no threat, or maybe because he or she has never heard of it.

Stage 1 concerns are typified by a teacher seeking to find out something about the innovation in general terms.

Management concerns are usually exhibited by inexperienced users. Research[14] indicates that management concerns are at a maximum after the first usage of an innovation. Logistics, for example, is a major concern.

The "consequences" stage indicates that the teacher's concern is beginning to shift toward the learner and away from the self. They wonder how the students are being affected by the innovation thus far.

"Collaboration" concerns are generally those of coordinating personnel rather than of teachers.[15] Teachers are too busy to be concerned about how cooperation with other teachers might make them more effective. But it happens!

A teacher or supervisor with "refocusing" concerns is at the refinement stage. They are ready for changing the innovation or abandoning it for an even more effective one.

The Research and Development Center for Teacher Education has a Concerns Questionnaire that is designed to measure the Stages of Concern of individual teachers. A quick-scoring device is also available.

**Figure 11-1**

Stages of Concern

| Stage | Definition | Typical Expression of Concern |
|---|---|---|
| *Awareness* | Little concern about or involvement with the innovation is indicated. | "I am not concerned about it." |
| *Informational* | A general awareness of the innovation and interest in learning more detail about it is indicated. The person is interested in a selfless manner in substantive aspects of the innovation such as general characteristics, effects, and so on. | "I would like to know more about it." |
| *Personal* | The individual is uncertain about the demands of the innovation, his or her inadequacy to meet these demands, and his or her role with the innovation. This includes analysis of his or her role in relation to the reward structure of the organization, decision making, and consideration of potential conflicts with existing structures or personal commitment. Financial or status implications of the program for self and colleagues may also be reflected. | "How will using it affect me?" |
| *Management* | Attention is focused on the processes and tasks of using the innovation and the best use of information and resources. Issues related to efficiency, organizing, managing, scheduling, and time demand are utmost. | "I seem to be spending all my time getting material ready." |
| *Consequences* | Attention focuses on impact of the innovation on students in his or her immediate sphere of influence. The focus is on relevance of the innovation for students, evaluation of student outcomes, including performance and competencies, and changes needed to increase student outcomes. | "How is my use of this procedure affecting my students?" |
| *Collaboration* | The focus is on coordination and cooperation with others regarding use of the innovation. | "I am concerned about relating what I am doing with what other teachers are doing." |
| *Refocusing* | The focus is on exploration of more universal benefits from the innovation, including the possibility of major changes of replacement with a more powerful alternative. Individual has definite ideas about alternatives to the proposed or existing form of the innovation. | "I have some ideas about something that would work even better." |

Original concept from G. E. Hall, R. C. Wallace, Jr., and W. A. Dossett, *A Developmental Conceptualization of the Adoption Process Within Educational Institutions* (Austin: Research & Development Center for Teacher Education, University of Texas, 1973).

Measurement described in G. E. Hall, A. G. George, and W. L. Rutherford, *Measuring Stages of Concern About the Innovation: A Manual for Use of the SoC Questionnaire* (Austin: Research & Development Center for Teacher Education, University of Texas, 1977).

Reprinted with permission.

It is proposed that by using this questionnaire or some similar procedure (individual teacher interviews, for example), staff development personnel will be able to determine the level of intervention appropriate for each individual participant.

The CBAM model provides a taxonomy of interventions, shown in Figure 11-2, which can assist staff development personnel in determining how to address specific diagnosed stages of concern.

Gene E. Hall,[16] one of the originators of the concepts contained in the CBAM model, along with a colleague, has designed a grid showing typical responses from three levels of the taxonomy appropriate for each stage of concern. It is given in Figure 11-3.

Staff development personnel may utilize these materials with a fair degree of confidence since researchers at the Research and Development Center report that the stages have been initially verified, that measurement procedures have been developed, and that they have been used extensively in research and practice.[17]

**Levels of Experience Impact**

A number of related models have been used in attempts to construct a taxonomy of the impact that inservice sessions may have on participants. Those of Joyce and Showers,[18] and Loucks and Zigarmi[19] will be reviewed as will be that of Harris, Bessent, and McIntyre.[20]

This model development has been based on the premise that any one inservice activity, by its very nature, has a degree of potential to have an impact on learning of various kinds. Harris,[21] for example, feels that when an activity is characterized by a distinctive set of components, utilized with specific procedures, along with skillful leadership and conducive conditions, then unique outcomes can be expected. However, it is worth noting, with respect to this idea, that it has been stated that no matter how skillfully delivered, a lecture is unlikely to produce new skills in the listeners.[22]

Harris believes that a demonstration, if well organized, planned, and presented, is more likely to help participant-observers comprehend relationships between teaching materials and techniques for their use than would a series of readings about the same inservice aspects. He also feels that role playing is more likely to give a sense of spontaneous application of skills and knowledge to a given context than would a written exercise about such application.[23]

It seems reasonable to expect that if activities vary widely on a number of characteristics that make a difference in impact, then impact levels are likely to be quite different.

Harris, Bessent, and McIntyre[24] formulated an experience impact grid in an attempt to show how various inservice activities have varying levels of experience impact. Here, experience impact means that the learner is more likely to interact with the learning situation in such a way that the experience will have some impact that will affect the subsequent behavior of the participant-learner. This grid is shown in Figure 11-4.

### Figure 11-2
### Levels of Interventions

**Policy:** A policy is a rule or guideline that directs the procedures, decisions, and actions of an organization and the individuals within it. Policies usually affect most, if not all, of the individuals in the organization and are in effect for extended periods of time (years).
   *Example:* Teachers will be provided with inservice training in the use of each new curricular program during the contractual day.

**Game Plan:** A game plan is the overall plan or design for the interventions that are taken to implement the improvement. It encompasses all aspects of the implementation effort, lasts the full time period of the change process, and affects all persons who are directly or indirectly involved.
   *Example:* After the principal provides an initial awareness and information session, teachers will attend three day-long inservice sessions providing training in how to use the objective-referenced math program. These sessions will be scheduled throughout the first year of implementation.

**Strategy:** A strategy is a framework for action; it translates theory at the game plan level into concrete action. Strategies cover a large portion of the change process time period and impact most, if not all, users.
   *Example:* Training sessions will be held each month throughout the course of the change effort for administrators and teachers.

**Tactic:** A tactic operationalizes strategies. A tactic is a series of actions intentionally undertaken to affect attitudes or use of the educational improvement. Tactics cover a shorter time period than a strategy and affect many innovation users but not necessarily all of them.
   *Example:* Several times during the first half of the year, the principal and teachers will view videotapes of teachers using a new reading program.

**Incident:** An incident is the singular occurrence of an action or event. Incidents may be one-of-a-kind happenings, or they may aggregate into tactics and strategies. Incidents usually cover a very small amount of time and can be targeted at one or more individual.
   *Example:* The principal will give suggestions to one teacher about how to improve his or her use of the new science lab.

From G. E. Hall, P. Zigarmi, and S. M. Hord, *A Taxonomy of Interventions: The Prototype and Initial Testing* (Austin: Research & Development Center for Teacher Education, University of Texas, 1979). Reprinted with permission.

**Figure 11-3**

**Staff Development Interventions Targeted Toward Stages of Concern**

| STAGE OF CONCERN | LEVEL OF INTERVENTION | | |
|---|---|---|---|
| | **Incident** | **Tactic** | **Strategy** |
| *Awareness* | Decision maker says use is a priority. | Several announcements in newsletters, memos and meetings are made about the innovation. | A dissemination plan is implemented that entails policy announcements, resource allocations and very general descriptive information about the innovation and how it is related to system needs. |
| *Informational* | Descriptive brochure is provided. | Innovation overview workshop (1–2 hours) is conducted. | Potential users are involved in planning, selecting, and developing the innovation. |
| *Personal* | Supervisor says, "It is okay to have self concerns." | Meeting is held with decision makers where resource supports and rewards for use are described. | A six-month series of preimplementation steps, including bulletins, small-group meetings, and initial use training are conducted to build confidence and enthusiasm for first use. |
| *Management* | Counselor empathizes with early user about the extra time involved in sorting things out. | A one-day "how to do it" workshop is held with content that is paced along with how far the early users are. | A few experienced users are given released time during the first year of implementation to conduct "comfort and caring" sessions on a "when called" basis. |
| *Consequence* | A staff developer sends a recent article on a unique adaption of the innovation. | A refinement oriented workshop is held that provides training in a technique for more flexible teaching behavior with the innovation. | A program of inservice sessions designed to add other components to innovation is offered to selected experienced users. |
| *Collaboration* | One user's work is changed to one that is closer to another's so that they may work together. | An organizational development workshop on teaming is offered. | Policies are changed and a special released time planning period is established. |
| *Refocusing* | The user takes a trip to a field site to see a possible replacement to the "old" innovation. | A few users form a study committee to explore major refinements in the innovation. | An innovation development process is initiated that will lead toward the creation of a more advanced innovation. |

Reprinted with permission. The Research and Development Center for Teacher Education at the University of Texas at Austin, U.S.A.

## Figure 11-4
### Experience Impact of Activities

| Activity | Control of Content | | Two-Way Communication | |
|---|---|---|---|---|
| Lecture | | X | | ⎫ |
| Illustrated lecture | | X | | ⎬ Low Experience Impact |
| Demonstration | | X | | ⎬ |
| Observation | | X | | ⎭ |
| Interviewing | X | | | ⎫ |
| Brainstorming | X | | | ⎬ High Experience Impact |
| Group discussions | X | | | ⎬ |
| Buzz sessions | X | | | ⎭ |
| Role playing | X | X | X | ⎫ |
| Guided practice | X | X | X | ⎭ |

From B. M. Harris, E. W. Bessent, and K. E. McIntyre, *Inservice Education: A Guide to Better Practice* (Englewood Cliffs, N.J.: Prentice-Hall, 1969), p. 35. Reprinted with permission.

These authors also created a model for determining the impact of particular inservice activities on various objectives as categorized by Bloom's[25] taxonomy. This model is given in Figure 11-5.

In a related research survey undertaken by Joyce and Showers,[26] the realization that the level of experience impact would vary was further strengthened. That survey, involving over two hundred teachers, showed that the outcomes of inservice training can be classified into at least four levels of impact, with no difference as to whether the inservice was focusing on reteaching old skills or teaching new ones:

1. *Awareness.* The importance of an area is realized and focusing on it begins.
2. *Acquisition of concepts and organized knowledge.* Concepts provide intellectual control over relevant content.
3. *Learning principles and skills.* Principles and skills are tools for action. As awareness of the area develops, one can develop the skills necessary to act on it.
4. *Ability to apply principles and skills to problem solving.* The new teaching strategies are used, integrated into teacher's style, and combined with others in teacher's repertoire.

These authors say that only after the fourth level is reached will there be any impact on students in the teachers' classrooms.

**Figure 11-5**

**Inservice Design Grid**

| ACTIVITIES | OBJECTIVES |||||| 
|---|---|---|---|---|---|---|
|  | Knowledge | Comprehension | Application | Synthesis | Values and Attitudes | Adjustment |

Lecture
Illustrated lecture
Demonstration
Observation
Interviewing
Brainstorming
Group discussions
Buzz sessions
Role playing
Guided practice

*Cognitive Objectives* — *Broad Spectrum Objectives* — *Affective Objectives*

| Cognitive Domain | Affective Domain |
|---|---|

From B. M. Harris, E. W., Bessent, and K. E. McIntyre, *Inservice Education: A Guide to Better Practice* (Englewood Cliffs, N.J.: Prentice-Hall, 1969), p. 37. Reprinted with permission.

Joyce and Showers also analyzed about two hundred studies where researchers attempted to investigate effectiveness of various kinds of training methods. They feel that it is difficult to determine the level of impact because of three major factors:

1. Most studies were not designed to measure levels of impact on the incremental value of each training component but on differences between treatment and comparison groups.
2. Conclusions nearly always addressed the issue of whether skills were acquired and demonstrated. The question of transfer at the classroom level was addressed in relatively few studies.
3. No single study used all training components or measured effects at all levels of impact.

These authors state that the results of studies of inservice training are remarkably consistent. Teachers learn the designated concepts and are able to demonstrate the new skills and strategies. However, they state that a very important set of conditions have to be in place for that to occur, namely, the provision of opportunity for some combination of modeling, practice, and feedback. We shall return to a discussion of these ideas.

### Level of Use

The CBAM model has a second dimension that can be utilized in assessing the involvement of people with respect to an innovation. (An innovation, with respect to the present discussion, can be any aspect of curriculum, instruction, or school management that is of interest to the inservice personnel. It does not have to be an absolutely and entirely new approach to any aspect of schooling.) This second component is called level of use (LoU). This part of the CBAM model focuses on the behavior and performance of the individual who is engaged in implementing the specific innovation that is of interest. The level of use component of the model contains eight classifications. The identified levels and their definitions are exhibited in Figure 11-6.

The essential point to note is that as individuals become more familiar with an innovation, they become more skilled and coordinated in its use, and more sensitive to its effect on students. The behavior and performance of individuals change over time with respect to their actual use of the specific innovation of interest.

The people at the Research and Development Center for Teacher Education also describe seven categories of use for each LoU, namely, knowledge, acquiring information, sharing, assessing, planning, status reporting, and performing. Descriptors of indicators have been provided for each level and category. These descriptors can help inservice personnel determine with a very high degree of accuracy the present status of a teacher with respect to an inservice thrust. These seven categories of use, their definitions, and descriptors for each LoU are given in the paragraphs that follow. (*Note:* This material was originally prepared as a result of the Procedure for Adopting Educational Innovations Project, Research and Development Center for Teacher Education, University of Texas at Austin, 1975, N.I.E. contract number NIE-C-74-0087, and is reprinted with permission of the Research and Development Center for Teacher Education from G. E. Hall, S. F. Loucks, W. L. Rutherford, and B. W. Newlove, "Levels of Use of The Innovation: A Framework for Analyzing Innovation Adoption," *The Journal of Teacher Education*, Vol. 26, no. 1 (1975), pp. 52–56.)

*Knowledge.* This category of possible use refers to that which the user knows about characteristics of the innovation, how to use it, and the consequences of its use. This is cognitive knowledge related to using the innovation, not feelings or attitudes.

| | |
|---|---|
| *Level 0 (nonuse).* | Knows nothing about this or similar innovations or has only very limited general knowledge of efforts to develop innovations in this area. |
| *Level 1 (orientation).* | Knows general information about the innovation such as origin, characteristics, and implementation requirements. |

Figure 11-6

Levels of Use of the Innovation

| Level of Use | Definition of Use | Typical Behaviors of Level |
|---|---|---|
| 0  Nonuse | State in which the user has little or no knowledge of the innovation and no involvement with the innovation and is doing nothing toward becoming involved. | No action is being taken with respect to the innovation. |
| Decision Point A: | Takes action to learn more detailed information about the innovation. | |
| 1  Orientation | State in which the user has recently acquired or is acquiring information about the innovation and/or has recently explored or is exploring its value orientation and its demands upon user and user system. | The user is seeking out information about the innovation. |
| Decision Point B: | Makes a decision to use the innovation by establishing a time to begin. | |
| 2  Preparation | State in which the user is preparing for first use of the innovation. | The user is preparing to use the innovation. |
| Decision Point C: | Changes, if any, and use are dominated by user needs. | |
| 3  Mechanical Use | State in which the user focuses most effort on the short-term, day-to-day use of the innovation with little time for reflection. Changes in use are made more to meet user needs than client needs. The user is primarily engaged in a stepwise attempt to master the tasks required to use the innovation, often resulting in disjointed and superficial use. | The user is using the innovation in a poorly coordinated manner and is making user-oriented changes. |
| Decision Point D-1: | A routine pattern of use is established. | |
| 4A  Routine | Use of the innovation is stabilized. Few, if any, changes are being made in ongoing use. Little preparation or thought is being given to improving innovation use or its consequences. | The user is making few or no changes and has an established pattern of use. |

160

| Decision Point D-2: | Changes use of the innovation based on formal or informal evaluation to increase client outcomes. |
|---|---|
| 4B Refinement | State in which the user varies the use of the innovation to increase the impact on clients within the immediate sphere of influence. Variations are based on knowledge of both short- and long-term consequences for clients. The user is making changes to increase outcomes. |

| Decision Point E: | Initiates changes in use of innovation based on input of and in coordination with what colleagues are doing. |
|---|---|
| 5 Integration | State in which the user is combining own efforts to use the innovation with related activities of colleagues to achieve a collective impact on clients within their common sphere of influence. The user is making deliberate effort to coordinate with others in using the innovation. |

| Decision Point F: | Begins exploring alternatives to or major modifications of the innovation currently in use. |
|---|---|
| 6 Renewal | State in which the user reevaluates the quality of use of the innovation, seeks major modifications of or alternatives to present innovation to achieve increased impact on clients, examines new developments in the field, and explores new goals for self and the system. The user is seeking more effective alternatives to the established use of the innovation. |

This information is a composite compiled from information contained in the following documents: G. E. Hall, Concerns-Based Inservice Teacher Training: An Overview of the Concepts, Research and Practice; "Paper presented at the conference on School-Focused Inservice Training, Bournemouth, England, March 2–3, 1978 (R&D Center for Teacher Education, Report #3057, University of Texas at Austin); and S. F. Loucks and P. Zigarmi, Effective Staff Development for the Process of Innovation;" Educational Concerns, Vol. 8, no. 2 (Winter 1981), pp. 4–8. The information is based on materials related to the CBAM project at the Research and Development Center for Teacher Education, the University of Texas at Austin. Used with permission.

161

*Level 2 (preparation).* Knows logistical requirements, necessary resources and timing for initial use of the innovation and details of initial experiences for clients.

*Level 3 (mechanical use).* Knows on a day-to-day basis the requirements for using the innovation. Is more knowledgeable on short-term activities and effects than long-range activities and effects of use of the innovation.

*Level 4A (routine).* Knows on a day-to-day basis the requirements for using the innovation. Is more knowledgeable about short-term activities and effects than about long-range activities and effects of use of the innovation.

*Level 4B (refinement).* Knows cognitive and affective effects of the innovation on clients and ways for increasing impact on clients.

*Level 5 (integration).* Knows how to coordinate own use of the innovation with colleagues to provide a collective impact on clients.

*Level 6 (renewal).* Knows of alternatives that could be used to change or replace the present innovation that would improve the quality of outcomes of its use.

*Acquiring Information.* Solicits information about the innovation in a variety of ways, including questioning resource persons, corresponding with resource agencies, reviewing printed materials, and making visits.

*Level 0 (nonuse).* Takes little or no action to solicit information beyond reviewing descriptive information about this or similar innovations when it happens to come to personal attention.

*Level 1 (orientation).* Seeks descriptive material about the innovation. Seeks opinions and knowledge of others through discussions, visits, or workshops.

*Level 2 (preparation).* Seeks information and resources specifically related to preparation for use of the innovation in own setting.

*Level 3 (mechanical use).* Solicits management information about such things as logistics, scheduling techniques, and ideas for reducing amount of time and work required for user.

*Level 4A (routine).* Makes no special effort to seek information as a part of the ongoing use of the innovation.

*Level 4B (refinement).* Solicits information and materials that focus specifically on changing use of the innovation to affect client outcomes.

*Level 5 (integration).* Solicits information and opinions for the purpose of collaborating with others in use of the innovation.

*Level 6 (renewal).* Seeks information and materials about other innovations as alternatives to the present innovation or for making major adaptions in the innovation.

***Sharing.*** Discusses the innovation with others. Shares plans, ideas, resources, outcomes, and problems related to the innovation.

*Level 0 (nonuse).*     Is not communicating with others about the innovation beyond possibly acknowledging that the innovation exists.

*Level 1 (orientation).*     Discusses the innovation in general terms and/or exchanges descriptive information, materials, or ideas about the innovation and possible implications of its use.

*Level 2 (preparation).*     Discusses resources needed for initial use of the innovation. Joins others in preuse training and in planning for resources, logistics, schedules, and so on in preparation for first use.

*Level 3 (mechanical use).*     Discusses management and logistical issues related to use of the innovation. Resources and materials are shared for purposes of reducing management, flow and logistical problems related to use of innovation.

*Level 4A (routine).*     Describes current use of the innovation with little or no reference to ways of changing use.

*Level 4B (refinement).*     Discusses own methods of modifying use of the innovation to change client outcomes.

*Level 5 (integrating).*     Discusses efforts to increase client impact through collaboration with others on personal use of the innovation.

*Level 6 (renewal).*     Focuses discussion on identification of major alternatives or replacements for the current innovation.

***Assessing.*** Examines the potential or actual use of the innovation or some aspect of it. This can be a mental assessment or can involve actual collection and analysis of data.

*Level 0 (nonuse).*     Takes no action to analyze the innovation, its characteristics, possible use, or consequences of use.

*Level 1 (orientation).*     Analyzes and compares materials, content, requirements for use, evaluation reports, potential outcomes, strengths, and weaknesses for purpose of making a decision about the use of the innovation.

*Level 2 (preparation).*     Analyzes detailed requirements and available resources for initial use of the innovation.

*Level 3 (mechanical use).*     Examines own use of the innovation with respect to problems of logistics, management, time, schedules, resources, and general reactions of clients.

*Level 4A (routine).*     Assesses use of the innovation in global terms without reference to making changes. Specific evaluation activities are limited to those that are administratively required with little attention paid to findings for the purpose of changing use.

*Level 4B (refinement).*   Assesses use of the innovation for the purpose of changing current practices to improve client outcomes.

*Level 5 (integration).*   Appraises collaborative use of the innovation in terms of client outcomes and strengths and weaknesses of the integrated effort.

*Level 6 (renewal).*   Analyzes advantages and disadvantages of major modifications or alterations to the present innovation.

*Planning.* Designs and outlines short- and/or long-range steps to be taken during the process of innovation adoption (i.e., aligns resources, schedules activities, meets with others to organize and/or coordinate use of the innovation).

*Level 0 (nonuse).*   Schedules no time and specifies no steps for the study or use of the innovation.

*Level 1 (orientation).*   Plans to gather necessary information and resources as needed to make a decision for or against use of the innovation.

*Level 2 (preparation).*   Identifies steps and procedures entailed in obtaining resources and organizing activities and events for initial use of the innovation.

*Level 3 (mechanical use).*   Plans for organizing and managing resources, activities, and events related primarily to immediate ongoing use of the innovation. Planned-for changes address managerial or logistical issues with a short-term perspective.

*Level 4A (routine).*   Plans intermediate- and long-range actions with little projected variation in how the innovation will be used. Planning focuses on routine use of resources, personnel, and the like.

*Level 4B (refinement).*   Develops intermediate- and long-range plans that anticipate possible and needed steps, resources, and events designed to enhance client outcomes.

*Level 5 (integration).*   Plans specific actions to coordinate own use of the innovation with others to achieve increased impact on clients.

*Level 6 (renewal).*   Plans activities that involve pursuit of alternatives to enhance or replace the innovation.

*Status Reporting.* Describes personal stand at the present time in relation to use of the innovation.

*Level 0 (nonuse).*   Reports little or no personal involvement with the innovation.

*Level 1 (orientation).*   Reports presently oriented self to what the innovation is and is not.

*Level 2 (preparation).*   Reports preparing self for initial use of the innovation.

*Level 3 (mechanical use).* Reports that logistics, time, management, resource organization, and so on are the focus of most personal efforts to use the innovation.

*Level 4A (routine).* Reports that personal use of the innovation is going along satisfactorily with few if any problems.

*Level 4B (refinement).* Reports varying use of the innovation to change client outcomes.

*Level 5 (integration).* Reports spending time and energy collaborating with others about integrating own use of the innovation.

*Level 6 (renewal).* Reports considering major modifications of or alternatives to present use of the innovation.

*Performing.* Carries out the actions and activities entailed in operationalizing the innovation.

*Level 0 (nonuse).* Takes no discernible action toward learning about or using the innovation. The innovation or its accouterments are not present or in use.

*Level 1 (orientation).* Explores the innovation and requirements for its use by talking to others about it, reviewing descriptive information and sample materials, attending orientation sessions, and observing others using it.

*Level 2 (preparation).* Studies reference materials in depth, organizes resources and logistics, and schedules and receives skill training in preparation for initial use.

*Level 3 (mechanical use).* Manages innovation with varying degrees of efficiency. Often lacks anticipation of immediate consequences. The flow of actions in the user and clients is often disjointed, uneven, and uncertain. When changes are made, they are primarily in response to logistical and organizational problems.

*Level 4A (routine).* Uses the innovation smoothly with minimal management problems; over time, there is little variation in pattern of use.

*Level 4B (refinement).* Explores and experiments with alternative combinations of the innovation with existing practices to maximize client involvement and to optimize client outcomes.

*Level 5 (integration).* Collaborates with others in use of the innovation as a means for expanding the innovation's impact on clients. Changes in use are made in coordination with others.

*Level 6 (renewal).* Explores other innovations that could be used in combination with or in place of the present innovation in an attempt to develop more effective means of achieving client outcomes.

Since I have barely scratched the surface of these important and useful concepts, I would strongly recommend that you obtain detailed information from the Research and Development Center for Teacher Education at the University of Texas at Austin.

## A FINAL WORD

In this chapter, I have created a context in which to discuss inservice activities. In the next chapter we shall examine components that can make the sessions effective and meaningful. We will also examine appropriate postsession activities.

# CHAPTER 12

## THE SESSIONS AND FOLLOW-UP

The inservice session is a basic unit of inservice staff development for teachers. A session will be directed at a specific client group, selected or self-selected, and its purpose will normally be the satisfaction of one or several specific predetermined, articulated objectives. It will take place at a particular place and at a particular time. It will utilize particular specifically determined and specifically selected activities, materials, and approaches. This is the "make it or break it" level of staff development. This is "in the trenches"; this is "where it's at"! This is where the theory and models, the research and synthesis, and the extrapolations and projections are put to the test.

At an earlier point in this examination, extensive effort was directed at needs assessment. We shall return briefly to some of the issues raised there. You may wish to refer back to that section to refresh your memory. The inservice sessions should be based on specific information about the teacher-clients to be served: their numbers, their formal academic-professional backgrounds, their experiences, their perceptions of their inservice needs, their specific teaching or administrative assignments, their diagnosed needs, and the specific strategies that have been determined to be of most positive long-term impact.

### OBJECTIVES AND EXPECTATIONS

The inservice sessions should be goal oriented. That is, both the trainer group and the client group should have clearly in mind what objectives are in focus and, to some degree, should have common understandings respecting the extent to which these objectives are expected to be satisfied. If the objectives or goals are not specified and well understood, the trainers may address one set of objectives while the teacher-participants may have expectations of satisfying a different set of objectives. It is important that all concerned have common understandings respecting the objectives of the specific inservice sessions.

It is also worth noting that the goals may indeed be well understood, but they may be unrealistic in scope, or breadth, or both. Too much may be attempted in one session and too much may be hoped for. Effects that, realistically, should be expected to manifest themselves only in the long term and after a series of sessions may be expected after only one session. If the objectives and expectations of the sessions are unrealistic, then there will likely be a perception of failure, whereas the sessions might be perceived as successes if the commonly held objectives and expectations are realistically obtainable. The appropriateness and mutual understanding of objectives constitute crucial considerations that cannot be overemphasized.

It is important that you relate the objectives of the individual inservice sessions to the needs of the teacher-clients. While various individual teachers may have varying and divergent needs, and while you cannot be expected to address wide-ranging needs of a number of people in one inservice session, you will need to demonstrate that the objectives of each session do, in fact, relate in a logical fashion to the needs of each participant. It will not be sufficient merely to address some immediate, short-term, or superficial needs. A successful inservice session will address significant objectives related to well-articulated intermediate or long-term goals.

Discuss with the participants exactly what the purposes of the session are and how it was determined that these specific purposes were appropriate. It may be necessary to outline briefly the process that has been utilized to determine the appropriate session objectives. You could mention, for example, the needs assessment, the discussion with teachers, the teachers who assisted in the planning, and the feedback from teachers as planning was progressing. Remind the participants, subtly, that these sessions are the results of their involvement in the decision making, and the result of consultation with them. This will assist them in establishing and reinforcing their "ownership" of the sessions and will, therefore, contribute to the sessions' success.

It may be useful to address the degree of specificity of the objectives that might be necessary for inservice sessions. You are probably familiar with the notions of developing behavioral objectives as espoused by Mager.[1] The objectives that I am advocating are not necessarily quite as specific as the performance, condition, and standard criteria as espoused by him. His approach, while useful in its appropriate situation, has limitations when applied to inservice education for teachers. Harris has outlined three specific limitations when Mager-style objectives are utilized for teacher inservice:

1. Certain learning outcomes (performances) cannot be so clearly specified in advance.
2. Such explicit statements of outcomes tend to encourage preoccupation with fragments of a larger, more complex performance.

## THE SESSIONS AND FOLLOW-UP

3. Such statements tend to give importance to those outcomes that are more easily observable and undervalue those that are difficult to detect.[2]

A number of other limitations may be added:

4. It is difficult to prescribe the outcome with respect to affective or attitudinal objectives.
5. Some objectives, especially psychomotor ones, develop over a period of time, and others seem to develop by stages or plateaus rather than by constant progression.
6. The objectives may be met. However, the "evidence" may manifest itself differently in different individuals, or even differently in the same individual at different times and under different conditions.

### THE COMPONENTS OF AN INSERVICE EXPERIENCE

Because an inservice staff development "session" may carry connotations of an event taking place within specific time limits, it may be wiser to speak in terms of an inservice experience, realizing that the totality of the experience may be designed to be completed over a period of time, utilizing a variety of "sessions" of the time-constrained variety. A number of authors[3] have outlined implementation processes and have designed planning guides. Joyce and Showers,[4] with this emphasis in mind, have listed and described five components of staff development "sessions." They are outlined as follows:

1. *Theory.* Presentation of theory or description of skill or strategy.
2. *Demonstration.* Modeling or demonstration of skills or models of teaching. Teachers need to see the strategy demonstrated with children.
3. *Practice.* Practice in simulated and classroom settings.
4. *Feedback.* Structured and open-ended feedback (provision of information about performance). Teachers need to be able to practice the new strategy with feedback under protected (success-oriented) conditions.
5. *Classroom application.* Coaching for application (hands-on, in-classroom, assistance with the transfer of skills and strategies to the classroom). Teachers need help in transferring the new strategy to their actual classroom situations until the new strategy feels normal and comfortable.

These components are now discussed in more detail.

### Theory

The theory component of an inservice experience includes the rationale, the theoretical base, verbal descriptions, and media presentations. It is not unusual to find many inservice sessions dealing with theory almost exclusively.

Mackay[5] states that only about 1 percent of teachers are able to gain skill acquisition if they have had exposure to the theory only. Joyce and Showers state that "presentation of theory can raise awareness and increase conceptual control of an area to some extent.... It is not powerful enough alone to achieve much impact beyond the awareness level, but... it is an important component."[6] In other words, the theory component is a necessary but insufficient aspect of inservice staff development sessions. It is important that it be provided, but it is only the first component and cannot stand alone.

**Modeling or Demonstration**

This component involves the modeling of the teaching strategy, skill, or procedure either through live demonstration or through the utilization of other techniques, such as videotaped presentations of the new procedures in actual classroom (i.e., "realistic") settings. Modeling may occur as many times as you feel it necessary. This is especially true if the modeling is available in a media format that lends itself to individual rerun. The individual teacher may desire several repetitions to develop the confidence that he or she needs to try out the new approach in his or her classroom situation. According to Joyce and Showers, this is precisely why some of the related research is flawed. That is, because too few instances of modeling have occurred for successful transfer of sometimes quite complex models of teaching. These authors state that modeling appears to have significant effect on both teacher awareness of a new technique, and on knowledge of it. Modeling can also assist in the mastery of the theory. That is, in Piaget's terms, it is a concrete operations example. These authors state, "Some teachers can transfer skills to the classroom after observing demonstrations. However, most teachers are unlikely to be able to transfer skills unless it is accompanied by other components."[7] With respect to this point, Mackay[8] estimates that maybe 10 percent of teachers can transfer skills to the classroom after experiencing both the theory and the modeling components.

**Practice Under Simulated Conditions**

This stage involves trying out the new skills or strategies under conditions that are in some significant and critical respects similar to those conditions that the teacher will meet in actual classroom practice. With respect to level of impact after this stage has been reached, Joyce and Showers state that practice is a very efficient way of acquiring skills and strategies after the teacher has achieved awareness and knowledge. It is a very effective way to develop competence in a wide variety of classroom techniques. Mackay claims that approximately 25 percent of teachers are able to transfer skills to the classroom after theory, modeling, and simulation practice have all been done.[9]

This is the "How do I do it" phase of inservice, the phase where teachers are provided an opportunity to become actively involved. This phase will include "hands-on" activities with the materials and participation in the exercises and experiences that are to be used with the students. These are the "dry runs," which, combined with appropriate feedback, help teachers to anticipate problems that might be encountered when they attempt to implement the new teaching notions into their regular teaching repertoire.

### Feedback

Structured feedback involves using a procedure for observing teachers in a real situation. Feedback can be provided in a wide variety of ways. By the utilization of tape recordings and videotapes, for example, the teacher is able to provide his or her own feedback. Feedback can be provided by colleagues in the teacher's school or by outside "experts." The feedback may be regular or intermittent, and it may be associated with other aspects or components of the staff development sequence. Joyce and Showers feel that feedback has "reasonable power for the acquisition of skills and their transfer to the classroom situation."[10] They emphasize, however, that feedback probably needs to be both regular and consistent. According to Mackay's estimates, if components discussed so far are utilized, up to 75 percent of teachers will be able to make the skills transition to classroom practice. Joyce and Showers estimate that as many as 90 percent of teachers can make the skills transfer.[11] They emphasize that feedback should be structured, implying that open-ended feedback may not profit many teachers, although it may be a useful method to develop awareness. The feedback provided by some time-on-task instruments, for example, or the related "interaction analysis" techniques of Flanders[12] could serve to point out to teachers the importance and value of specific aspects of classroom practice.

### Coaching for Application

The coaching for application component includes providing assistance to teachers in their attempts to analyze both the content to be taught and the methodologies and materials to be utilized. They will also need aid in designing specific lessons to help the students to adapt to the new approaches that the teacher will be using. A number of authors, including Joyce and Showers,[13] feel that it will be necessary to provide this kind of direct coaching to many teachers while they are attempting to apply the new methods, skills, and instructional models. It is not important who does the coaching—colleagues, administrators, supervisory personnel—as long as the person providing the assistance is competent at the coaching task. It is important that teachers have the opportunity to receive protected practice. That is, they must be allowed opportunity to practice in a nonthreatening situation where they can receive assurance that it's O.K. if they don't "get it right" the first time they go solo. Such situations would *never* constitute evaluation sessions, and teachers must be assured that they will not be "evaluated" when they are engaging in such practice sessions.

## THE IMPORTANCE OF THESE COMPONENTS

The major thrust of my comments is that the social and psychological environment in which staff development takes place has implications for the success of the activity. This position receives the support of another author pair, Loucks and Zigarmi, who state, "As a rule, staff development activities that generate or take place in a low-threat, comfortable setting in which there is a degree of psychological 'safety' for the teacher are most conducive to change."[14] These authors feel that a teacher will be more open to new learnings when he or she is in an environment that includes other teachers who have the same or similar concerns, problems, and solutions. They feel that during a learning experience it is important that teachers be able to "acknowledge" that they have needs without any fear of teacher evaluation consequences.

It appears that all these components are necessary for a great many teachers in a variety of teacher inservice situations. In relation to this, Joyce and Showers state that for most staff development activities, it is probably wise to include most or maybe all these training components. These authors feel that by using such methods, the majority of teachers will be able to expand their repertoire to the point where they will be able effectively and efficiently to utilize a much greater variety of teaching approaches and curricular models. If any of the components are neglected or omitted, fewer teachers will progress to the point where they are able to transfer the new methodologies and ideas to their classroom situations. And, of course, the classroom is the only level that has significant meaning if the schooling experiences of students are going to improve. They state, for example, that little is likely to be accomplished even if the coaching is done, if the theory, observation of demonstration, and practice with feedback components are neglected.[15]

## CONSOLIDATION AND LONG-TERM MAINTENANCE

The literature generally ceases to pursue the process of staff development after the stage has arrived when the teachers have gone home from the inservice group "sessions," except for some comment on coaching for application and vague statements about continuous follow-up. Little appears about the nature of the desired changes in the long term. The literature clearly indicates that it is very difficult to bring about significant long-term, sustained change in in-classroom practice and that where such change is successful, it is only when the effort to bring it about is sustained over a long period of time. The general indictment that inservice is a disaster, or a waste of time at best, may be due to the fact that a simplistic assumption is made by staff development personnel and their administrators. That assumption is that teachers are able to make the transfer to their everyday classroom situations and that little, if anything, needs to be done after "the sessions" are over.

It has been my experience that even when teachers feel that the "sessions" have been "good sessions," and even after the trainers have received compliments on their presentations and raves about the wonderful ideas that have been presented, there still remains a strong likelihood that teachers will go back to their classrooms and continue to instruct classes using almost exactly the same methodologies, techniques, and materials, with the same approaches, attitudes, and assumptions as was the situation before the inservice sessions were held. Furthermore, this is true even when the teacher-participants have participated in the planning for the inservice; after they have expressed their ideas about the kinds of activities that were to be included in the inservice sessions; after needs assessment had been conducted; after teacher colleagues (peer group) have been presenters; after sessions have been held during "prime time"; after teachers have received released time with pay, with all expenses covered; and when teachers have been able to arrive home no later than if they had spent the day in their regular classrooms. In other words, when all the favorable conditions, as isolated by researchers, have been met, many teachers make no identifiably significant changes in their methods of instruction. Surely something is still missing!

I choose to call that frequently missed element *therapy*, calling to mind the continuous exercises in which a newly released hospital patient might have to engage to ensure complete recuperation and recovery. Loucks and Zigarmi's[16] efforts constitute an exception in the literature. They authored the only significant literature items that I found on long-term maintenance. They have identified this therapy stage as consisting of two substages: implementation and maintenance.

**The Classroom Implementation Stage (Consolidation)**

This stage is to be distinguished from the inservice implementation stage that is the topic of the entire chapter. Inservice implementation refers to the delivery of the new learning experience to the teacher. The classroom implementation stage is a substage of the therapy stage that is a substage of the inservice implementation stage. It is the stage during which the teacher is implementing the desired innovations into his or her normal routine of classroom instructional practice until the new technology becomes "second nature" to the teacher.

During this stage, the teacher is mastering the new behaviors needed to utilize the new approaches naturally and smoothly, integrating them into normal daily practice. It is to be expected that a teacher's first attempts are going to be somewhat uncoordinated as he or she wrestles with the insecurity and the absence of familiar crutches. The teacher will have difficulty incorporating the new structures into his or her planning, indicative of a mechanical level of usage. According to Loucks and Zigarmi, teacher concerns at this stage are often management related, as each component of the new procedures is used for the first time with real students in the reality of the teacher's regular classroom. A teacher will need help when meeting problems associated with first usage of the new programs and procedures with students. Your own teaching experience will help you realize that students readily detect teacher insecurity. You know, too, that teachers detect such student awareness. All this can create some rather awkward moments and possible painful experiences for the teacher. The teacher will probably want to retreat to the security of "tried and proven" old ways of doing things. Maybe the students would prefer that, too, since they also have to adjust to new ways of doing things, with new expectations and new demands on them. If the teacher is not able to receive help at this stage, the new ideas may be mutated and may be changed beyond recognition, as the teacher grasps at known ground to survive.

***One-on-One Practice*** It is obvious, then, that there must be opportunity for follow-up. This is not a pedantic, nice-sounding, vague generality to get staff development people (and authors!) off the methodological hook. This means that there must be formal, structured, planned opportunity for the innovating teachers to ask questions and raise issues associated with the "beginning practice" stage of an innovation. The teacher must be able to admit that things aren't going as well as was expected and that the glowing predictions of the staff development people, especially of the program developers, have not become manifest. It cannot be a "call me if you are in need" approach, nor can it be a "I'll get back to you when I can" situation. This follow-up must be available to address the unique needs, fears, problems, worries, and support requirements of the teacher as the difficulties are being experienced. It is likely that this has to be one-on-one practice with group sessions of little or no value. The teacher may need individual explanations about the utilization of the new curricular materials, conferences about individual children who are not responding, or maybe a full-fledged demonstration lesson taught with the teacher's regular class in the regularly scheduled time period, with only the materials and resources that the teacher would normally have available.

It may be unwise, and even dysfunctional, to have a group session at this point. Teachers having difficulty would find support from each other that the new methods were not working and the pressure on the staff developers to abandon the effort would be great. Even if they didn't succeed in getting approval to abandon the attempt, they would probably convince each other that the effort was doomed to failure. If they begin to think this way, and if they know that other teachers in the same situations think this way, the effort is probably doomed. Self-fulfilling prophetic phenomena take effect.

I have seen this occur on numerous occasions. Even if teachers don't meet face to face, they will phone each other seeking confirmation that this is all a bad idea. And, to make matters worse, the complaints go all the way to one's superordinates (e.g., principals or superintendents) who, anxious that teachers not become upset, may order the effort abandoned just when one is on the cliff edge of success. Sometimes the superordinate may simply withhold support or funds, all the while not even admitting to what he is doing. Politics will have its day, and the "superordinate petty politicians" are just as vulnerable to pressure as any other politician. To make matters even worse, the staff development personnel may be blamed for the lack of success by the very superordinate who withheld overt moral and material support!

You can avoid this scenario by having the necessary one-on-one assistance available—and then hope, and pray if you are so inclined. Maybe you should pray, anyhow, just in case. Staff development and inservice teacher education can be a lonely and thankless job.

***Continuous Assessment of Needs*** While inservice sessions may be based on a needs assessment, bear in mind that it may probably be only the most generalized needs that are addressed. Loucks and Zigarmi suggest that there should be continuous assessment of needs. There are several reasons for this. It can be expected that since the inservice sessions were designed for a group, individual teachers probably expressed felt needs that were not addressed by the sessions. Additionally, change is an evolutionary process with new needs arising over time. Teachers need an opportunity to express concerns and needs as they arise—needs associated with comfort, security, and belongingness, for example, or needs arising from the desire for new or further information, insecurity with perceived prerequisite skills, and attitude conflict. But, further than this, the teacher may have participated in the inservice sessions with expectations that his or her individual expressed needs on the original needs assessment were to be addressed, only to find that such was not the case. The teacher may be struggling with resentments, frustrations, and outright anger because the inservice didn't live up to expectations. The trainer should be available and should initiate contact with teachers to determine and isolate needs and to attempt to respond to the needs in a manner that is perceived as satisfying by the teacher. It would be even more desirable if the trainer or other supervisory personnel were able to detect teacher problems and address them before they had reached the teacher's level of awareness.

*Positive Feedback Is Needed* In spite of what has been said up to this point, which may seem a little contradictory, we must not assume that teachers, in their attempts to bring about change in their classrooms, are completely different as learners from adolescents, as learners, in a particular learning experience. Most adults, if attempting to learn a new skill, will quickly find reasons not to pursue the endeavor if the experience is painful. Consider, for example, the extreme reluctance of adults to begin to play a musical instrument if they have never played before, or to sing, or to engage in an art activity. They excuse themselves with statements such as "I can't draw a straight line with a ruler," as if art consisted of straight lines! I, for example, was a dismal failure as a hockey player, a rather devastating failing in my native macho-hockey-country-Canada. I found all sorts of excuses to avoid practice, feigned illness during competitions, and was mercifully dropped from the team. There was certainly a loss of face among peers, especially of the opposite sex. But that was much more bearable than demonstrating incompetence on the ice. In almost precisely the same way, teachers will need moral support and understanding and will need to be given assurance that it is normal to experience rough spots, difficulties, and problems; that this is the nature of the change process. Giving birth to a baby is certainly engaging in a process of change, but it is certainly not brought off without a certain amount of pain and discomfort—or so I have been told, and so I have observed! Teachers need positive feedback to help them build a sense of mastery and accomplishment. According to Loucks and Zigarmi, this is essential if commitment is to remain high.

*Supportive and Compatible Supervisors* In addition to the staff development people, the school administrator is crucial at this stage because he or she may have to develop supportive and compatible administrative and supervisory structures to facilitate the innovation. Timetabling changes may be necessary, for example. Maybe the innovating teacher needs to be relieved of corridor and playground supervision duties for a period of time, or maybe the teacher should have a lesser teaching load for a semester. Other major or minor facilitative procedures may be needed, depending on the nature of the change effort and the teachers concerned.

There is a tendency for staff development people to be available only for the inservice sessions, hence focusing most attention on activities of a type that can be conducted in the short term, usually with groups. Because of this, many innovations are not adequately implemented at the classroom level. Sometimes, district priorities are such that the inservice personnel have to move on to work with other groups. With respect to this, Loucks and Zigarmi state that "many innovative efforts are lost once teachers have settled back into their classrooms and district efforts are focused elsewhere."[17] There is clearly a role for inservice trainers even when the innovation is assumed to be routine.

**Long-Term Maintenance**

To assure the continued use of an innovation, Loucks and Zigarmi suggest that attention needs to be maintained on two related aspects: ongoing administrative support and ongoing opportunities for problem solving.

*Ongoing Administrative Support* Studies reviewed by Loucks and Zigarmi appear to be unanimous in the call for strong administrative support from both the local administration and from district-level administration. It seems necessary that administrators continue to exhibit empathy with the teachers in their efforts and to conduct themselves in such fashion that it is obvious that the innovation maintains a priority status.

Administrators will exhibit this empathy and priority by ensuring that requisite supplies and materials are available and by providing adequate training to those teachers who are new to the innovation. The principal must, for example, attempt to determine ongoing teacher needs and must expedite the addressing of these needs.

*Ongoing Opportunities for Problem Solving* Loucks and Zigarmi call this aspect "perhaps the most effective staff development activity during the maintenance phase."[18] It is important that administrators arrange for time for participating teachers to share their experiences, their successes, and their failures. However, in my opinion and experience, this should not occur until and unless both school and district administrators have expressed and overtly articulated their commitment to the "innovation." I have observed administrators who have deliberately arranged such "sharing and commiseration" sessions to foster disgruntlement, hence providing them with an excuse to abandon the effort after they had either lost their initial commitment and enthusiasm (maybe the publicity faded!) or were responding to other needs or pressures.

It is also important that opportunities be provided for participating teachers to make suggestions and to seek to solve problems that might otherwise prevent the continuation of the innovation.

## THE SESSIONS AND FOLLOW-UP

### The Refining Phase of Inservice

An innovation may become a routine part of a teacher's repertoire, but efforts may not be made to refine the ideas, procedures, techniques, or materials. Because new curricular efforts may materialize, because new changes may be attempted, and because there are other demands on teacher time and energy, any one innovation may lose its profile. This is especially true if no concerns are raised with respect to it or if its status is not reviewed occasionally.

Loucks and Zigarmi suggest that there are five activities that can support and foster the refinement and long-term health of an inserviced innovation. They are discussed briefly:

1. *Opportunities for self-observation.* After an innovation becomes a routine aspect of a teacher's repertoire, the teacher is no longer concerned about the change aspects of an innovation or about its daily classroom management. Energies can now be directed to the effect of the innovation on students. Teachers need, at this stage, techniques to monitor and evaluate their own performance.

2. *Individualization.* Continued staff development with respect to a particular innovation should be addressed to particular needs of individual teachers.

3. *Opportunity for choice.* When the teacher has internalized the innovation and is consciously operating in a monitoring, evaluating, refining mode, the teacher himself or herself is probably the best judge of what he or she needs with respect to that innovation. The staff development people will be colleagues and collaborators at this stage, assisting in the assessment of needs and providing individual options that the teacher may or may not choose to do.

4. *Opportunities for leadership.* Since the teacher has now accumulated considerable experience with the innovation in a practical hands-on way, he or she is probably in a better position than the original trainer to deliver the "hands-on" practical aspects of the innovation to other teachers. Besides, the teacher has probably developed significant creative uses of the innovation and may be delighted at the expressed confidence implicit in being asked to lead an inservice session. (This has been my experience when I have, for example, chosen the classrooms of particular teachers as sites for inservice sessions. The host teacher has invariably felt complimented and proud that his or her classroom was chosen as an example of "approaching the ideal.") Also, as has been shown earlier, the teacher's colleagues will likely perceive him as being a more "legitimate" trainer than the original.

5. *Administrative support.* The continued support of local and district administration is always a critical element. Administrative support, assistance, and overt encouragement are always important to the continued status profile of a particular innovation. Because concomitant changes can compete for teachers' time and energy, it is important that only one innovation be implemented at a time and that it be well along in the

maintenance phase before another, possibly competing, innovation is begun.

## A FINAL WORD

The discussion has clearly now gone beyond simple inservice (if inservice can ever be considered simple!) and has moved into the area of ongoing supervision. Observations three or five years after an initial staff development initiative may reveal that the particular innovation has died, not because there was anything intrinsically wrong with any of the components, but simply because other priorities arose. The teacher may have met problems and, rather than admit failure, simply reverted to prior behaviors. This happened to a teacher for whom I had supervisory responsibility. She attempted particular creative painting activities as a part of the art program. She was concerned about the mess that children created. She decided not to seek assistance, and she quietly dropped that component from her art program, in spite of the fact that painting was a legally mandated component of the curriculum.

There is a constant, ongoing long-term need for a clinical type of supervision if inservice activity and staff development efforts are to be effective. A program of consistent, ongoing, long-term supportive classroom visitation and clinical supervision is the context in which staff development efforts take place. That is probably the most important assumption on which the staff development enterprise rests.

# CHAPTER 13

## EVALUATING YOUR EFFORTS

We are always concerned that we are successful in our educational efforts. Sometimes the evidence of our success or failure is determined only in the long term, and even then only by sometimes very vague measures of indeterminate criteria. It doesn't have to be that way in our inservice staff development efforts.

This chapter will serve several functions. It will provide some new perspectives on staff development; it will provide some degree of summary and synthesis of the whole book through a presentation of evaluative instruments; it will provide a number of approaches to planning and evaluating staff development; and it will provide a number of instruments that you can readily adapt to your own staff development purposes.

### PREPARING FOR EVALUATION

As a high school principal I sometimes said to teachers that if they didn't know how they were going to evaluate a unit or chapter before they had "taught" it, then one could question whether they knew what their objectives were. While I was probably off-base, particularly with respect to affective kinds of objectives, there was no doubt that teachers' evaluations revealed what they considered to be of most importance. What was also revealed were the particular biases of the people doing the evaluating.

The situation with staff development is not really different. Various people, operating on sometimes unique sets of assumptions, having had unique sets of experiences, approach staff development from a variety of perspectives. Sometimes, they have formulated sets of planning guidelines and evaluative instruments to assist them with their task.

It is a useful practice to determine your evaluative criteria before you begin staff development. Your evaluative criteria will then likely reflect your objectives fairly consistently. If you wait until after the various inservice staff development activities to decide on a priority-ranked listing of evaluative criteria, chances are that these criteria will reflect what actually took place in the staff development activities rather than what you intended before the sessions occurred.

There is also the advantage that a good evaluative criteria listing can be used as planning and operating guidelines, and vice versa.

Before you begin the process of evaluation, it would be useful to decide for yourself why the evaluation is being done. The ultimate recipients of the evaluation results will no doubt influence what and how you evaluate.

For example, is the evaluation for purposes of improving future staff development attempts? If so, you may wish to examine questions such as the following: Are the aims and objectives appropriate? Was the content and level of treatment too advanced or too elementary, relevant or irrelevant? Was the total effort too long? Did participants get bored or tired? Were the materials appropriate? Were the facilities adequate?

Is your evaluation designed to determine if participants have attained predetermined objectives? Or is the object of the evaluation to provide good publicity or a good image for you or your school or your district or your subject area or your grade level? Are you attempting to provide the necessary evidence so that you will continue to enjoy administrative support and permissions for future staff development efforts? Or are your efforts designed to support your bid for a promotion?

Your evaluation efforts may be designed for any combination of these or other purposes. Whatever your purposes, they will determine what you choose to observe, what you choose to measure, the methods of measurement, and maybe your methods of analysis.

If the major objective in evaluating staff development efforts is teacher development, then you may choose to focus on teacher knowledge, attitudes, and behavior (e.g., classroom skills). You will also need to predetermine, in at least some intuitive way, your criteria of success. That is, what will you accept as evidence that your efforts have been successful or less so? You may also choose to form a small committee of prospective participants to assist you in deciding how to evaluate the staff development efforts.

Initial teacher reaction to staff development activity may be very positive, and you may be justifiably pleased with yourself. But will you have succeeded if teachers don't engage in the new desired teaching practice? We now have returned to a question posed at the beginning of the book. "When has the staff development been delivered?" Can you be satisfied that the innovation has been inserviced if it doesn't result in certain predetermined student outcomes?

I hasten to add that not all your staff development efforts will be of such nature that its outcomes will be measurable, at least in the short term. Consider, for example, the delivery of stress management sessions or conflict management activities or other interpersonal communication efforts to your teachers. The results of such efforts will likely become evident, but in subtle ways over an extended period of time. Yet we will continue to offer such inservice in spite of lack of evidence of success because, based on the personnel development literature, we believe that such training and self-awareness is intrinsically good for teachers and students, and because we believe that there will be positive outcomes even if we can't measure them. We are prepared to operate on a degree of faith. In such instances, we will probably decide that any kind of formal evaluation procedure is not warranted. However, we may still seize opportunities to engage participants in conversation to try to satisfy our natural curiosity and our desire to be useful. We will probably ask them if they enjoyed the experience and if they think the sessions will be of benefit to them. Subsequent to the sessions we will probably ask if the efforts have been of value and if the teachers would like follow-up efforts. Such informal methods still constitute defensible forms of evaluation.

The point is that evaluation has to be for a purpose, to determine if certain predetermined objectives have been met. To engage in evaluation of staff development activity without knowing why it is being done or what the criteria of success are, is probably to engage in a useless exercise.

## ASSUMPTIONS AND BELIEFS ABOUT STAFF DEVELOPMENT

Many of the authors to whom reference has been made in this book, and other authors as well, have made statements relative to inservice staff development of teachers. It is on these statements of belief that most of the existing ISSD methods and techniques are based. The list that follows is drawn from a number of sources, particularly Harris.[1] It contains some of the assumptions and beliefs that have been stated in the literature:

1. People can and will learn on the job.[2]
2. People tend to view each projected learning outcome as appropriate or inappropriate from an internal frame of reference.[3]
3. People experience satisfaction from learning that is clearly perceived as appropriate.[4]
4. Participants should be actively involved in solving real problems.
5. People learn from doing.
6. Learning takes place when people receive data and when they have an opportunity to interact with that data.[5]
7. People respond positively to the opportunity to work from their strengths.[6]
8. People are more effective when they feel good about themselves.[7]
9. Success is built upon success.[8]
10. People need feedback on their own behavior to make efficient use of experiences for learning.[9]

11. People need cognitive organizers to make efficient use of feedback in guided learning.[10]
12. People seem better able to apply new learnings and refine their skills, and continue growing as they get feedback and support from others.[11]
13. People tend to want to learn some things at some times, under certain conditions, at certain costs, but not all things, at all times, under all conditions and costs.[12]
14. Human support systems encourage movement toward renewal.[13]
15. Participants should be involved in decision making about the design, implementation, and evaluation of their own programs.[14]
16. People are capable of learning anything if the time, conditions, and motivations (rewards) are adequate,[15] but not any combination of these.[16]
17. Shared decision making increases involvement.[17]
18. People learn best those things they perceive to be meaningful.[18]
19. People need direct intervention in accomplishing some learning outcomes, but not others.[19]
20. People have developmental as well as situational and personal needs that learning can help satisfy.[20]
21. People's needs are met partially by learning. They have other needs too. To deal with higher-order needs, lower-order needs must be at least partially met.[21]
22. People must learn to survive in the long run. But they do not have to learn to survive in the short run; instead, they can cope, resist, endure.[22]
23. People will benefit from self-initiated and self-directed inservice. People are their own instruments for growth; they do not sabotage their own projects.[23]
24. People learn in active states under conditions of mild arousal, attentiveness, and stress.[24]

## GUIDELINES FOR STAFF DEVELOPMENT

A number of authors have formulated sets of guidelines respecting staff development. By far the most comprehensive set of guidelines gleaned from the literature is that of Harris.[25] It is presented here with some abridgement and adaption. (See Figure 13-1.)

Another outstanding contribution to the literature respecting guidelines for ISSD is that provided by the National Inservice Network.[26] Its professionals worked for some time on the formulation of a comprehensive set of guidelines for quality practices in ISSD and reported in July 1980. Because of its comprehensive nature, its summary of major findings is given here in its entirety. (See Figure 13-2.)

**Figure 13-1**

**A Set of Principles for Staff Development**

*Clients Served*

1. All personnel within a designated target organization or operating unit should be provided opportunities for inservice education.
2. No client should be required to participate in a specific program or session if for no other reason than that it serves the convenience of scheduling, planning, or funding.
3. Different client groups (or individuals) should be recognized within any given program of ISSD.
4. Individuals or groups are designated as clients on the basis of rational and explicit relationships between individual needs and program goals.
5. Groupings of clients are developed to facilitate optimum learning and to assure transfer.

*Timing Inservice*

6. Time frames normally allocated for inservice programs, for client participation in planning, designing, and evaluating, are part of the normal work load and assignment schedule of personnel.
7. Special events, requiring substantial variations in the normal work load and assignment of personnel, should be utilized sparingly.
8. Time allocations allow for continuity of inservice.
9. Time allocations allow for flexible use of time as needed to design an appropriate and necessary variety of activities.

*Involvement*

10. Clients should have opportunities to serve selectively in roles as planners, designers, managers, presenters, and evaluators of ISSD programs or sessions as well as being trainees.
11. Clients should be provided with opportunities for making choices among alternatives within ISSD program plans.
12. All personnel involvement should be by virtue of competence needed or offered rather than because of desire to control or to serve self-interest.
13. Client perceptions of needs in relation to job realities are among the various criteria for determining involvement.

*Locale(s) for Inservice*

14. The locations selected for training activities should be determined by training requirements rather than by arbitrary preferences of trainees or administering officials.
15. The use of remote locations should be an open option for any inservice activity or program to be determined by cost/benefit analysis in comparison with local alternatives.
16. When resources needed for training are not available locally or can be more economically utilized at a remote location, program plans and regulations should facilitate their judicious use.

*Continued*

**Figure 13-1 (continued)**

*Resources*
17. Time should be provided for client participation in planning and evaluation activities that are sufficient to meet urgent needs and are adequate to assure quality programs.
18. Personnel, programs, materials, and other resources of various institutions, should be shared.
19. Costs associated with full participation in ISSD should be fully defrayed without personal expense to clients.

*Locus of Control and Decision Making*
20. Those most directly affected should be the most completely involved in decisions regarding those portions of the operation that affect them.
21. Control over various operations should be retained as close to the people responsible as is commensurate with economy and efficiency.
22. Decision making should involve all who have responsibility as well as those who have a contribution to make.
23. Decisions should be guided by law, explicit policy statements, planning documents, and the dictates of research on good practice.

*Scope of Planning*
24. Program plans should be clearly related to larger efforts (larger organizational units, larger goals, longer timetables, etc.).
25. Each school district, school, and other related unit should have a comprehensive plan of ISSD within which subunits can plan their operations.
26. Program schedules and timetables should provide for continuity both within the program and among related programs or other operations.

*Systematic Planning*
27. Program planning should continue as implementation and process evaluation indicate needs for change requirements and additions.
28. Program plans should include statements of objectives that are specific in identifying kinds of performance changes anticipated.

*Designing for Learning*
29. The design of activity sequences and materials for use should provide for some differentiated experiences even when common goals, objectives, and needs are being served.
30. The activities and materials should be designed to assure active, meaningful, and purposeful experiences as much as possible.
31. A great variety of activities should be planned. They should be as task oriented and as reality based as possible.

### Figure 13-1 (continued)

*Content for Learning*
32. Objectives should be selected to reflect both organizational development needs and those of individual clients.
33. Objectives for inservice programs should identify performance outcomes that are directly related to (a) job realities, (b) the improvement of important performances, and (c) affective aspects to the extent they are relevant.

Adapted from B. M. Harris, *Improving Staff Performance Through Inservice Education.* (Boston, Allyn & Bacon, 1980). Used with permission.

### Figure 13-2
### Quality Practices in Inservice Education

**Quality practice in inservice education recognizes that programs must be integrated into and supported by the organization within which they function.**

A formally adopted written plan of inservice for the district or agency should be prepared. It should describe all components of a comprehensive system. This plan can then be used as a basis for evaluation and ongoing planning, for communication purposes, and for building support for the program.

—The inservice education program is an integral part of the total organizational system within which it functions.
—Written policy exists to support the inservice education program.
—The assumptions and the theoretical rational underlying the inservice program are explicitly stated.
—The inservice education program design describes the organizational role, responsibility, and support for planning, implementation, and evaluation of the program.
—Procedures exist to assure the program of adequate fiscal, material, staff, and facility resources.
—Federal, state, and local policies pertaining to the inservice education program are studied by planning participants.
—The inservice program design includes plans for facilitating the implementation of quality practices throughout the system.
—The inservice program design is long range and provides for ongoing implementation, support, and evaluation.
—Information about inservice activities is systematically communicated to all audiences concerned.

**Quality practices in inservice education are designed to result in programs that are collaborative.**

Collaborative approaches to inservice programs are the most effective. Including participants, students, and the community in program planning, delivery, and evaluation can result in increased motivation.

—The inservice education program provides opportunities for all school personnel to act as participants.
—Personnel from agencies involved in or affected by the inservice education program are included in the planning process.

*Continued*

**Figure 13-2 (Continued)**

—All groups that are affected by the inservice education program, including parents and students, have a voice in decisions regarding the program.
—Inservice activities include students as teachers/learners whenever possible.
—Procedures exist to assure inclusion of community resources for the inservice education program.
—Participants and others affected by the inservice education program are major providers of data for evaluation.

**Quality practices in inservice education are designed to result in programs that are needs based.**

Inservice education is a support service for the total educational system. It draws its legitimacy from the contribution it makes to strengthening the system's programs and services for students.
—The inservice education program design recognizes the vital importance of the participants' perceptions of the need for the training proposed.
—An assessment of the strengths and needs of the prospective participants and the system is part of the inservice program design.
—Inservice programs goals are derived primarily from a set of educational goals for students, including students with handicaps.
—Inservice content and strategies are drawn from and designed to meet the assessed needs of students, personnel and organizations.
—Programs include activities to meet the needs of leadership personnel, with special attention to building principals.

**Quality practices in inservice education are designed to result in programs that are responsive to changing needs.**

Responsive inservice, built upon indentified needs, meets those needs and is adaptable to ongoing changes in programs, personnel, and conditions. It is planned and delivered in ways that recognize the findings of research on innovation and change theories.
—The inservice program design defines a dynamic and continuous process that is flexible and responsive to changing needs and new requirements.
—Inservice activities are individualized, insofar as possible, to meet the needs and goals of individual participants.
—The inservice program design includes goals that are designed to reduce undue stress and to increase both competence and morale among program participants.
—Inservice providers are selected on the basis of qualifications for specific tasks.
—Inservice activities make use of peer-teaching strategies and participant-created materials, whenever appropriate.
—On-site demonstrations with students are included when appropriate to the inservice education experience.
—Participants are provided with positive feedback on their progress and with follow through consultation that is kept separate from the system's personnel evaluation procedures.

Reproduced with permission of National Inservice Network, School of Education, Indiana University, Bloomington.

We now turn to a number of sets of planning guidelines formulated by various other authors.

Lawrence[27] advocated a set of guidelines consisting of seven basic principles, presented here in abridged form:

1. There should be individualized ISSD programs.
2. Teachers should take an active role.
3. ISSD should include demonstration, trial, and feedback.
4. Teachers should have the opportunity to provide each other with mutual assistance.
5. ISSD programs should be an integral part of an overall long-term staff development program rather than one-shot short-term affairs.
6. Teachers should be able to choose at least some of the goals and activities rather than having all activities entirely preplanned and preselected.
7. Those ISSD activities that are self-initiated and self-designed tend to be successful.

Another series of generalizations has been formulated by several professors of education at Western Washington State College.[28] Six of these guidelines follow:

1. Teachers are more likely to benefit if they can choose the goals and activities that they wish to pursue rather than having to participate in a totally preplanned program.
2. School-based programs have more influence than do college-based programs.
3. ISSD objectives should be specified and articulated.
4. Programs that have different training experiences are more likely to accomplish their objectives than are programs having few objectives required of all teachers.
5. The goals and needs of teachers should be congruent with those of the school if staff development efforts are to improve significantly the aspects of the school being focused on.
6. Training is likely to be effective if adequate time is provided within the regular work schedule (i.e., during prime time).

This group at Western Washington State College has also prepared a model of planning for staff development. An adapted version is given in Figure 13-3.

Another useful set of planning guidelines has been prepared by Edelfelt.[29] He presents his guidelines in a questionnaire. (See Figure 13-4.)

Wlodarczyk[30] has prepared a listing of characteristics of effective staff development activities. (See Figure 13-5.)

Mackay[31] has added to this listing. He says that staff development activities will be more successful if they have the following additional characteristics:

## Figure 13-3
## An Inservice Planning Model

A. *Agreeing on Purposes*

   1. Local definition of ISSD.
   2. Who is responsible for staff development?
   3. Limiting factors?
   4. Role of teachers?
   5. Resources?
   6. Rewards?

B. *Planning a Program*

   1. Needs assessment.
   2. Community involvement.
   3. Objectives?
   4. Content?
   5. Method of instruction?
   6. Trainers?
   7. How are alternatives provided for?
   8. How will program be monitored?
   9. Criteria for assessing progress?

C. *Evaluating the Plan.* Critical areas are

| | |
|---|---|
| 1. Collaboration. | 9. Individualization. |
| 2. Needs assessment. | 10. Content. |
| 3. Teacher role. | 11. Long- and short-term goals. |
| 4. Teacher determination of goals. | 12. Delivery systems. |
| 5. Resources | 13. Participation. |
| 6. Rewards and incentives. | 14. Community involvement. |
| 7. Implementation. | 15. Program monitoring. |
| 8. Benefits and liabilities. | 16. Follow-up procedures. |
| | 17. Support structures. |

Used with permission of Western Washington State College.

## Figure 13-4
## Survey of Criteria for Local Inservice Education Programs

Instructions: In columns A and B, for each statement on the left, circle the response that best reflects your perception:

1 = Never or almost never
2 = Sometimes
3 = Frequently
4 = Always or almost always

In column C, for each statement on the left, circle the response that best reflects your judgment of the appropriateness of the item as a criterion for a local inservice education program:

1 = Very inappropriate
2–9 = Gradations from very inappropriate to very appropriate
10 = Very appropriate

|  | A<br>What Is | B<br>What Should Be | C<br>Appropriateness of Item |
|---|---|---|---|

**Decision Making**

1. Decision making processes are based on cooperation among all major interest groups, that is, school district, college/university, and teacher organization.    1 2 3 4    1 2 3 4    1 2 3 4 5 6 7 8 9 10

2. Decisions are made by the people who are affected, and the decisions are made as close as possible to the situation where they will be operative.    1 2 3 4    1 2 3 4    1 2 3 4 5 6 7 8 9 10

3. The cooperation of major interest groups is based on a concept of parity for each group.    1 2 3 4    1 2 3 4    1 2 3 4 5 6 7 8 9 10

4. Explicit procedures exist to assure fairness in decision making.    1 2 3 4    1 2 3 4    1 2 3 4 5 6 7 8 9 10

5. There are policies (e.g., in a collective-bargaining agreement) relating to inservice education.    1 2 3 4    1 2 3 4    1 2 3 4 5 6 7 8 9 10

6. Inservice education programs are institutionalized.    1 2 3 4    1 2 3 4    1 2 3 4 5 6 7 8 9 10

**Relationship to the Program of the School**

7. Inservice education is directly related to curriculum development.    1 2 3 4    1 2 3 4    1 2 3 4 5 6 7 8 9 10

8. Inservice education is directly related to instructional improvement.    1 2 3 4    1 2 3 4    1 2 3 4 5 6 7 8 9 10

*Continued*

**Figure 13-4 (Continued)**

| | A<br>What Is | B<br>What Should Be | C<br>Appropriateness of Item |
|---|---|---|---|
| 9. Inservice education is based on the needs of students. | 1 2 3 4 | 1 2 3 4 | 1 2 3 4 5 6 7 8 9 10 |
| 10. Inservice education is based on the needs of teachers. | 1 2 3 4 | 1 2 3 4 | 1 2 3 4 5 6 7 8 9 10 |
| 11. Inservice education is based on the needs of school program. | 1 2 3 4 | 1 2 3 4 | 1 2 3 4 5 6 7 8 9 10 |
| 12. Inservice education is a part of a teacher's regular teaching load. | 1 2 3 4 | 1 2 3 4 | 1 2 3 4 5 6 7 8 9 10 |
| 13. The techniques and methods used in inservice education are consistent with fundamental principles of good teaching and learning. | 1 2 3 4 | 1 2 3 4 | 1 2 3 4 5 6 7 8 9 10 |
| 14. Research/evaluation is an integral part of inservice education. | 1 2 3 4 | 1 2 3 4 | 1 2 3 4 5 6 7 8 9 10 |
| 15. All those who participate in inservice education are engaged in both learning and teaching. | 1 2 3 4 | 1 2 3 4 | 1 2 3 4 5 6 7 8 9 10 |

**Resources**

| | | | |
|---|---|---|---|
| 16. Time is available during regular instructional hours for inservice education. | 1 2 3 4 | 1 2 3 4 | 1 2 3 4 5 6 7 8 9 10 |
| 17. Adequate personnel are available from the school district and college/university for inservice education. | 1 2 3 4 | 1 2 3 4 | 1 2 3 4 5 6 7 8 9 10 |
| 18. Adequate materials are available. | 1 2 3 4 | 1 2 3 4 | 1 2 3 4 5 6 7 8 9 10 |
| 19. Inservice education makes use of community resources. | 1 2 3 4 | 1 2 3 4 | 1 2 3 4 5 6 7 8 9 10 |
| 20. Funds for inservice education are provided by the local school district. | 1 2 3 4 | 1 2 3 4 | 1 2 3 4 5 6 7 8 9 10 |
| 21. Inservice education is paid for by state funds provided for that purpose. | 1 2 3 4 | 1 2 3 4 | 1 2 3 4 5 6 7 8 9 10 |

**Commitment to Teacher Education**

| | | | |
|---|---|---|---|
| 22. Professional growth is seen as a continuum from preservice preparation through career-long professional development. | 1 2 3 4 | 1 2 3 4 | 1 2 3 4 5 6 7 8 9 10 |

## Figure 13-4 (Continued)

| | A<br>What Is | B<br>What Should Be | C<br>Appropriateness of Item |
|---|---|---|---|
| 23. The inservice education program reflects the many different ways that professionals grow. | 1 2 3 4 | 1 2 3 4 | 1 2 3 4 5 6 7 8 9 10 |
| 24. The inservice education program addresses the many different roles and responsibilities that a teacher must assume. | 1 2 3 4 | 1 2 3 4 | 1 2 3 4 5 6 7 8 9 10 |
| 25. Inservice education is related to research and development. | 1 2 3 4 | 1 2 3 4 | 1 2 3 4 5 6 7 8 9 10 |
| 26. The respective strengths of the school district, the college/university, the teacher organization, and the community are used in the inservice education program. | 1 2 3 4 | 1 2 3 4 | 1 2 3 4 5 6 7 8 9 10 |
| 27. Internship and student teaching experiences are used for analysis and study in the inservice education program. | 1 2 3 4 | 1 2 3 4 | 1 2 3 4 5 6 7 8 9 10 |
| 28. Inservice education is available to all professional and nonprofessional personnel. | 1 2 3 4 | 1 2 3 4 | 1 2 3 4 5 6 7 8 9 10 |
| **Rewards** | | | |
| 29. There is a reward system for teachers, administrators, and college/university personnel and others who engage in inservice education programs. | 1 2 3 4 | 1 2 3 4 | 1 2 3 4 5 6 7 8 9 10 |

Used with permission of R. A. Edelfelt.

## Figure 13-5

### Characteristics of Effective Staff Development Activities

1. *Involvement in planning objectives.* Staff development activities tend to be more effective when participants have taken part in planning the objectives and the activities. Objectives planned by the participants are perceived as more meaningful with a higher degree of clarity and acceptance.

2. *Active building principal involvement.* Staff development activities in which the building principal is an active participant have proven over a period of time to be more effective. Active involvement means that the building principal needs to be a participant in all the activities in which his or her teachers are involved.

3. *Time for planning.* Whether the staff development activities are mandated or whether participation is voluntary, participants need time away from their regular teaching or administrative responsibilities to plan objectives and subsequent activities.

4. *District administrative support.* For staff development activities to be effective, district-level support needs to be visible.

5. *Expectations.* Participants in staff development activities should know what they will be able to do when the experience is over and how the experience will be evaluated. Participants should also know what will be expected of them during the activities.

6. *Opportunity for sharing.* Staff development activities in which participants share and provide assistance to one another are more apt to attain their objectives than are activities in which participants work alone.

7. *Continuity.* Staff development activities that are thematic and linked to a staff development plan or a general effort of a school are usually more effective than is a series of one-shot approaches on a variety of topics.

8. *Expressed needs.* Effective staff development activities are based on a continuous assessment of participants' needs—as needs change, the activity should be adjusted accordingly.

9. *Opportunity for practice.* Staff development activities that include demonstrations, supervised tasks, and feedback are more likely to accomplish their objectives than are those activities that expect participants to store up ideas and skills for use at a later time.

10. *Active involvement.* More successful staff development activities are those that provide the participant with a chance to be actively involved. When "hands-on" experiences with materials, active participation in exercises that will later be used with students, and involvement in small-group discussions are used, participants are more likely to apply learnings when they return to their schools or school districts.

11. *Opportunity for follow-up.* Staff development activities are more successful if participants know there is an opportunity to become involved in follow-up sessions.

12. *Opportunity for choice.* If a participant has chosen to become involved in an activity, there is a far greater likelihood that the experience will be more meaningful. A meaningful series of alternative activities should also be offered within a staff development program that is planned over a period of time.

13. *Building on strengths.* People like to be recognized as valued, competent, liked, and needed. Staff development activities that view each participant as a resource are often more responsive to participants' needs.

14. *Content.* More successful staff development activities appear to be those that are geared toward a relatively narrow grade-level range, a specific topic, or a specific set of skills, so that when the participant leaves the activity, he or she has a plan that is ready for immediate use or a set of instructional materials that translates the ideas presented into practice.

### Figure 13-5 (Continued)

15. *The presenter.* More successful staff development activities are those in which the presenter has been able to come at the subject from the participant's point of view. The presenter's expertise also plays a role, as does his or her ability to convey genuine enthusiasm for the subject.

16. *Individualization.* Staff development activities that have different educational experiences for participants at different stages of their development are more apt to obtain their objectives than programs in which all participants engage in common activities.

17. *Number of participants.* Some presentations are as effective with one hundred participants as they are with ten. However, for staff development activities requiring personal contact, informality, and an interchange of ideas, seven to ten participants appears to be optimal. There are exceptions and variations based on the skill of the presenter, the organization of the activity, and the nature of the topic.

18. *The learning environment.* As a general rule, more successful staff development activities take place within a low-threat, comfortable setting in which there is a degree of psychological safety." Openness to learning appears to be enhanced when peers can share similar concerns, highs and lows, problems and solutions.

19. *The physical facility.* Accessibility of supporting materials, appearance of the facility, room temperature, lighting, auditory and visual sources of distraction, and many other physical factors have subtle but sometimes profound effects on the success of the staff development activity.

20. *Time of day and season.* Staff development activities that take place at the end of a school day have a smaller chance of being successful than do those offered when participants are fresh. Further, staff development activities are less likely to be successful when they are scheduled at times of the year when seasonal activities, such as parent conferences and holiday celebrations, occur.

---

This listing of effective staff development characteristics was compiled by Dr. Steven Wlodarczyk, assistant superintendent of schools, South Windsor, Conn., in cooperation with the National Staff Development Council. Used with permission.

---

comprehensive evaluation, model instructional behaviors, sound principles of adult learning, accommodation of needs of all levels of staff, built on preservice training.

As we have seen earlier, Harris[32] has devoted considerable attention and effort to developing guidelines for inservice sessions. He has done a unique task, the results of which are presented here with some abridgement and adaptation.

His set of guidelines for planning inservice is important because careful detailed plans provide certain assurances. Barrera[33] states that careful plans assure

1. That the best possible design has been developed.
2. That all materials and arrangements have been provided for.
3. That the design can be communicated to others who need to be involved.
4. That the session leaders will be guided to implement the session designed.
5. That the design can be reused with minor variations with another client or group.

Harris's guidelines provide for all these assurances. His listing is given in Figure 13-6.

Another useful planning and evaluation document has been provided by the Oregon State Department of Education. It has prepared a questionnaire to elicit teachers' interests and needs with respect to inservice education. A set of principles is implicit in the questions. It is left to you to determine the "appropriate" response to the, by now, familiar staff development statements. (See Figure 13-7.)

The literature does not contain very much respecting the evaluation of the postsession aspects of staff development. Generally, this kind of instrument is found in the clinical supervision literature. One such instrument is Kindsvatter and Wilen's[34] Conference Category System Analysis Form, given in Figure 13-8. This form will assist a supervisor to evaluate his conferences with teachers, an essential component of the postsession phase of staff development.

The last instruments given here were prepared by the New York Department of Education.[35] It has provided two very useful questionnaires, one for inservice sessions participants and one for observers.

## IN CONCLUSION

The implementation of inservice staff development for teachers is likely to fail if it is conceived in simplistic terms. ISSD is an enterprise affecting a very sensitive aspect of the lives of teachers. Human behavior is complex. Therefore, it would probably be futile to apply rigidly any of the formulations or models or listings that have been presented in this discourse. It is important to keep in mind that a model is nothing more than an analogy focusing on one or several specific aspects of a multifaceted behavioral complex.

With respect to definitive formulations and guidelines, the jury is still out and will be out for some time, at least until substantially more "hard," substantive, research findings have become available. This can be interpreted as a statement of encouragement that school districts and individual educators get involved in primary research in this area. There could be immediate, even if limited, benefit.

## Figure 13-6

### Guidelines for Preparing an Inservice Plan

**A. Statement of the problem**

1. The educational problem to which the session is related is clearly identified.

2. The problem is described in concrete terms related to the real situation...and its importance is made clear.

3. The problem is defined in terms that make it at least partially responsive to inservice education, as distinguished from curriculum development, and so on.

4. The problem is translated into needs for improved performance of teachers.

**B. Client specified**

5. The individuals or groups toward which the activities will be directed are clearly specified. Clients are described in terms of background of training, experience, prior involvement with problem, and so on (i.e., with whom are you dealing? Knowing about them will assist.).

6. The relationship of these clients to the problem is indicated. Similarities or differences in attitudes, skills, and knowledge related to the problem are described or estimated.

7. The rationale for focusing upon these clients instead of others is presented.

**C. Goals and objectives**

8. The major outcome(s) anticipated from the session(s) is(are) specified...in observable terms where possible. Portions of the problems or needs not addressed are noted.

9. The anticipated outcomes are specified. They should clearly be related to major outcomes and should be expressed in performance terms if possible. Specific objectives reflect differentiated needs of participants.

10. The goals and objectives selected are the most important as well as the most realistic ones. Specific objectives are selected to deal with the problem in a truly significant way.

**D. Schedule of events**

11. A master calendar of events indicates dates for preplanning, implementing, and follow-up.

12. An agenda for the session clearly indicates the timetable of activities. Careful, realistic allocations of time are designated for each activity.

13. Sequences, allocations, activities, and relationships among them are shown.

**E. Description of procedures**

14. Each activity specified in the session agenda (item 12) is fully described, as to what happens, the objectives in focus, the sequence, the materials used, the special arrangements, persons involved, simultaneous events, and special problems to consider.

15. The selection of each activity is justified in terms of the specific objective focus and special conditions limiting activity selection.

16. Illustrations of materials, displays, room arrangements, and so on are included to clarify procedures of special kinds.

17. Alternative procedures or variations that might be required are described.

**F. Evaluation**

18. A set of evaluation procedures is clearly described. Evaluation of outcomes related to objectives is provided for. Evaluation of affective, skill, and cognitive outcomes is included where appropriate. Processes as well as outcomes are evaluated.

*Continued*

## Figure 13-6 (Continued)

19. Appropriate, objective instruments are decided on for each aspect of the evaluation. Where possible they should be pretested. Instruments are simple enough for practical administration. Decisions are made respecting what the objectives of evaluation are and if the chosen instruments are adequate.

20. Any analytical evaluation procedures should be predetermined, with any tables prestructured and procedures described.

### G. Follow-up plans

21. Follow-up plans are outlined and/or described in sufficient detail to show continuity toward full resolution of the problem.

22. Immediate next steps are carefully detailed to guide both clients and leaders.

### H. Exhibits

23. Materials to be used are illustrated. Handouts, advance information, name tags, work sheets, tapes, transparencies, questionnaires, instruments, bibliographies, and lists of material are included.

24. Equipment and special physical facilities arrangements are listed with sources clearly designated.

25. Resource persons are clearly designated including all pertinent communications relating to each (curriculum vitae, addresses, phone numbers, assignment sheets, etc.).

26. A budget is prepared showing all expenses and clearly detailing cash outlay costs.

---

Adapted from B. M. Harris, *Improving Staff Performance Through Inservice Education* (Boston: Allyn & Bacon, 1980), pp. 62–64. Used with permission.

# Figure 13-7
## Attitude Toward Inservice Inventory

| Statements | Strongly agree | Agree | Uncertain | Disagree | Strongly disagree |
|---|---|---|---|---|---|
| 1. The teacher should have the opportunity to select the kind of inservice activities that he or she feels will strengthen his or her personal competence. | | | | | |
| 2. The real test of an inservice program is whether it helps the teacher to cope with his professional tasks more successfully. | | | | | |
| 3. ISSD must allow for individual teacher interest. | | | | | |
| 4. Teachers *need* to be involved in developing purposes, activities, and evaluation methods for ISSD programs. | | | | | |
| 5. The primary purpose of ISSD is to upgrade teachers' performance. | | | | | |
| 6. One of the most important evaluative criteria for ISSD programs is whether the teacher uses the training in his or her classroom. | | | | | |
| 7. One of the best motivators is the opportunity to become acquainted with new teaching practices or innovative programs. | | | | | |
| 8. If more teachers were involved in planning, commitment would be greater. | | | | | |
| 9. Each teacher should participate. | | | | | |
| 10. More small-group activities should be provided during ISTE. | | | | | |
| 11. All teachers should be required to attend. | | | | | |
| 12. Many ISSD programs are not relevant to teacher-felt needs. | | | | | |
| 13. Implementation of ideas depends on principal's support and interest. | | | | | |
| 14. ISSD should relate to direct classroom problems. | | | | | |
| 15. Most teachers do not like to attend ISSD activities. | | | | | |
| 16. Should be in the school where the teacher works. | | | | | |
| 17. Should be during the school day. | | | | | |
| 18. Transfer to classroom with respect to most ISSD is minimal. | | | | | |
| 19. ISSD is more effective when total school staff is involved in *one* activity. | | | | | |
| 20. Most ISSD activities do not seem well planned. | | | | | |
| 21. Most ISSD activities arise from a study of the needs and problems of teachers. | | | | | |
| 22. Most ISSD activities are virtually useless. | | | | | |
| 23. Objectives of ISSD are always specific. | | | | | |
| 24. Orientation for new teachers is adequate. | | | | | |
| 25. There is adequate follow-up to determine the effects of ISSD. | | | | | |
| 26. I would prefer a three-hour night session. | | | | | |

Used with permission of the State Department of Education, Salem, Ore.

## Figure 13-8
## Conference Category System Analysis Form

|  | Analysis Scales | |
|---|---|---|
|  | **Occurrence** | **Effectiveness** |
| Supervisor _____ | 1. Not evident | 1. Not effective |
|  | 2. Slightly evident | 2. Slightly effective |
| Teacher _____ | 3. Moderately evident | 3. Moderately effective |
|  | 4. Quite evident | 4. Quite effective |
| Date _____ | N. Not applicable | N. Not applicable |

| Categories (parts A and B correspond to occurrence and effectiveness in the analysis scale) | A. Occurrence | B. Effectiveness |
|---|---|---|
| 1. CLIMATE: A. Supervisor makes comments specifically intended to affect the climate. B. Supervisor's statements release tension and contribute to productive communication. This includes expressions of support and encouragement, stated in a comfortable, relaxing tone. | | |
| 2. TARGET SETTING: A. Supervisor designates intended conference content. B. Supervisor explains the purpose of the conference, possible outcomes, and items to be included. The teacher is given the opportunity to approve these and suggest others. The resulting agenda is attended to in the conference. | | |
| 3. QUESTIONING: A. Supervisor employs questions as an essential means of pursuing conference targets. B. Supervisor uses a questioning strategy thoughtfully and purposefully to encourage the teacher to reflect, analyze, and evaluate. Questions that focus, probe, clarify, that transcend the obvious and mundane, are posed. | | |
| 4. COMMENTARY: A. Supervisor clarifies ideas and provides information and suggestions. B. Supervisor remarks are descriptive rather than judgmental. Pertinent information is provided incisively. Comments are appropriate and substantive. | | |
| 5. PRAISE: A. Supervisor praises and encourages when opportune. B. Praise is used judiciously and authentically to commend teacher ideas and performance. Praise is specific in most instances. | | |
| 6. NONVERBAL: A. Communication other than through voice occurs. B. Supervisor has a pleasant facial expression, smiles as appropriate. Speech is accompanied by gestures. Nonverbal behavior communicates interest and enthusiasm. Touching may occur if appropriate. | | |
| 7. BALANCE: A. Communication occurs in both directions. Supervisor is a patient and attentive listener. Supervisor elicits ample teacher involvement, usually talks less than the teacher. | | |
| 8. SENSITIVITY: A. Supervisor acts on the teacher's behalf. B. Supervisor is alert to emotional and conditional factors, to verbal and nonverbal cues, and responds appropriately often with climate building comments. Supervisor avoids self-serving behavior. | | |
| 9. CLOSURE: A. Supervisor uses a culminating technique. B. Supervisor reviews, or causes the teacher to review, the major outcomes of the conference: understandings, solutions, plans, and especially commitment. | | |

Reprinted with permission of the Association for Supervision and Curriculum Development. Copyright 1981 by the Association for Supervision and Curriculum Development. All rights reserved.

# APPENDICES

A. Addresses of Agencies Having a
   Staff Development Focus

B. Resources

# APPENDIX A

## ADDRESSES OF AGENCIES HAVING A STAFF DEVELOPMENT FOCUS

Adult Education Association of the United States of America
810 Eighteenth Street, N.W.
Washington, DC 20006

American Association of Colleges of Teacher Education
One Dupont Circle, N.W.
Suite 610
Washington, DC 20036

American Society for Training and Development
Suite 305
600 Maryland Avenue, S.W.
Washington, DC 20024

Appalachia Educational Laboratory
P.O. Box 1348
Charleston, WV 25325

Association for Continuing Professional Education
402 Graham Hall
Northern Illinois University
DeKalb, IL 60115

Association for Supervision and Curriculum Development
225 N. Washington St.
Alexandria, VA 22314

Canadian Association for Adult Education
29 Prince Arthur Avenue
Toronto, Ont., Canada M5R 1B2

Certified Consultants International
Box 573
Brentwood, TN 37027

Council for Educational Development and Research
Suite 206
1518 K Street, N.W.
Washington, DC 20005

ERIC Document Reproduction Service
4827 Rugby Ave.
Bethesda, MD 20014

Far West Laboratory for Educational Research and Development
1855 Folsom St.
San Francisco, CA 94103

International Council for Adult Education
29 Prince Arthur Ave.
Toronto, Ont., Canada M5R 1B2

Mid-continent Regional Educational Laboratory
2600 South Parker Road
Building 5, Suite 353
Aurora, CO 80014

National Association for Public and Continuing Education
1201 16th St., N.W.
Suite 429
WAshington, DC 20036

National Council on Community Services and Continuing Education
One Dupont Circle, N.W.
Suite 410
Washington, DC 20036

National Council of State Directors of Adult Education
1201 16th St., N.W.
Suite 429
Washington, DC 20036

National Dissemination Center
123 Huntington Hall
Syracuse University
Syracuse, NY 13210

National Education Association
1201 16th St., N.W.
Washington, DC 20036

National Home Study Council
1601 18th St., N.W.
Washington, DC 20009

National Inservice Network
Indiana University School of Education
2853 East Tenth St.
Cottage L
Bloomington, IN 47405

National Institute of Adult Education
19B De Montfort St.
Leicester, England LE1 7GE

National Institute of Education
555 New Jersey Ave., N.W.
Washington, DC 20208

National School Public Relations Association
1801 North Moore St.
Arlington, VA 22209

National Staff Development Council
5198 Westgate Drive
Oxford, OH 45056

Northwest Regional Educational Laboratory
300 S.W. Sixth Avenue
Portland, OR 97204

The Network Inc.
290 South Main St.
Andover, MA 01810

Research for Better Schools
444 North Third St.
Philadelphia, PA 19123

The Research and Development Center for Teacher Education
College of Education
University of Texas at Austin
Austin, TX 78712

Southwest Educational Development Laboratory
211 East Seventh St.
Austin, TX 78701

# APPENDIX B
## RESOURCES

Resources for awakening the creative response faculties and for preventing or combatting perceptual blindness:

Adams, J. L. *Conceptual Blockbusting: A Guide to Better Ideas* (1974). Order from W. W. Norton & Company, 500 Fifth Avenue, New York, N.Y. 10036. ISBN: 0-393-95054-99.

McKim, R. H. *Experiences in Visual Thinking* (1972). Order from Brooks/Cole Publishing Company, Inc., Calif. 94002. ISBN: 0-8185-0031-X. (A Division of Wadsworth, Inc. 7625 Empire Drive, Florence, KY 41042.)

Von Oech, R. *A Whack on Side of the Head: How to Unlock Your Mind for Innovation* (1983). Order from Warner Books, Inc., 666 Fifth Avenue, New York, N.Y. 10103.

*A Kick in the Seat of the Pants* (1986). Order from Harper & Row, Publishers, Inc., 10 East 53rd St., New York, N.Y. 10022.

Resources for improving your interpersonal relations and communications:

Griffin, K., and Patton, B. R. *Fundamentals of Interpersonal Communication* (1971). Order from Harper & Row, Publishers, Inc., 10 East 53rd St., New York, N.Y. 10022.

Berne, E. *Games People Play* (1983). Order from Ballantine Books, a division of Random House, Inc., 201 East 50th St., New York, N.Y. 10022. ISBN: 0-345-30207-9.

Resources for determining characteristics of effective schools and teachers and for helping schools and teachers to become effective:

Bedley, G. *How Do You Recognize a Good School When You Walk into One?* (1984), (hundreds of practical ideas), and *Climate Creators* (1982). Order both from People Wise Publications, 14252 East Mall, Irvine, Calif. 92714

*Evaluating Teacher Performance* (1978). Order from Educational Research Service, Inc., 1800 North Kent St., Arlington, Va. 22209. An excellent resource.

Flanders, N. A. *Analyzing Teaching Behavior* (1970). Addison-Wesley Publishing Company, Reading, Mass. 01867, ISBN: 0-201-02052-1.

Keiley, E. A. *Improving School Climate: Leadership Techniques for Educators* (1980). Order from the National Association of Secondary School Principals, 1904 Association Drive, Reston, Va. 22091. ISBN: 0-8821-115-3.

Mitsakos, C. L. *Mirrors for the Classroom: A Guide to Observation Techniques for Teachers and Supervisors* (1980). A monograph, Mr. Mitsakos is assistant superintendent of schools, Andover, Mass. 01810.

Squires, D. A., Huitt, W. G., and Segars, J. K. *Effective Schools and Classrooms: A Research-Based Perspective* (1983). Order from Association for Supervision and Curriculum Development, 225 North Washington St., Alexandria, Va. 22314.

Resources for creating better staff development experiences:

Dr. Madeline Hunter's *Theory into Practice* books:
*Retention*
*Teach More—Faster*
*Motivation*
*Reinforcement*
*Teach for Transfer*
*Improved Instruction*
Order from TIP Publications, P.O. Box 514, El Segundo, Calif. 90245.

*Life Styles Inventory* Order from Human Synergistics, 39819 Plymouth Road, Plymouth, Mich. 48170. An experience!

*Adventures in Attitudes* Order from Personal Dynamics, Inc., 5186 W. 76th St., Minneapolis, Minn. 55435. Another worthwhile experience!

*Models of Teaching and Coaching for Impact.* A set of eleven 30-minute videotapes with Dr. Bruce Joyce. May be purchased separately. Order from Teacher Effectiveness Associates, 35 Dudley Court, Bethesda, Md., 20914

*M.O.S.T.* (Motivational Opportunities for Successful Teaching). Order from Universal Dimensions, Inc., 4063 N. 16th St., Suite #4, Phoenix, Ariz. 85016. Videotape presentations. Preview tape available.

*Teachers Teaching Writing.* A set of six videotape presentations with suggested pre- and postviewing activities. May be purchased separately. Preview available. Order from Association for Supervision and Curriculum Development, 225 North Washington St., Alexandria, Va. 22314. ASCD has a number of excellent staff development resources. Ask for its MEDIA catalog.

*STERN Personality and Environment Indices.* Order from Evaluation Research Associates, P.O. Box 6503, Teall Station, Syracuse, N.Y. 13217.

Resources to assist you in achieving a greater understanding of the teacher as an adult learner:

Knox, A. B. *Adult Development and Aging* (1977). Order from Jossey-Bass, Inc., Publishers, 433 California St., San Francisco, Calif. 94104.

Krupp, J. A., *Adult Development: Implications for Staff Development* (1981), and *The Adult Learner: A Unique Entity* (1982). Order both from Adult Development and Learning, 40 McDivitt Drive, Manchester, Conn. 06040.

Sheehy, G. *Passages* (1981). Order from E. P. Dutton & Company, Inc., 201 Park Avenue South, New York, N.Y. 10003. ISBN: 0-553-20138-7 (a Bantam book).

Resources in the general area of continuing education and adult development:

Rochte, N. C. *Recurrent Education: A Resource Guide* (1975), and *Recurrent Education: Annotations* (1975). Order both from John H. Russel Center for the Study of Higher Education, College of Education, University of Toledo, Toledo, Ohio 43606.
The two sources just listed, together, constitute what is probably the most comprehensive existing guide to the literature on continuing education. They have a worldwide focus.

*Resources for Continuing Education Managers.* Dean and Director, 331 Madison Avenue, New York, N.Y. 10017. Ask for current edition.

# NOTES

## CHAPTER ONE

1. A. M. Nicholson and B. R. Joyce, *The Literature on Inservice Education: ISTE Report III* (Syracuse, N.Y.: National Dissemination Center, Syracuse University, 1976), p. 79.
2. *Ibid*.
3. L. Carrol, *Alice in Wonderland* and *Through the Looking Glass* (London: Bancroft Books, 1973).
4. National Education Association, *Inservice Education of Teachers, Research Summary 1966-S1*, (Washington, D.C.: NEA, Research Division, 1966). ERIC Clearing House on Teacher Education (ERIC: ED 022 728).
5. R. A. Edelfelt, *Inservice Teacher Education—Sources in the ERIC System*, (Washington, D.C.: January 1975); and R. A. Edelfelt and M. Johnson, *Rethinking Inservice Education* (Washington, D.C.: National Education Association, 1975). (ERIC: ED 099 308).
6. S. J. Yarger, "About the Naming of an Orphan—A Letter to a Friend," *Journal of Teacher Education*, Vol. 30, no. 1 (January–February 1979), p. 11.
7. D. C. Orlich, "Inservice Education: A Problem or a Solution," *Science and Children*, February 1984, pp. 33–35. One estimate suggests that there is one inservice person for every eight teachers in American schools, and Moore and Hyde estimate that up to 6 percent of school district budgets are spent on inservice activities. See D. Moore, and A. Hyde, *Rethinking Staff Development: A Handbook for Analyzing Your Program and Its Costs* (New York: The Ford Foundation, 1978).
8. Hite, Howey, *Planning Teacher Inservice Education Promising Alternatives*. Washington, D.C.: American Association of Colleges for Teacher Education; ERIC Clearinghouse on Teacher Education, May, 1977. (ERIC: ED 137 229).
9. F. H. Wood and S. R. Thompson. Guidelines for Better Staff Development, *Educational Leadership*, February 1980, p. 375.

10. M. C. Rist, "When All Else Fails, Import Teachers," *The Executive Educator*, October 1984, pp. 24–37.

11. *Ibid.*

12. Newfoundland is the easternmost province of Canada, consisting of the Island of Newfoundland and Labrador, which is on the Canadian mainland.

13. R. K. Crocker, *Continuing Teacher Education: Views from the Profession* (St. John's: Memorial University of Newfoundland, 1981), p. 27.

14. *Ibid.* p. 29.

15. *Ibid.*

16. F. Cramm and E. J. Cluett, *Recent Employment Trends: Beginning Teachers 1977–79 and 1978–79* (St. John's: Memorial University of Newfoundland, 1979).

17. *New Directions for Federal Programs to Aid Mathematics and Science Teaching* (Washington, D.C.: U.S. General Accounting Office, 1983).

18. Nicholson and Joyce, *The Literature on Inservice Education*, p. 36.

19. *Ibid.*, p. 29.

20. D. W. Champaign, "Does Staff Development Do Any Good?" *Educational Leadership*, Vol. 37, no. 5 (February 1980), p. 401.

21. National School Public Relations Association, *Inservice Education: Current Trends in School Policies and Programs* (Arlington, Va.: NSPRA, 1975), p. 53.

22. J. Ryor, "Three Perspectives on Inservice Education," *Journal of Teacher Education*, Vol. 30, no. 1 (January–February 1979), p. 14.

23. National Education Association, *Inservice Education of Teachers*, p. 3.

24. *Ibid.*, p. 4.

25. T. Calhoun, "Throwaway Teachers," *Educational Leadership*, Vol. 32, no. 5 (Feburary 1975), p. 310.

26. Champaign, *"Does Staff Development Do Any Good?"* p. 400.

27. National Science Teachers Association, *NSTA News-Bulletin*, February 1982.

28. "Math Shortage," *Education Digest*, November 1982, p. 67.

29. Rist, "When All Else Fails."

30. L. Gubser, "Is the New Technology Education's Last Hope?" *Tech Trends*, Vol. 30, no. 2 (February–March 1985), p. 12.

31. "Teacher Shortages," *Education Digest*, November 1980, p. 69.

32. "Teacher Shortages" *Educational Digest*, February 1982, p. 66.

33. "Math Shortage" *Education Digest*, November 1982, p. 67.

34. "Academic Decline," *Education Digest*, February 1983.

35. "Education Students," *Education Digest*, September 1982, p. 71.

36. Gubser, *"Is the New Technology Education's Last Hope?"* p. 15.

37. *Ibid.*, p. 12.

38. Wood and Thompson, *"Guidelines for Better Staff Development,"* p, 374.

39. "Education Students."

40. "Teacher Shortages."

## CHAPTER TWO

1. E. A. Kelley and E. A. Dillon, "Staff Development: It Can Work for You, *NASSP Bulletin*, Vol. 62, no. 417 (April 1978), 1–8.

# NOTES

2. B. Joyce and B. Showers, "Improving Inservice Training: The Messages of Research," *Educational Leadership*, February 1980, p. 379.

3. H. J. James, *Evaluation of a Junior High School Inservice Program Designed to Help Teachers Provide for Pupils' Individual Differences in Reading Ability*, Unpublished doctoral dissertation, University of Miami, Coral Gables, Fla., 1969.

4. J. L. Steele and J. L. Caffey, *Implementing and Evaluating Inservice Programs for Teachers*, paper presented at the annual meeting of the IRA Southeastern Regional Conference, Jacksonville, Fla., February 18–21, 1976 (ERIC: ED 133 697).

5. W. C. Heeney, and C. R. Ashbaugh, *Observed Individualization of Instruction by Vocational and Non-vocational Teachers*, 1976, p. 110. Austin, Tx: Dept. of Education Administration, University of Texas. (ERIC: ED 118 996).

6. B. Scriven, "Inservice Education and Secondary Teachers," *Administrators Bulletin*, 1978, p. 4.

7. W. J. Smyth, "Clinical Supervision: A Reality-Centered Mode of Inservice Education, *Educational Technology*, Vol. 20, no. 3 (March 1980), pp. 31–34.

8. R. K. Wade, "What Makes a Difference in Inservice Teacher Education? A Meta-analysis of Research," *Educational Leadership*, December 1984–January 1985, p. 36.

9. Kelley and Dillon, "Staff Development."

10. D. W. Champaign, "Does Staff Development Do Any Good?" *Educational Leadership*, Vol. 37, no. 5 (February 1980), p. 401.

11. D. N. Aspy and F. N. Roebuck, "From Humane Ideas to Humane Technology and Back Again Many Times," *Education*, Vol. 95, no. 2 (1975).

12. P. Berman and M. W. MacLaughlin, *Federal Programs Supporting Educational Change VIII. Implementing and Sustaining Innovation* (Santa Monica, Calif.: The Rand Corporation, May 1978), pp. v–x.

13. F. H. Wood and S. R. Thompson, "Guidelines for Better Staff Development," *Educational Leadership*, February 1980, p. 375.

14. Wade, "What Makes a Difference in Inservice Teacher Education?" p. 36.

15. B. R. Joyce, K. R. Howey, and S. J. Yarger, *Issues to Face: ISTE Report* (Syracuse, N.Y.: National Dissemination Center, College of Education, Syracuse University, 1976, p. 1.

16. *Ibid.*, p. 2.

17. J. L. Brim and D. Tollet, "How do Teachers Feel About Inservice Education?" *Educational Leadership*, Vol. 31 (March 1974), pp. 521–525.

18. B. A. Ainsworth, "Teachers Talk About Inservice Education," *Journal of Teacher Education*, Vol. 27, no. 2 (Summer 1976), pp. 107–109.

19. B. Joyce and L. Peck, *Inservice Teacher Education Report II: Interviews* (Syracuse, N.Y.: National Dissemination Center, College of Education, Syracuse University, 1977).

20. P. Zigarmi, I. Betz, and D. Jensen, "Teacher Preferences in and Perceptions of Inservice," *Educational Leadership*, Vol. 34 (April 1977), pp. 545–551.

21. R. K. Crocker, *Continuing Teacher Education: Views from the Profession* (St. John's: Memorial University of Newfoundland, 1981), p. 27.

22. Wood and Thompson, "Guidelines for Better Staff Development," p. 374.

23. Joyce, Howey, and Yarger, *Issues to Face*, p. 2.

24. Wood and Thompson, "Guidelines for Better Staff Development," p. 374.

25. P. Coleman, "Professional Development: A Status Report," paper presented at the Work Study Symposium of OISE. Northwestern Center Thunder Bay, Ontario, April 12, 1976. (ERIC: ED 147 938).

26. Wood and Thompson, "Guidelines for Better Staff Development," p. 375.

27. Wade, "What Makes a Difference in Inservice Teacher Education."
28. G. M. Sparkes, "The Trees of the Forest? A Response to Ruth Wade," *Educational Leadership*, December 1984–January 1985, pp. 55–58.
29. Wood and Thompson, "Guidelines for Better Staff Development," p. 375.
30. J. Ryor, "Three Perspectives on Inservice Education." *Journal of Teacher Education*, vol. 30, no. 1 Jan.–Feb. 1979, p. 14.
31. Wood–Thompson, p. 375.
32. Ryor, "Three Perspectives," p. 14.
33. Joyce, Howey and Yarger. *Issues to Face*, p. 8.
34. Ryor, "Three Perspectives."
35. Joyce, Howey and Yarger, *Issues to Face*, p. 12.
36. W. Irving, *Rip Van Winkle and The Legend of Sleepy Hollow*. New York, The Macmillan Co., 1925.

## CHAPTER THREE

1. R. N. Bush, "Curriculum-Proof Teachers: Who Does What for Whom?" in L. J. Rubin, ed., *Improving Inservice Education: Proposals and Procedures for Change* (Boston: Allyn & Bacon, 1971), pp. 33–70.

## CHAPTER FOUR

1. B. R. Joyce, K. R. Howey, and S. J. Yarger, *Issues to Face: ISTE Report I* (Syracuse, N.Y.: National Dissemination Center, Syracuse University, 1976), p. 50.
2. A. M. Nicholson and B. R. Joyce, *ISTE Report III: The Literature on Inservice Education* (Syracuse, N.Y.: The National Dissemination Center, Syracuse University, 1976), p. 45.
3. *Ibid.*, p. 45.
4. E. A. Kelley, ed., *Personnel Managemenet for Schools* (Lincoln: Department of Educational Administration, Teachers College, University of Nebraska-Lincoln, 1975), p. 57.
5. E. A. Dillon, *Position paper on staff development*, presented at the National Staff Development Council of Urban School Districts National Convention, 1972.
6. W. J. Smyth, "Clinical Supervision: A Reality-Centered Mode of Inservice Education," *Educational Technology*, Vol. 20, no. 3 (March 1980), p. 31.
7. L. C. Burello and T. Orbaugh, "Reducing the Discrepancy Between the Known and the Unknown in Inservice Education," *Phi Delta Kappan*, Vol. 63, no. 6 (1982), p. 386.
8. L. L. Jones and A. E. Hayes, "How Valid Are Surveys of Teacher Needs?" *Educational Leadership*, February 1980, pp. 390–392.
9. L. L. Jones, "Elementary School Reading: Relationships Among Teacher Background, Needs, Knowledge, and Hindrances to Effective Reading Instruction," Ph.D. dissertation, University of North Carolina at Chapel Hill, 1976, p. 391.
10. Jones and Hayes, "How Valid Are Surveys of Teacher Needs?"
11. Smyth, "Clinical Supervision," p. 31.
12. D. Burrell, "Teachers Center: A Critical Analysis," *Educational Leadership*, Vol. 33, no. 6 (March 1976), p. 422.

NOTES 211

13. Nicholson and Joyce, *ISTE Report III*, p. 17.
14. R. A. Luke, *Teacher-Centered Inservice Education: Planning and Products* (Washington, D.C.: National Education Association, 1980), p. 19.
15. A. L. Jefferson, "The Failings of Inservice Education," *The Canadian School Executive*, October 1982, p. 34.
16. Luke, *Teacher-Centered Inservice Education*.
17. Jefferson, "The Failings of Inservice Education."
18. National School Public Relations Association, *Inservice Education: Current Trends in School Policies and Programs* (Arlington, Va.: NSPRA, 1975), p. 19.
19. Jones, *Elementary School Reading*; and Jones and Hayes, "How Valid Are Surveys of Teacher Needs?" Both documents refer to the same research effort.
20. R. L. Ryan, "An Analysis of Some of the Relationships Between Management Style of Junior and Senior High School Principals and Teacher Job Satisfaction and Productivity," master's thesis, Memorial University of Newfoundland, St. John's, 1980, pp. 38–50.
21. Burello and Orbaugh, "Reducing the Discrepancy Between the Known and the Unknown."
22. K. R. Howey, S. J. Yarger, and B. R. Joyce, *Improving Teacher Education* (Washington, D.C.: Association of Teacher Educators, 1978), p. x.
23. R. K. Crocker, *Continuing Teacher Education: Views from the Profession* (St. John's: Memorial University of Newfoundland, 1981).
24. Howey, Yarger, and Joyce, *Inproving Teacher Education*, p. 48.
25. J. D. Inglis, R. B. Carroll, and J. R. Gress, "Teacher Corps Program, 1979, The University of Toledo/Springfield Local Schools," *An Initial Assessment of Year Two Activities*, January 1981; *An Assessment of Spring, 1981, Staff Development Activities*, July 1981; *An Assessment of Winter, 1982, Staff Development Activities* (Toledo, Ohio: College of Education, University of Toledo).
26. Howey, Yarger, and Joyce, *Improving Teacher Education*, p. 48.
27. P. Coleman, "*Professional Development: A Status Report*," paper presented at the Work-Study Symposium of OISE, Northwestern Center, Thunder Bay, Ontario, April 12, 1976, p. 5.
28. G. E. Dickson and R. W. Saxe, *Partners for Educational Reform and Renewal: CBTE, IGE and the Multi-Unit School* (Berkeley, Calif.: McCutcheon, 1973), p. 16.
29. Coleman, "Professional Development," p. 6.
30. Howey, Yarger, and Joyce, *Improving Teacher Education*.
31. W. R. Borg, M. L. Kelley, P. Langer, and M. Gall, *The Mini-Course: A Microteaching Approach to Teacher Education* (Berkeley Hills, Calif.: Macmillan Educational Services, 1970), p. 192.
32. Coleman, "Professional Development," pp. 8–9.
33. B. Rosenshine and N. Furst, "Research on Teacher Performance Criteria," in B. O. Smith, ed., *Research in Teacher Education: A Symposium* (Englewood Cliffs, N.J.: Prentice-Hall, 1971), p. 54.
34. E. W. Roberson, *Effects of Teacher Inservice on Instruction and Learning* (Tucson, Ariz.: EPIC Evaluation Center, 1969); D. J. Strickler, "*Teacher Behavior and Pupil Performance Related to a Training Program for Inservice and Preservice Teachers Based on Minicourse 18: Teaching Reading on Decoding*," Doctoral dissertation, State University of New York, Buffalo, 1972; M. L. Wilson, *Variables Related to the Professional Growth of Teachers*, 1977 and Borg, et al., *The Mini-Course*. (ERIC: ED 137 302).

## CHAPTER FIVE

1. National Commission on Excellence in Education; *A Nation at Risk: The Imperative for Educational Reform* (Washington, D.C. U.S. Government Printing Office, April 1983).

2. G. Dorman, J. Lipsitz, and P. Verner, "Improving Schools for Young Adolescents," *Educational Leadership*, March 1985, pp. 44–49; N. E. Curran, "Teacher Self-concept as a Predictor of Inservice Needs," doctoral dissertation, University of Missouri-Columbia, 1980; R. Hersh, "How Effective Is Your School?" *Instructor*, October 1982, pp. 34–35; G. T. Houlihan, "Using the Right Variables in Measuring School Effectiveness," *NASSP Bulletin*, October 1983, pp. 9–15; C. V. Sapone, "A Research Review—Perceptions on Characteristics of Effective Schools," *NASSP Bulletin*, October 1983, pp. 66–70; and T. R. Sizer, "Common Sense," *Educational Leadership*, March 1985, pp. 21–22.

3. G. A. Bedley, *How Do You Recognize a Good School When You Walk into One?* (Irving, Calif.: People-Wise Publications, 1985).

4. D. A. Squires, E. G. Huitt, and J. K. Segars, *Effective Schools and Classrooms: A Research-Based Perspective* (Alexandria, Va.: Association for Supervision and Curriculum Development, 1983, pp. 46–55 and 61–65).

5. M. Rutter, B. Maugham, P. Mortimer, J. Ouston, and A. Smith, *Fifteen Thousand Hours: Secondary Schools and Their Effects on Children* (Cambridge, Mass.: Harvard University Press, 1979).

6. C. M. Edwards andd J. J. English "Professional Growth Incentives: A Career Ladder that Works," unpublished paper on 1983–1985 pay-for-performance and staff development study, Orange County Public Schools, Orange, Va. 22960. Presented at the National Staff Development Conference, Williamsburg, Va., December 13, 1984.

7. For example; B. S. Bloom, *Human Characteristics and School Learning* (New York: McGraw-Hill, 1976).

8. R. F. Mager, *Preparing Instructional Objectives* (Palo Alto, Calif.: Fearon, 1962).

9. L. W. Lezotte and B. A. Bancroft, "Growing Use of the Effective Schools Model for School Improvement," *Educational Leadership*, March 1985, p. 26.

10. See, for example, *1984*, by George Orwell, (Harmondsworth, Middlesex: Penguin Books, 1956) and *Brave New World*, by Aldous Huxley (New York, N.Y.: Harper & Brothers, 1946).

11. P. Evans, "Presentation at National Staff Development Conference at Williamsburg, Va., December 13, 1984.

12. Mastery Learning Corporation, 85 Main St., Watertown, Mass. 02172.

13. Sapone, "A Research Review."

14. Sizer, "Common Sense," p. 22.

15. Betty MacPhail Wilcox and Jim Guth address some of these issues in their article, "Effectiveness Research and School Administrator—Both Sides of the Coin," *NASSP Bulletin*, October 1983, pp. 3–8.

16. S. J. Gould, *The Mismeasure of Man* (New York: W. W. Norton, 1981).

17. H. Gardner, *Frames of Mind* (New York: Basic Books, 1983).

18. J. Naisbett, *Megatrends* (New York: Warner, 1982), p. 83.

19. C. W. Beegle, untitled paper presented at the National Staff Development Conference, Williamsburg, Va., December 13, 1984, p. 14. Professor Beegle is at the School of Education, University of Virginia, Charlottesville.

## CHAPTER SIX

1. M. L. Berge, R. E. Harris, and C. B. Walden, "Inservice Education Programs of Local School Systems," in N. B. Henry ed., *Inservice Education for Teachers, Supervisors and Administrators, Part I* (Chicago: the National Association for the Study of Education, 1957), pp. 197–223.

2. R. A. Edelfelt, *Inservice Teacher Education—Sources in the ERIC System* (Washington, D.C.: ERIC Clearinghouse on Teacher Education, January 1975). (ERIC: ED 099 308).

3. R. A. Edelfelt, ed., *Inservice Education: Criteria for and Examples of Local Programs* (Bellingham: Western Washington State College, 1977).

4. F. T. Sobol, *What Variables Appear Important in Changing Traditional Inservice Training Procedures*, (Washington, D.C.: Bureau of Educational Personnel Development, HEW, 1971), pp. 6–7 (ERIC: ED 083 146).

5. B. R. Joyce and B. Showers, "Improving Inservice Training: The Messages of Research," *Educational Leadership*, February 1980, pp. 379–385.

6. A. M. Nicholson and B. R. Joyce, *ISTE Report III: The Literature on Inservice Education* (Syracuse, N.Y.: National Dissemination Center, Syracuse University, 1976), pp. 15–17.

7. *Ibid.*, p. 16.

8. *Ibid.*, p. 17.

9. B. R. Joyce, K. M. McNair, R. Diaz, M. D. McKibbin, I. T. Waterman, and M. G. Baker, *ISTE Report II: Interviews* (Syracuse, N.Y.: National Dissemination Center, Syracuse University, 1977), p. 3.

10. Nicholson and Joyce, *ISTE Report III*, pp. 57–58.

## CHAPTER SEVEN

1. L. J. Bishop, *Staff Development and Instructional Improvement Plans and Procedures* (Boston: Allyn & Bacon, 1976), pp. 29–31.

2. L. W. Downey, *The Task of Public Education: The Perceptions of People* (Chicago: University of Chicago, 1960).

3. G. D. Kuh, T. Orbaugh, and K. Byers. *Designing and Conducting Needs Assessment in Education* (Bloomington: National Inservice Network, School of Education, Indiana University, 1981), p. 8.

4. M. Scriven, and J. Roth, "Needs Assessment: Concept and Practice," in S. Anderson and C. Coles, eds., *Exploring Purposes and Dimensions* (San Francisco: Jossey-Bass, 1978).

5. D. L. Stufflebeam, *Needs Assessment in Evaluation*, paper presented at the meeting of the American Educational Research Association, Evaluation Conference, San Francisco, September 1974.

6. W. A. Firestone, "Participation and Influence in the Planning of Educational Change, *The Journal of Applied Behavioral Science*, Vol. 13, no 2 (1977), pp. 167–183.

7. C. B. Derr, "O D Won't Work in Schools," *Education and Urban Society*, Vol. 8 (1976), pp. 227–261.

8. S. Rath and R. Hagans, *Collaboration Among Schools and Business and Industry: An Analysis of the Problems and Some Suggestions for Improving the Process* (Portland, Ore.: Northwest Regional Educational Laboratory, 1978).

9. R. L. Ackoff, "The Corporate Raindance," *The Wharton Magazine*, Winter 1977, pp. 36–41.
10. M. C. Erly and J. D. Greenberg, "*Customizing a Needs Assessment Process for Planning Staff Development: A Model of Collaboration*," paper delivered at the International Seminar for Teacher Education in the 80's and 90's, Digby Stuart College, Roshampton, Surrey, England, April 13–19, 1984.

## CHAPTER NINE

1. A. M. Nicholson and B. R. Joyce, *ISTE Report III: The Literature on Inservice Education* (Syracuse, N.Y.: National Dissemination Center, College of Education, Syracuse University, 1976), p. 16.
2. *Ibid.*, p. 17.
3. *Ibid.*, p. 18.
4. See, for example, W. G. Ward, *A Review of the Literature and Research on Inservice Training for Teachers with an Emphasis on Vocational and Technical Teachers* (Stillwater, OK: Oklahoma State Dept. of Vocational and Technical Education, Div. on Research, Planning and Education. Nov. 1972). (ERIC: ED 073 244) and F. T. Sobol, *What Variables Appear Important in Changing Traditional Inservice Training Procedures?* (Washington, D.C.: Bureau of Educational Personnel Development, HEW, 1971) (ERIC: ED 083 146).
5. Nicholson and Joyce, *ISTE Report III*, p. 18.
6. D. L. Hartenbach, "A Synthesized Model for Inservice Programs: A Focus on Diffusion," doctoral dissertation, University of Northern Colorado, Greeley, 1981.
7. R. L. Bieber, "A Study of Decision Making for Inservice Teacher Education," doctoral dissertation, Washington State University, Pullman, 1978.
8. S. Y. O. Bunday, "Teacher Attitudes and Behaviors as Related to One-Day Inservice Education," doctoral dissertation, University of Northern Colorado, Greeley, 1978.
9. M. D. Morrison, "The Effect of an Intensive Inservice Program in Modifying the Questioning Behavior of Teachers and Students in Secondary School Social Studies Classes," doctoral dissertation, West Virginia University, Morgantown, 1978.
10. B. T. Atkins, "Impact of Certain Selected Types of Technical Assistance on Participants Following an Inservice Program," doctoral dissertation, University of Michigan, Ann Arbor, 1981.
11. T. C. Meadows, "The Effect of Selected Variables on Elementary Teachers Ratings of Science Inservice Workshops," doctoral dissertation, the University of Texas at Austin, 1978.
12. G. Lawrence, D. Baker, P. Elzie, and B. Hanson, *Patterns of Effective Inservice Education* (Tallahassee: University of Florida, Department of Education, 1974).
13. J. E. Doyle, "The Effect of Teacher Inservice Training on Teachers' Knowledge of the Basic Characteristics of the Lecture, Guided Discussion and Demonstration Methods," doctoral dissertation, University of Iowa, Iowa City, 1981.
14. C. M. Hess, "Three Methods of Teaching Metric Measurements and Their Cognitive and Affective Effects on Preservice Elementary Teachers," doctoral dissertation, Pennsylvania State University, University Park, Penn. 1978.
15. W. N. Cox, "A Study of Teacher Effectiveness Training upon Secondary School Teachers and their Students," doctoral dissertation, The College of William and Mary, Williamsburg, Va., 1978.

16. R. P. Longobardi, "The Effects of Teacher Training on the Moral Development of Their Students," doctoral dissertation, Boston College, Boston, 1981.

17. J. W. Moore, "A Study of the Relationships Between Types of Inservice Teacher Training and the Degree of Implementation of Affective Educational Programs," doctoral dissertation, Saint Louis University, St. Louis, MO, 1977.

18. L. P. Rodriguez, "Effects of an Inservice Treatment of Teacher Perception of Self and School Climate," doctoral dissertation, Arizona State University, Tempe, 1981.

19. F. J. Friederwitzer, "The Development, Implementation, and Evaluation of a Model Inservice Program in the Teaching of Measurement Concepts to Third, Fifth and Sixth Grade Elementary School Teachers," doctoral dissertation, Rutgers University, Camden, N.J., 1981.

20. Nicholson and Joyce, *ISTE Report III*, p. 21.

21. Hess, "Three Methods of Testing Metric Measurements."

22. R. J. Garmston, "The Effect of Different Inservice Treatments on the Reading Gains of Primary Children: A Study in Cost Effectiveness," doctoral dissertation, University of Southern California, Los Angeles, 1979.

23. Doyle, "The Effect of Teacher Inservice Training."

24. D.A. Young, "An Investigation of the Effectiveness of a Secondary Teacher Inservice Program in Individualizing Instruction Techniques and Career Education Concepts," doctoral dissertation, University of Maryland, College Park, Maryland, 1980.

25. J. H. Kearns, "An Inservice Model for Improving Elementary Science Teaching," doctoral dissertation, University of North Carolina, Chapel Hill, N.C., 1981.

26. J. Mandelbaum, "A Study of the Relationships of an Inservice Program in Music and Movement to Opportunities for Creativity in Selected Kindergartens," doctoral dissertation, New York University, New York City, 1978.

27. E. W. Roberson, *Effects of Teacher Inservice on Instruction and Learning* (Tucson, Ariz.: EPIC Evaluation Center, 1979).

28. N. A. Flanders, *Analyzing Teacher Behavior* (Don Mills, Ontario: Addison-Wesley, 1970).

29. E. A. Kelley and E. A. Dillon, "Staff Development: It Can Work for You," *NASSP Bulletin*, Vol. 62, no. 417 (April 1978), pp. 1–8.

30. D. Jensen, L. Betz, and P. Zigarmi, "If You Are Listening to Teachers, Here Is How You Will Organize Inservice," *NASSP Bulletin*, Vol. 62, no. 417 (April 1978), pp. 9–14.

31. *Ibid.*

32. A. M. E. Cheatly, "Teacher Inservice and Professional Development in the Urban School Divisions of Metropolitan Winnipeg," doctoral dissertation, University of North Dakota, Grand Forks, 1977.

33. B. M. Schroedinger, "The Effect and Use of Identified Criteria for Effective Inservice Teacher Education and Teacher Attitudes Toward Inservice," doctoral dissertation, University of Idaho, Moscow, 1977.

34. Lawrence et al., *Patterns of Effective Inservice Education*.

35. N. E. Curran, "Teacher Self-Concept as a Predictor of Inservice Needs," doctoral dissertation, University of Missouri-Columbia, 1980.

36. B. R. Joyce, K. M. McNair, R. Diaz, M. D. McKibbin, I. T. Waterman, and M. G. Baker, *ISTE Report II: Interviews* (Syracuse, N.Y.: National Dissemination Center, College of Education, Syracuse University, 1977).

37. Jensen, Betz, and Zigarmi, "If You Are Listening."

38. W. G. Monahan and H. E. Miller, *Planning and Developing Inservice Education*, (Iowa City: Iowa University Center for Research into School Administration, 1970) (ERIC: ED 045 611).

39. Joyce et al., *ISTE Report II*, p. 24.

40. B. A. Ainsworth, "Teachers Talk About Inservice Education," *Journal of Teacher Education*, Vol. 27, no. 2, (Summer 1976), pp. 107–109.

41. J. L. Brim and D. Tollett, "How Do Teachers Feel About Inservice Education?" *Educational Leadership*, Vol. 31 (March 1974), pp. 521–525.

42. L. C. Burrello and T. Orbaugh, "Reducing the Discrepancy Between the Known and the Unknown in Inservice Education," *Phi Delta Kappan*, Vol. 63, no. 6 (1982), p. 386.

43. P. J. Sireno, L. Devlin and R. Stephens, *Assisting Industrial Arts Teachers in Integrating Occupationally-Oriented Activities into Their Existing Instructional Programs: Final Report* (Kirksville, Mo.: Northeastern State University, 1976).

44. J. H. Davis, *A Study of the Inservice Education Program of Elementary School Teachers in Knoxville City Schools* (Knoxville: University of Tennessee, 1977).

45. L. J. Rubin, *A Study of the Continuing Education of Teachers*, (Santa Barbara, CA: Center for Coordinated Education, University of California; N.Y.: Ford Foundation, 1969). p. 49 (ERIC: ED 036 487).

46. Nicholson and Joyce, *ISTE Report III*, p. 21.

47. Joyce et al., *ISTE Report II*.

48. *Ibid.*

49. M. L. Wilson, *Variables Related to the Professional Growth of Teachers*, 11–12. (ERIC: ED 137 302).

50. L. L. Jones, "Elementary School Reading: Relationships Among Teacher Background, Needs, Knowledge and Hindrances to Effective Reading Instruction," doctoral dissertation, University of North Carolina at Chapel Hill, 1976.

51. R. Davis, "An Exploratory Study of the Espoused Theories of Beginning Reading Held by Teachers and Their Theories-in-Use in Teaching Beginning Reading, masters dissertation, Queens University, Kingston, Ont., July 1982.

52. C. M. Henson, "A Comparison of a Faculty-Planned Inservice Program Versus a District-Planned Inservice Program," doctoral dissertation, St. Louis University, St. Louis, Mo., 1978.

53. G. M. Ingersoll, "Assessing Inservice Training Needs Through Teacher Response," *Journal of Teacher Education*, Vol. 27 (Summer 1969), pp. 169–173.

54. R. L. Evans, D. M. Byrd, and T. M. Coleman, "Responsive Teacher Inservice Needs Assessment in an Urban Setting," paper presented at the American Educational Research Association Annual Meeting, Toronto, March 1978. (ERIC: ED 152 731).

55. H. M. Clar, "Teacher Attitudes Towards Inservice Education: An Exploration," doctoral dissertation, University of Northern Colorado, Greeley, 1978.

## CHAPTER TEN

1. M. Hruska, "Reconceptualizing Inservice: A Teacher Designed Staff Development Program," doctoral dissertation, University of Massachusetts, Amherst, 1978. Dr. Merrita Hruska Cooke is the former director of the Amherst Area Teacher Center. She is now director of the Child Study Program of the Amherst Regional Schools, Amherst, Massachusetts.

2. R. L. Ryan, "Analysis of Some of the Relationships Between Management Style of Junior and Senior High School Principals and Teacher Job Satisfaction and Productivity," master's dissertation, Memorial University of Newfoundland, St. John's, 1980. See the review of research.

3. B. R. Joyce, K. M. McNair, R. Diaz, M. D. McKibbin, I. T. Waterman and M. G. Baker, *ISTE Report II: Interviews* (Syracuse, N.Y.: National Dissemination Center, College of Education, Syracuse University, 1977), p. 49.

4. *Ibid.*, p. 14.

5. A. M. Nicholson and B. R. Joyce, *ISTE Report III: The Literature on Inservice Education* (Syracuse, N.Y.: National Dissemination Center, College of Education, Syracuse University, 1976), p. 16.

6. J. R. Berry and M. Murfin, "Meeting Barriers to Inservice Education," *Educational Leadership*, March 1960, pp. 341–355.

7. *Ibid.*, 354.

8. National Education Association *Inservice Planning Manual. Info Item Educators Digest/No. 5070* (Washington, D.C.: NEA; Columbus: Ohio Education Association, Instruction and Professional Development Division). Document undated.

9. F. T. Sobol, *What Variables Appear Important in Changing Traditional Inservice Training Procedures?* (Washington, D.C.: Bureau of Educational Personnel Development, HEW, 1971), (ERIC: ED 083 146).

10. F. H. Wood and S. R. Thompson, "Guidelines for Better Staff Development," *Educational Leadership*, February 1980, pp. 374–378.

11. H. J. James, "Evaluation of a Junior High School Inservice Program Designed to Help Teachers Provide for Pupils' Individual Differences in Reading Abilities," doctoral dissertation, University of Miami, Coral Gables, Fla., 1969.

12. *Ibid.*, p. 32; and Joyce et al., *ISTE Report II*.

13. Joyce et al., 1977, *Ibid.*, 54.

14. A. L. Jefferson, "The Failings of Inservice Education," *The Canadian School Executive*, October 1980, p. 34.

15. L. C. Burello and T. Orbaugh, "Reducing the Discrepancy Between the Known and the Unknown in Inservice Education," *Phi Delta Kappan*, Vol. 63, no. 6, 1982, p. 386.

16. Joyce *ISTE Report II*, p. 15.

17. Jefferson, "The Failings of Inservice Education."

18. B. A. Ainsworth, "Teachers Talk About Inservice Education," *Journal of Teacher Education*, Vol. 27, no. 2 (Summer 1976), pp. 107–109.

19. D. Jensen, L. Betz, and P. Zigarmi "If You Are Listening to Teachers, Here Is How You Will Organize Inservice," *NASSP Bulletin*, Vo. 62, no. 417 (April 1978), pp. 9–14.

20. National Educational Association and Ohio Education Association, *Inservice Planning Manual*, p. 4.

21. D. Westby-Gibson, *Inservice Education—Perspectives for Educators*, (Berkley, Calif.: Far West Laboratory for Education Research and Development, 1967), p. 4. (ERIC: ED 015 161).

22. *Inservice Education of Teachers: Research Summary 1966-S1*, ERIC: ED 022 728 (Washington, D.C.: National Education Association, Research Division, 1966), adapted from p. 5.

23. Wood and Thompson, "Guidelines for Better Staff Development," adapted from p. 377.

24. Joyce et al., *ISTE Report II*, p. 3.

25. *Ibid.*, p. 15.

## CHAPTER ELEVEN

1. R. V. Urick, D. M. Pendergast, and S. B. Hillman, "The Preconditions for Staff Development," *Educational Leadership*, Vol. 38, no. 7 (April 1981), pp. 546–549.

2. For example, P. Berman and M. W. McLaughlin, *Federal Programs Supporting Educational Change*. Volume 4. *The Findings in Review* (Santa Monica, Calif.: The Rand Corporation, 1975).

3. M. Alexander, "Organizational Norms," in J. E. Jones and J. W. Pfeiffer, eds., *The 1977 Annual Handbook for Group Facilitators* (La Jolla, Calif.: University Associates, 1977).

4. E. Locke, "Toward a Theory of Task Motivation and Incentives," *Organizational Behavior and Human Performances*, Vol. 3 (1968), pp. 159–189.

5. B. R. Joyce, K. R. Howey and S. J. Yarger, *Issues to Face: ISTE Report I* (Syracuse, N.Y.: National Dissemination Center, Syracuse University, 1976).

6. R. K. Crocker, *Continuing Teacher Education: Views from The Profession* (St. John's: Memorial University of Newfoundland, 1981).

7. Joyce, Howey and Yarger, *ISTE Report I*, pp. 19–20.

8. *Ibid.*, 23.

9. C. Rogers, "Toward Becoming a Fully Functioning Person," in *Perceiving, Behaving, Becoming* (Washington, D.C.: Association for Supervision and Curriculum Development, 1962).

10. F. F. Fuller, "Concerns of Teachers: A Developmental Conceptualization," *American Educational Research Record*, Vol. 6, no. 2 (1969), pp. 207–226.

11. G. E. Hall, R. C. Wallace, and W. A. Dossett, *A Developmental Conceptualization of the Adoption Process Within Educational Institutions* (Austin: Research and Development Center for Teacher Education, University of Texas at Austin, 1973).

12. G. E. Hall, "Concerns-Based Inservice Teacher Training: An Overview of the Concepts, Research and Practice," paper presented at the conference on School-Focused Inservice Training, March 2–3, 1978, Bournemouth, England (R & D Center for Teacher Education Report No. 3057, University of Texas at Austin); and S. M. Hord and S. F. Loucks, *A Concerns-Based Model for the Delivery of Inservice* (Austin: Research and Development Center for Teacher Education, University of Texas at Austin, 1980).

13. A. H. Maslow, *Motivation and Personality* (New York: Harper & Row, 1954).

14. G. E. Hall, "The Concerns-Based Approach to Facilitating Change," *Educational Horizons*, Vol. 57, no. 4, (1979), pp. 202–208.

15. *Ibid.*

16. G. E. Hall and W. L. Rutherford *Client Concerns: A Guide to Facilitating Institutional Change* (Austin: Research and Development Center for Teacher Education, University of Texas at Austin, 1980).

17. S. F. Loucks and P. Zigarmi, "Effective Staff Development," *Educational Considerations*, Vol. 8, no. 2 (Winter 1981), pp. 4–8.

18. B. R. Joyce and B. Showers, "Improving Inservice Training. The Messages of Research," *Educational Leadership*, February 1980, pp. 379–385.

19. Loucks and Zigarmi, "Effective Staff Development,"

20. B. M. Harris, E. W. Bessent, and K. E. McIntyre, *Inservice Education: A Guide to Better Practice* (Englewood Cliffs, N.J.: Prentice-Hall, 1969).

21. B. M. Harris, *Improving Staff Performance Through Inservice Education* (Boston: Allyn & Bacon, 1980).

22. L. Flock, "Retirement: For Some It's Only Temporary," *Austin American Statesman*, November 11, 1976, p. B1.

23. Harris, *Improving Staff Performance*, p. 75.
24. Harris, Bessent and McIntyre, *Inservice Education*.
25. B. Bloom, *Taxonomy of Educational Objectives,* Handbook 1: *Cognitive Domain* (New York: David McKay, 1956).
26. Joyce and Showers, "Improving Inservice Training."

## CHAPTER TWELVE

1. R. Mager, *Preparing Instructional Objectives* (Palo Alto, Calif.: Fearon, 1962).
2. B. M. Harris, *Improving Staff Performance Through Inservice Education* (Boston: Allyn & Bacon, 1980), p. 48.
3. S. F. Loucks and P. Zigarmi, "Effective Staff Development," *Educational Considerations*, Vol. 8, no. 2 (Winter 1981), pp. 4–8; and Harris, *Improving Staff Performance*.
4. B. R. Joyce and B. Showers, "Improving Inservice Training: The Messages of Research; *Educational Leadership*, February 1980, pp. 379–385.
5. J. Mackay, personal notes taken from his talk at the Program Coordinators' Special Interest Council Workshop at Corner Brook, Newfoundland, April 26, 1982.
6. Joyce and Showers, "Improving Inservice Training," p. 382.
7. *Ibid.*
8. Mackay, personal notes.
9. *Ibid.*
10. Joyce and Showers, "Improving Inservice Training," p. 384.
11. *Ibid.*
12. N. A. Flanders, *Analyzing Teacher Behavior* (Reading, Mass.: Addison-Wesley, 1970).
13. Joyce and Showers, "Improving Inservice Training"; and B. R. Joyce and B. Showers, "The Coaching of Teaching," *Educational Leadership*, October 1982, pp. 4–9.
14. Loucks and Zigarmi, "Effective Staff Development."
15. Joyce and Showers, "The Coaching of Teaching," p. 5.
16. Loucks and Zigarmi, "Effective Staff Development."
17. *Ibid.*, p. 6.
18. *Ibid.*

## CHAPTER THIRTEEN

1. B. M. Harris, *Improving Staff Performance Through Inservice Education* (Boston: Allyn & Bacon, 1980), p. 10.
2. A. H. Maslow, *The Farther Reaches of Human Nature* (New York: Viking Press, 1951), p. 380, quoted by Harris, *Improving Staff Performance*.
3. Harris, *Improving Staff Performance*.
4. L. J. Rubin, "A Study of the Continuing Education of Teachers, Part I," *Instructor Development* (General Learning Corporation), Vol. 1, no. 6 (March 1970) and Vol. 1, no. 8 (May 1970), quoted by Harris, *Improving Staff Performance*.
5. J. Mackay, perosnal notes taken from his talk at the Program Coordinators Special Interest Council Inservice, Corner Brook, Newfoundland, April 26, 1982; and M. Hruska, "Reconceptualizing Inservice: A Teacher Designed Staff Development Program," doctoral thesis, University of Massachusetts, Amherst, 1978.

6. Mackay, personal notes.
7. *Ibid.*
8. Hruska, *Reconceptualizing Inservice.*
9. B. S. Bloom, *Human Characteristics and School Learning* (New York: McGraw-Hill, 1976), p. 5, quoted by Harris, *Improving Staff Performance.*
10. E. E. Lohman, "Differential Effects of Training on the Verbal Behavior of Student Teachers—Theory and Implications," paper presented to the American Education Research Association, New York, February 16–18, 1967, quoted by Harris, *Improving Staff Performance.*
11. Hruska, *Reconceptualizing Inservice.*
12. Harris, *Improving Staff Performance.*
13. Hruska, *Reconceptualizing Inservice.*
14. *Ibid.*
15. Bloom, *Human Characteristics and School Learning.*
16. Harris, *Improving Staff Performance.*
17. *Ibid.*
18. *Ibid.*
19. *Ibid.*
20. Maslow, *The Farther Reaches of Human Nature,* p. 5.
21. Maslow, pp. 299–306.
22. Harris, *Improving Staff Performance.*
23. Hruska, *Reconceptualizing Inservice.*
24. C. M. Fuir, "The Reluctant Student: Perspectives on Feeling States and Motivation," Chapter 6 in L. M. Berman and J. A. Roderick, eds., *Feeling, Valuing, and the Art of Growing: Insights into the Affective* (Washington, D.C.: Association for Supervision and Curriculum Development, 1977), p. 138, quoted by Harris, *Improving Staff Performance.*
25. Harris, *Improving Staff Performance,* pp. 157–159.
26. National Inservice Network, *Quality Practices in Inservice Education* (Bloomington: School of Education, Indiana University, 1980).
27. G. Lawrence et al., *Patterns of Effective Inservice Education* (Tallahassee: Department of Education, University of Florida, 1974), pp. 14–17.
28. Western Washington State College, *Planning an Inservice Program: A Process Guide* (Bellingham: Western State College, Washington, January 1977); and *A Generic Model for Inservice Education: A Monograph,* 1977, (Bellingham, Wa.: Western Washington State College, January 1977). (ERIC: ED 152 688).
29. R. A. Edelfelt, ed., *Inservice Education: Criteria for and Examples of Local Programs* (Bellingham: Western Washington State College, 1977).
30. S. Wlodarczyk, assistant superintendent of schools, South Windsor, Conn., in cooperation with the National Staff Development Council.
31. Mackay, personal notes.
32. Harris, *Improving Staff Performance.*
33. R. M. Barrera, *Catching the Kinks in Staff Development Programs* (San Antonio, Tex: Inter-Cultural Development Research Association, 1976).
34. R. Kindsvatter and W. W. Wilen, "A Systematic Approach to Improving Conference Skills," *Educational Leadership,* April 1981, pp. 525–529.

# INDEX

# A

Active listening/unstructured interview, 70
Activities, as a defect in ISSD:
  options and choices in learning, 13
  unrelated and impersonal, 13
Activities, characteristics of effective staff development, 192-93
Administrative commitment, failure of inservice activities and, 142
Administrative evaluation-staff interview, 79, 122-23
Administrators:
  data collection from, 69
  as inservice trainers, 134
  support from, 176, 177-78
Agencies having a staff development focus, addresses of, 201-3
American Council on Education, 8
American Federation of Teachers, 27
Archival research, use of, 74-76
Arizona State Department of Education, 50-52
Assessing, a category of use, 163-64

Assignments, teacher training versus teaching, 5-8
Attitudes:
  changing, 127
  as an inservice prerequisite, 147
  needs and, 62, 63
  success of inservice activities and, 140
  toward inservice inventory, 197
Attrition rates, ISSD and, 4
Audiences, needs assessment for target, 64
Audiotapes, use of, 128
Awareness:
  as an inservice prerequisite, 147
  level of experience impact and, 157
  level of intervention and, 156
  as a stage of concern, 152, 153

# B

Back to the basics, 45
Barrera guidelines for staff development, 193

Bedley, Gene, 37
Behavior modification focus, 151
Brainstorming:
   experience impact on, 157
   impact of, on various objectives, 158
Buzz sessions:
   experience impact on, 157
   impact of, on various objectives, 158

# C

Case studies, use of, 76
CBAM. *See* Concerns-Based Adoption Model
CBTE (Competency-based teacher education), 31, 45
CCSSO (Council of Chief State School Officers), 8
Change:
   colleague/associate relations and, 148
   Concerns-Based Adoption Model and, 151
   creativity/innovation and, 148
   ISSD and educational, 4
   leadership, 148
   organizational/personal pride and, 148
   performance/excellence and, 148
   self-directed, 150
   teamwork/cooperation and, 148
   training/development and, 148
Checklist, use of a, 73
Chicago Mastery Learning, 47
Classroom application, a component of an inservice experience, 169, 171
Classroom implementation stage, sessions and follow-up and:
   continuous assessment of needs, 174-75
   description of, 173-74
   need for positive feedback, 175
   one-on-one practice, 174
   supportive and compatible supervisors, 175-76
Clients served, guidelines for ISSD regarding, 183
Coleman, James, 12

Coleman, Peter, 77
Collaboration:
   guidelines for ISSD regarding, 185-86
   level of intervention and, 156
   as a stage of concern, 152, 153
Colleague/associate relations, change and, 148
College courses, 149
Commission on Excellence, 33-34
Commitments:
   administrative, 142
   as an inservice prerequisite, 148
   for staff development, 22-23
Committees, use of, 76
Competencies, needs and, 62, 63
Competency-based teacher education (CBTE), 31, 45
Concepts, level of intervention and the acquisition of, 156
Concerns-Based Adoption Model (CBAM) project:
   assumptions about change, 151
   concept of Stages of Concern, 151-54
   level of use, 159-66
   levels of interventions, 154, 155
Concerns Questionnaire, 152, 154
Conference Category System Analysis Form, 194, 198
Consequences:
   level of intervention and, 156
   as a stage of concern, 152, 153
Consolidation, sessions and, 173-76
Consultants:
   failure of inservice activities and, 140
   as inservice trainers, 134
Content/skills:
   failure of inservice activities and, 140, 141
   level of intervention and, 156
   needs and, 62, 63
   substantive dimension of, 150
Context phase for staff development, 21
Continuing education, needs assessment instrument, 107-12
Cost of inservice activities:
   amount spent on, 3, 12
   defrayed, 184
   incentives and, 149
   successful programs and, 140, 141, 149

Council of Chief State School Officers (CCSSO), 8
Creativity/innovation, change and, 148
Credential orientation, description of, 58
Curriculum content, effective schools and, 34, 35

# D

Data collection for needs assessment, methods of:
 archival research, 74-76
 case studies, 76
 committees, 76
 observations, 73-74
 personal interviews, 70-71
 response forms, 71-73
 small-group meetings, 76
 sources for, 69
Decision-making processes:
 failure of inservice activities and, 142
 guidelines for ISSD regarding, 184
 innovations and, 177
Declining enrollments, ISSD and, 3-4
Delivery systems, as an inservice prerequisite, 148-49, 150
Demonstration(s):
 a component of an inservice experience, 169, 170
 experience impact of, 154, 157
 impact of, on various objectives, 158
Discussions:
 experience impact on group, 157
 impact of, on various objectives, 158
 use of guided, 129
District-level personnel, needs determined by, 25-26

# E

Edelfelt guidelines for staff development, 187, 189-91
Educational changes, ISSD and, 4

Educational malpractice, 7
Education vouchers, 45
Elementary school social climate questionnaire, 77, 80-82
Evaluation:
 failure of inservice activities and, 142
 phase for staff development, 24
 preparing for, 179-81
Experience impact, levels of, 154, 157

# F

Far West Laboratory for Education Research and Development, 143
Feedback, a component of an inservice experience, 169, 171
Films, use of, 128
Follow-up:
 as a defect in ISSD, 13, 16
 failure of inservice activities and, 142
 of sessions, 172-78
Fond du Lac school district staff inservice education needs assessment, 102-6
Foundations for staff development, 21-22
*Frames of Mind*, 47
Fuller, Francis, 151

# G

Game plan, a level of intervention, 155
Games, use of, 128
Gardner, H., 47
Goals:
 of Arizona State Department of Education, 50-52
 for effective schools, 35, 47
 failure of inservice activities and setting of, 142
 of sessions, 167-69
 of White Bear Lake (Minnesota) school district, 48-50

Gould, Stephen Jay, 47
Governance of ISSD, past and future of, 57
Governor's Task Force on Higher Education (Houston), 8
Group composition for staff development activities, 133
Guided practice:
  experience impact of, 157
  impact of, on various objectives, 158

# H

Hall, Gene E., 154
Handicapped children, specific need instrument and, 79, 120-21
Harris guidelines for staff development, 182-85, 194, 195-96
*How Do You Recognize a Good School When You Walk into One?*, 37, 38-39
Hunter, Madeline, 41-42

# I

Impetus and initiative phase for staff development, 22
Incentives, as an inservice prerequisite, 149
Incident, a level of intervention, 155
Individualization, innovations and, 177
Information:
  a category of use and acquiring, 162
  processing focus, 150
Informational:
  needs, 62, 63
  level of intervention and, 156
  as a stage of concern, 153
Innovation:
  definition of, 159
  long-term maintenance and, 176
  refining phase of, 177-78
Input into ISSD, 13, 14

Inservice, synonyms for, 1-2
Inservice design grid, 157, 158
Inservice education, stages of, 142
Inservice planning model, 188
Inservice staff development (ISSD):
  amount of money spent on, 3, 12
  assumptions and beliefs about, 181-82
  definition of, 2-3
  efficacy of, 9-11
  guidelines for, 182-98
  negative aspects of, 12-17
  prerequisites for, 147-51
  problems with information/research on, 136-39
  rationale for, 3-4
  substantive dimension of, 150
  teachers' views of, 12
  unions' views of, 14
Inservice staff development orientations:
  centralized approach to, 54
  centrally coordinated approach to, 54
  credential orientation, 58
  criteria for teacher inservice, 55
  decentralized approach to, 54
  job embedded orientation, 58
  job related orientation, 58
  professional organization related orientation, 58
  purposes and conditions of, 55, 56
  self-directed orientation, 58
  shifting emphasis in, 57
  value orientation, 59
Inservice staff development programs:
  criteria for successful, 126
  different methods of implementing, 128-29
  effectiveness of, 128-29
  group composition for, 133
  how to improve, 142-45
  preferences of teachers in, 131-33
  preferred content for, 134-35
  questions to be answered before implementing, 124-25
  scheduling of, 127-28
  stages in the delivery of, 126
  survey of criteria for local, 189-91
  teacher involvement in the planning of, 13, 130-31

# Index

Inservice staff development programs, failure of:
  administrative commitment and, 142
  consultants and, 140
  content/skills and, 140, 141
  decision-making processes and, 142
  evaluation and, 142
  follow-up and, 142
  goal setting and, 142
  leadership and, 140
  lectures and, 140
  locations of programs and, 141
  materials and equipment and, 140
  monetary compensation and, 141
  needs assessment and, 142
  participation problems and, 140
  poor planning and organization and, 141
  role of teachers and, 140, 141
  sufficient staff and, 140
  unions and, 141
Inservice trainers. *See* Trainers
Instructional staff, survey for, 78, 99-101
Instructional Theory into Practice (ITIP), 42
Instruction used in ISSD, 16
Interaction Analysis, 129
Interfaces, as an inservice prerequisite, 149
Interviewing:
  experience impact of, 157
  impact of, on various objectives, 158
Interviewing techniques, sources of information on, 71
Interviews, use of, 70-71
Iowa University Center for School Administration, 132
ISSD. *See* Inservice staff development
ITIP (Instructional Theory into Practice), 42

## J

Job embedded orientation, description of, 58

Job related orientation, description of, 58
*Journal of Teacher Education, The*, 3

## K

Knowledge, a category of use, 159, 162

## L

Lawrence guidelines for staff development, 187
Leadership:
  change and, 148
  failure of inservice activities and, 140
  innovations and, 177
Learning:
  as a defect in ISSD, 13
  effective schools and, 46-47
  guidelines for ISSD regarding, 184-85
  level of intervention and, 156
Lectures:
  experience impact of, 157
  failure of inservice activities and, 140
  impact of, on various objectives, 158
  use of, 128, 129
Level of use (LoU):
  categories of use, 159, 162-65
  definitions of the levels, 160-61
Levels of intervention, 154, 155
  stages of concern and, 156
Lincoln, Nebraska, junior high schools, teacher involvement in planning for ISSD in, 130
Location of programs:
  failure of inservice activities and, 141
  guidelines for ISSD regarding, 183
  incentives and, 149

## M

Mackay guidelines for staff development, 187, 193

Maine, survey of teacher preferences in staff development in, 132
Management:
 level of intervention and, 156
 personnel, 16
 as a stage of concern, 153
Materials and equipment, failure of inservice activities and, 140
Meta analysis, 137
Michigan school improvement project, 77-78, 83-96
Minimum competency testing, 45
*Mismeasure of Man, The*, 47
Modeling:
 a component of an inservice experience, 169, 170
 lack of, 14
Monetary compensation:
 failure of inservice activities and, 141
 incentives and, 149
Moral development, growth of, 127
Multimedia methods of teaching inservice, 129

# N

National Center for Educational Statistics (NCES), 8
National Council of Teachers of Mathematics, 8
National Education Association (NEA):
 criticism of inservice programs, 142
 study of why inservice programs fail by the, 140
 teaching as a profession, 7
 types of ISSD according to the, 2, 54
 ways to improve ISSD according to the, 143
National Inservice Network (NIN):
 guidelines for staff development, 182, 185-86
 specific need instrument, 79, 120-21
National Institute of Education, 8
National School Public Relations Association (NSPRA), 28-29
National Science Teachers Association, 7-8

*Nation at Risk, A*, 33-34
NCES (National Center for Educational Statistics), 8
NEA. *See* National Education Association
Needs assessment:
 of Arizona State Department of Education, 50-52
 attitudes, 62, 63
 competencies, 62, 63
 completion or partial completion of, 65
 content/skills, 62, 63
 criteria for determining, 65
 as a defect in ISSD, 13, 14-16
 definition of, 64-65
 delimiting, 60-63
 determined by district-level personnel, 25-26
 determined by teachers, 27-30, 66
 for effective schools, 47-48
 emphasis on individuals rather than on organizations, 64
 errors in, 64-66
 failure of inservice activities and, 142
 guidelines for ISSD regarding, 186
 informational, 62, 63
 methods of data collection for, 69-76
 model for, 67-68
 organization, 62, 63
 personal and interpersonal, 150
 planning for, 66-69
 political pressure and, 65
 positive and negative side effects and, 65
 process, 63
 rank ordering of, 65
 relationship between need areas and need categories, 63
 resources and utilization, 62, 63
 sessions and continuous, 174-75
 for staff development, 23
 strength analysis, 64
 target audiences for, 64
 teacher survey of, 134-35
 of White Bear Lake (Minnesota) school district, 48-50
 who plans for, 64
Needs assessment instruments, 65
 continuing education, 107-12

Index

from the Koll and Cozad collection, 78, 102-12
Michigan school improvement project, 77-78, 83-96
Portland consortium training complex:
  teacher survey instrument, 78, 113-16
school social climate questionnaire, 77, 80-82
specific need instrument, 79, 120-21
staff assessment of principal, 79, 122-23
staff development survey, 79, 117-19
for staff inservice education, 102-6
survey for instructional staff, 78, 99-101
telephone survey, 78, 97-98
"New Directions for Federal Programs to Aid Mathematics and Science Teaching," 6
New York Department of Education, 194
*New York Times, The*, 8
NIN. *See* National Inservice Network
NSPRA (National School Public Relations Association), 28-29

## O

Objectives, as a defect in ISSD, 13
Observations:
  experience impact of, 157
  impact of, on various objectives, 158
  use of, 73-74
  versus workshops, 129
Ohio Education Association, 140, 142
One-day inservice sessions, 127
Operational procedures, past and future of, 57
Orange County (Virginia) public school system, 42-44
Oregon State Department of Education, 194, 197
Organization. *See* Planning and organization
Organizational/personal pride, change and, 148

## P

Parents:
  data collection from, 69
  effective schools and the role of, 34, 36
  elementary school social climate questionnaire for, 81-82
Participation in ISSD:
  failure of inservice activities and, 140
  guidelines for, 183
  by parents, 34, 36
  by principals, 35, 36, 37, 40
  by students, 34, 36, 37, 40, 45-56
  by teachers, 13, 130-31
Performance/excellence, change and, 148
Performing, a category of use, 165
Personal:
  and interpersonal needs, 150
  interviews, use of, 70-71
  level of intervention and, 156
  as a stage of concern, 153
Personalistic focus, 150-51
Philosophy:
  as a defect in ISSD, 16-17
  for effective schools, 35, 36
  for staff development, 21
Plan, guidelines for ISSD regarding a written, 185
Planning and organization:
  a category of use, 164
  as a defect in ISSD, 12
  failure of inservice activities and poor, 141
  guidelines for ISSD regarding, 184, 195-96
  involvement of teachers in, 130-31
  model for, 18-21
  needs and, 62, 63, 64, 66-69
  phases of, 21-24
Policy, a level of intervention, 155
Politics:
  as a defect in ISSD, 14-16
  needs and, 65
Portland consortium training complex:
  teacher survey instrument, 78, 113-16
Practice, a component of an inservice experience, 169, 170-71

Portland consortium training complex, *continued*
Prairie du Chien school district continuing education needs assessment, 107-12
Principal(s):
  effective schools and the role of, 35, 36, 37, 40
  staff assessment of, 79, 122-23
Problem solving:
  level of intervention and, 156
  ongoing opportunities for, 176
Process, needs and, 63
Professional organization related orientation, description of, 58
Program delivery for staff development, 23-24
Program development for staff development, 23

## Q

Questionnaire(s):
  concerns, 152, 154
  Edelfelt guidelines for staff development, 187, 189-91
  elementary school social climate, 77, 80-82
  use of, 72-73

## R

Rand Corporation, 8
Readiness, as an inservice prerequisite, 147-48
Reading achievement, ISSD and effects on, 129
Readings, impact of, 154
Refocusing:
  level of intervention and, 156
  as a stage of concern, 152, 153
Reform, mandated by the courts, 7
Resources:
  guidelines for ISSD regarding, 184
  on staff development, 204-6

Resources and utilization, needs and, 62, 63
Response forms, use of, 71-73
Responsibilities, as a defect in ISSD, 13
Rogers, Carl, 150
Role playing:
  experience impact of, 154, 157
  impact of, on various objectives, 158
Ryor, John, 7, 13, 14

## S

Scheduling of inservice activities, 127-28, 140
School improvement survey, needs assessment instrument, 90-96
School social climate questionnaire, 77, 80-82
Schools, effective:
  characteristics of, 35-37, 40-41
  Commission on Excellence and, 33-34
  curriculum content and, 34
  good school checklist, 37, 38-39
  learning and, 46-47
  needs assessment and, 47-48
  research on, 45
  role of parents and, 34, 36
  role of principals and, 35, 36, 37, 40
  role of students and, 34, 36, 37, 40
  role of teachers and, 35, 36, 37, 40
  standards and expectations and, 34
  student outcomes and, 45-46
Self-appraisal inservice program, 129
Self-concerns, 152
Self-directed change, 150
Self-directed orientation, description of, 58
Self-observation, 177
Sensitivity training, 150
Sessions:
  components of, 169-71
  continuous assessment of needs and, 174-75
  follow-up of, 172-78
  importance of the components of, 171-72
  need for positive feedback, 175
  objectives and expectations of, 167-69

Index

supportive and compatible supervisors, 175-76
Sharing, a category of use, 163
Simon Fraser University, 77
Skinner, B.F., 151
Small-group meetings, use of, 76
Social interaction focus, 150
South Dakota:
　teacher involvement in planning for ISSD in, 130
　teacher preferences in staff development in, 132
Specific need instrument, 79, 120-21
Staff:
　assessment of principal, 79, 122-23
　development survey, 79, 117-19
　failure of inservice activities and sufficient, 140
　inservice education needs assessment instrument, 102-6
　as an inservice prerequisite, 149-51
　roles and responsibilities, 57
　survey needs assessment instrument, 83-89
*Staffing the Nation's Schools: A National Emergency,* 8
Stages of Concern (SoC):
　concerns about impact on learners, 152
　description of, 151, 153
　levels of intervention and, 156
　management concerns, 152
　self-concerns, 152
Stamina of teachers and success of inservice activities, 140
Standardized testing, 47
Standards/expectations, effective schools and, 34
Status reporting, a category of use, 164-65
Strategy, a level of intervention, 155
Strength analysis, needs assessment and, 64
Structured interview, 70
Students:
　data collection from, 69
　effective schools and the role of, 34, 36, 37, 40, 45-46
Substantive dimension of inservice, 150
Supervisors, supportive and compatible, 175-76

# T

Tactic, a level of intervention, 155
Teacher(s):
　characteristics of an effective, 42-43
　data collection from, 69
　demands made on, 6-7
　dissatisfaction in ISSD, 12
　effective schools and the role of, 35, 36, 37, 40
　elementary school social climate questionnaire for, 80
　failure of inservice activities and role of, 140, 141
　involvement in planning for ISSD by, 13, 130-31, 143
　ISSD trainers and the views of, 133-34
　learning of new skills by, 55, 58
　needs determined by, 27-30, 66
　oversupply of, 7-8
　shortages of, 4, 7-8
　staff development and the preferences of, 131-33
　survey instrument, 78, 113-16
　tuning/improving of present skills by, 55, 58
Teacher Corps, 12, 30
Teacher Needs Assessment Survey, 134-35
Teacher training:
　criteria for, 55
　ISSD and institutions for, 30-32
　problems with additional, 4-5
　teaching assignments versus, 5-8
Teaching:
　procedures for effective, 43-44
　as a profession, 7-8
　strategies, 42
Teamwork/cooperation, change and, 148
Telephone survey, needs assessment instrument, 78, 97-98
Tennessee, survey of teacher preferences in staff development, 132
T-groups, 150
Theory, a component of an inservice experience, 169-70
Timing inservice, guidelines for ISSD regarding, 183

Trainers, 17
    administrators as, 134
    consultants as, 134
    requirements of, 149-50
    teachers' views of, 133-34
Training/development, change and, 148
Training programs:
    effectiveness of, 158
    past and future, 57
Transactional analysis, 150
Trust and concern, promoting, as a defect in ISSD, 13

## U

Unions:
    failure of inservice activities and, 141
    views on ISSD, 14
U.S. General Accounting Office, 6
University of Idaho, teacher involvement in planning for ISSD and, 130-31
University of Maryland, 79
University of Texas (Austin), Research and Development Center for Teacher Education at, 151, 152, 154, 159
University of Toledo, 30
Unstructured interview, 70

## V

Value orientations, 59

Videotaped minicourses and programs, 128

## W

Western Washington State College:
    guidelines for staff development, 187
    model of planning for staff development, 188
White Bear Lake (Minnesota) school district, 48-50
Winnipeg, Canada, teacher involvement in planning for ISSD in, 130
Wlodarczyk guidelines for staff development, 187, 192-93
Workshops and courses:
    as a defect in ISSD, 12
    versus observation, 129

## X

## Y

Yarger, S.J., 3

## Z